THE
TRIALS OF
HANK JANSON

THE CLASSIC HANK JANSON

The first original Hank Janson book appeared in 1946, and the last in 1971. However, the classic era on which we are focusing in the Telos reissue series lasted from 1946 to 1953.

The following is a checklist of those books, which were subdivided into five main series and a number of "specials".

The titles so far reissued by Telos are indicated by way of an asterisk.

Pre-series books

When Dames Get Tough (1946) *
Scarred Faces (1946) *

Series One

1   This Woman Is Death (1948)
2   Lady, Mind That Corpse (1948)
3   Gun Moll For Hire (1948)
4   No Regrets For Clara (1949)
5   Smart Girls Don't Talk (1949)
6   Lilies For My Lovely (1949)
7   Blonde On The Spot (1949)
8   Honey, Take My Gun (1949)
9   Sweetheart, Here's Your Grave (1949)
10   Gunsmoke In Her Eyes (1949)
11   Angel, Shoot To Kill (1949)
12   Slay-Ride For Cutie (1949)

Series Two

13   Sister, Don't Hate Me (1949)
14   Some Look Better Dead (1950) *
15   Sweetie, Hold Me Tight (1950)
16   Torment For Trixie (1950)
17   Don't Dare Me, Sugar (1950)
18   The Lady Has A Scar (1950)
19   The Jane With The Green Eyes (1950)
20   Lola Brought Her Wreath (1950)
21   Lady, Toll The Bell (1950)
22   The Bride Wore Weeds (1950)
23   Don't Mourn Me Toots (1951)
24   This Dame Dies Soon (1951)

Series Three

25   Baby, Don't Dare Squeal (1951)
26   Death Wore A Petticoat (1951)

27   Hotsy, You'll Be Chilled (1951)
28   It's Always Eve That Weeps (1951)
29   Frails Can Be So Tough (1951)
30   Milady Took The Rap (1951)
31   Women Hate Till Death (1951) *
32   Broads Don't Scare Easy (1951)
33   Skirts Bring Me Sorrow (1951) *
34   Sadie Don't Cry Now (1952)
35   The Filly Wore A Rod (1952)
36   Kill Her If You Can (1952)

Series Four

37   Murder (1952)
38   Conflict (1952)
39   Tension (1952)
40   Whiplash (1952)
41   Accused (1952)
42   Killer (1952)
43   Suspense (1952)
44   Pursuit (1953)
45   Vengeance (1953)
46   Torment (1953) *
47   Amok (1953)
48   Corruption (1953)

Series Five

49   Silken Menace (1953)
50   Nyloned Avenger (1953)

Specials

A   Auctioned (1952)
B   Persian Pride (1952)
C   Desert Fury (1953)
D   Unseen Assassin (1953)
E   One Man In His Time (1953)
F   Deadly Mission (1953)

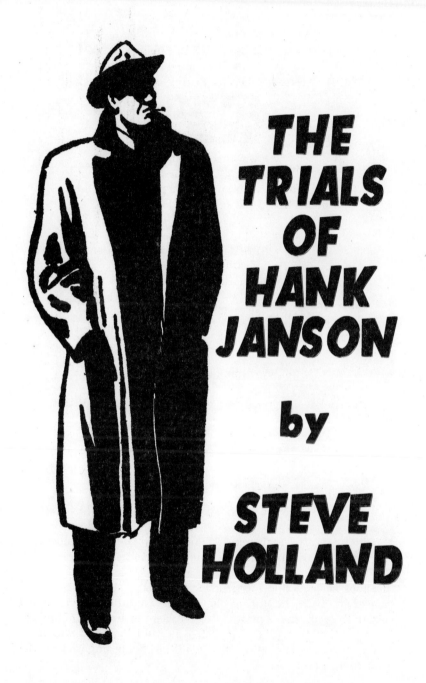

THE TRIALS OF HANK JANSON

by

STEVE HOLLAND

This edition first published in England in 2004
by Telos Publishing Ltd
61 Elgar Avenue, Tolworth, Surrey, KT5 9JP, England

www.telos.co.uk
Telos Publishing Ltd values feedback.
Please e-mail us with any comments you may have
about this book to: feedback@telos.co.uk

ISBN: 1-903889-84-7
Text © 2004 Steve Holland.

Cover by Reginald Heade
Silhouette device by Philip Mendoza
Cover design by David J Howe

www.hankjanson.co.uk

Internal design, typesetting and layout by David Brunt

The Hank Janson name, logo and silhouette device
are trademarks of Telos Publishing Ltd

Printed in India

1 2 3 4 5 6 7 8 9 10 11 12 13 14 15

British Library Cataloguing in Publication Data. A catalogue
record for this book is available from the British Library.

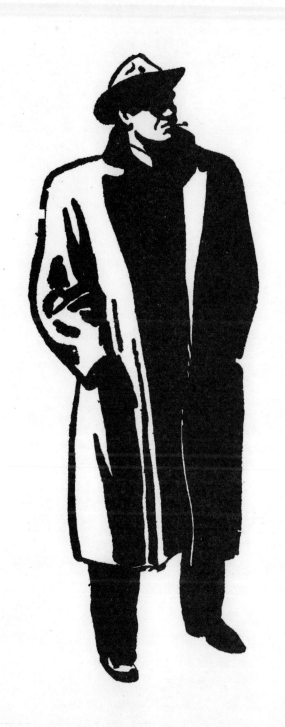

The Trials Of Hank Janson
is respectfully dedicated to
Derek Thomson
No.1 Hank Janson fan

CONTENTS

INTRODUCTION

Briefly successful, briefly notorious, Hank Janson might seem a strange choice of author to pluck from the darkness and push into the spotlight. To many people, Hank is just a fading memory, a purveyor of novels that, in their day, were "dirty books"; hot stuff that stirred more than just the imagination with their vivid portrayals of the violent, dark America that had grown out of the Prohibition era. This was an America filled with corrupt officials and cops, with hard-boiled criminals who would stop at nothing to make a buck, and with the exquisite dames they attracted – dames so beautifully captured in moments of sensual tension on the covers of the novels.

An erotic anxiety underpinned each novel. Typically, the cover would depict a stunningly attractive girl in a state of undress glancing fearfully at a point just outside the frame the artist had chosen for his canvas. In the pages within, Hank – the central character as well as the author – would be faced with violence, both physical and emotional, as he charted a course across the United States uncovering lurid headline stories as a crime reporter for the daily *Chicago Chronicle* newspaper. Hank narrated his tales with a breathless excitement that rushed his readers through more than fifty escapades in five years. Eight million copies of his novels sold to an audience that vicariously shared every kiss and every killing. 100,000 copies of each new novel thundered off the presses every six weeks into the hands of a voracious public.

Until, that is, Hank Janson was declared to be a writer of "obscene" publications. In January 1954, his publisher and distributor were brought before the Recorder of London at the Old Bailey where they were condemned as purveyors of filth and imprisoned. A warrant was issued for the arrest of the author.

To Stephen Frances – the true author of Hank Janson's sexually charged adventures – the official pronouncement that his work was depraving and corrupting stirred up only anger and resentment. For the next thirty-five years, Frances bitterly complained that Janson was not "found" guilty but "made" guilty; that the Janson novels were not obscene and were found so only because of misdirection by the judge, who allowed his personal beliefs to influence the jury against what he considered the "slide into the degeneracy of modern times," in which "the old standards of morals that you have known, [are] gradually slipping away from you and leaving you and your children a miserable inheritance."

The trial devastated the lives of all those involved with the books – in purely financial terms, fines sent Reginald Herbert Carter's publishing company New Fiction Press into liquidation; and Dr Julius Reiter, the distributor, later claimed the case had cost him £20,000. The fall-out from the trial affected the whole publishing scene that had grown up since the difficult days of paper rationing during the War; few were prepared to stand up for Hank Janson and his pulp novels, but when "respectable" publishers were subsequently called into the dock on similar charges of obscenity in the wake of the Janson trial, voices began to rise, from the letters page of *The Times* to the Houses of Parliament.

Few writers can be said to have had such an impact on literature. Without Janson, we might still be reading expurgated versions of *Lady Chatterley's Lover*, and *Fanny Hill* might be consigned to history.

Not that this was any comfort to Stephen Frances, because the changes that made it possible for Penguin to publish *Lady Chatterley's Lover* complete and unabridged in 1960 were at the cost of his own livelihood. Hank Janson was revived once his publisher and distributor were released from prison, but was never as popular again. The changes in the law that would have guaranteed his safety from another prosecution were slow in coming. Newsagents who had been persecuted in 1950-54 were nervous of stocking the titles, starving them of shelf space and sales. 350,000 books and magazines had been destroyed in 740 cases brought against supposedly obscene material. Hank Janson had been the subject of over 1,400 destruction orders alone.

The ghost of Hank Janson haunted Frances for the rest of his life. Only a few years before his death, and already frail from ill health, he still hoped that somehow he could see Hank vindicated, concocting a scheme that he hoped would publicise Hank and allow his author to claw his way out of poverty as writing the novels had done so many years earlier.

In 2004, Stephen Frances's legacy, and the legacy of Hank Janson has not been forgotten. Collectors are forever scouring second hand bookshops and auction houses both online and bricks and mortar for increasingly rare editions of his now highly priced and highly prized books. New fans are being given the chance to enjoy Janson's adventures through Telos Publishing's range of reprints, complete with original covers and text as originally presented. And online there is a wealth of information available through a dedicated website, created to share knowledge and information about the works of an author who was both self-effacing about his success, and who probably wrote more books in his lifetime than most authors could ever dream of matching.

Writing *The Trials Of Hank Janson* has been both a happy and sad experience. I've had a chance to re-read some of Steve Frances's books that have been on my shelves for over twenty years, and they've lost none of their power. Frances once confessed to having only "a limited literary ability," but, flawed as his novels admittedly are, he wrote instinctively, and no other British pulp writer of the time could beat Hank for telling emotionally compelling stories.

Steve Holland,
Colchester, 2004.

11

Acknowledgments

The Trials Of Hank Janson would have been impossible to write without the help of many people, and I would like to take this opportunity to give them my warmest thanks. In particular, I would like to thank: Derek Thomson who, nearly twenty-five years ago, introduced me to Hank Janson, and without whose encouragement and insight this book would never have seen the light of day; Stephen Reiter, who generously entrusted me with the court transcripts of his father's trial; and Jean Fowler, for her insights into working with Steve Frances when he was truly "the best of tough gangster writers".

My thanks also to Harry 'Hank' Hobson, Charles Jackson, Hector Kelly, Jim Moffatt, Mike Moorcock, Victor Norwood, Keith Roberts and Derek Vinter, who were all involved in bringing Hank Janson to life in one way or another as authors, editors and agents; and to all the following who offered help, information and support over the past twenty years: Roberto Pla Aragones, Leslie Bennie, Victor Berch, David and Rita Boyce, John Carpenter, Steve Chibnall, Ian Covell, John Davey, Maurice Flanagan, John Griffin, Peter Haining, Phil Harbottle, Ian Holt, Elaine Lewis and her son Mike, Bill Lofts, Prof J E Morpurgo, Roger Peacey, Jackie Reiter, Manel Sanroma, Leonard Shibko, Richard Skelly, Charles Skilton, Allan Tagg, Richard Williams, Neil Somerville of the BBC Written Archive Centre, Vi Bellamy of Companies House, Bruce Hunter and Tony Crouch of David Higham Associates, Sarah Paterson of the Imperial War Museum, Keith Bardwell of South Tyneside Metropolitan Borough Council, and the staffs of the British Film Institute, the British Library, the Commonwealth War Graves Commission, the London Borough of Camden Local History Library, the Public Records Office, and the Stoke-on-Trent City Archives at Hanley Library.

PART ONE

PRELUDE

CHAPTER ONE

LEARNING LIFE'S LESSONS

In the early, fog-clad morning of 21 March 1918, 6,000 heavy guns began to pound the British positions on the Western Front as the German Army began an onslaught to drive the British from the Somme. Fourteen divisions of General Byng's 3rd Army were dug in around Arras, and the position was thought to be safe. But to the south, the fifteen divisions of General Gough's 5th Army were defending a forty-mile front and had been stretched thin to take over French defensive positions. The French trench system was different from the British, relying more on artillery support, and with no reinforcements arriving, the British – trusting more in their infantry – had been unable to create the fall-back trench line they favoured. In England, Prime Minister Lloyd George was unconvinced that General Haig's Western Front campaign would drive the enemy troops out of France, and began removing Haig supporters from positions of power and starving his armies of much-needed labour. It was a decision that was to prove deadly.

The steady, terrifying bombardment of heavy guns began at 4.40 am. 3,000 mortars added to the thunder. Gas shells began to drop into the trenches. Two and a half hours later, the first wave of German infantry stormed the British lines, looming out of the fog, spectres of death to the British troops sweating and itching behind the Plexiglas lenses of their gas masks, firing blindly.

The Treaty of Brest-Litovsk, signed on 3 March, had signalled the end of the German war on the Russian front, and General Erich von Ludendorff, Germany's principal military strategist, had been able to move heavy artillery and machine guns captured deep within Russia swiftly from the Eastern Front by rail. He also brought in shock troops who were trained and prepared to tear through the British lines, relentlessly advancing over the trenches, leaving squads to occupy small pockets of resistance that were then broken by the second wave of infantry that followed.

From his safe position miles behind the line, Gough suddenly found himself cut off from the battle: communication lines were dead and his headquarters were under threat. As the fog began to lift around midday, the full devastation began to emerge. British planes took to the air against a larger German force, but dared not strafe the ground. Whose troops would they be killing? Gough requested and was granted two more divisions from General Headquarters, but the Western Front was broken. 21,000 British soldiers were taken prisoner that first day.

At the southern end of the British line, at St Quentin, the 47th (or 2nd London) Division were driven back by the German 18th Army. The Division was originally made up from the 4th, 5th and 6th London Brigades, later known as the 140th, 141st and 142nd Brigades respectively, whose men were mostly from South London. They, like the rest of the British 5th Army, were being forced chaotically back across the Somme, resisting valiantly but exposing a weakness in the Allied lines – a weakness that Ludendorff hoped to use to his advantage. Although there were no great military prizes behind the Somme, he believed that by hitting the Front where the British and French lines met, he could drive a wedge between the two, forcing the British to retreat north-west to cover the Channel ports and the French south-west to defend Paris. On 25 March, the Germans broke through and captured Bapaume and Noyon; another step towards their goal of taking Amiens. On 26 March, with German troops a full thirty miles behind the original lines of four days earlier, an emergency conference of Allied generals and politicians was held at Doullens to decide what response was possible. The gloomy meeting ended with Marshall Foch being given charge of the Allied armies.

By then, the German advance was slowing. French troops were moving up from the south to bring the Germans to a halt fifty miles from Paris, and Gough's troops of the 5th Army were holding a line on the Somme, although Gough himself was soon to be replaced by Sir Henry Rawlinson. By 1 April, British troops began moving forward again.

This was a moot point for Stephen Daniel Frances, a conscripted 25-year-old shop assistant, now Rifleman S/ 35243 with the 17th Battalion of the London Regiment, part of the 140th Brigade. He had been medically evacuated from the front line to Rouen and was not to become one of the 60,000 injured who recovered sufficiently to be returned to the front each month. He died on 27 March; his death certificate describes his cause of death simply and starkly: "Died of Wounds". He was buried in an extension to the St Server Cemetery, Block P, Plot 6, Row J. [1]

In France, over 100,000 infantry, mostly eighteen and nineteen year olds who had never seen action before, were shipped in through the Channel ports in two weeks to replace British mortalities.

In England, on 28 March, Stephen Daniel Frances junior turned one year old. Too young to celebrate his birthday. Too young to know that he had no cause to celebrate.

* * *

Although they shared the same name, father and son had rarely seen each other. Frances senior was working as a postman when he married May Isabel Abbott in January 1916. Both were 23 years old, both the children of cab drivers. The newly married couple moved to 77 Crampton Street, Newington Butts, a quarter mile from the Elephant and Castle, and, to earn a little extra now he was a family man, Frances senior became a hosier's assistant. His son was born fourteen months later at 41 Jeffreys Road, off the Clapham Road, in Stockwell.

---

[1] The account of the German advance in March 1918 is based on information from *A Short History of World War I* by James L Stokesbury (London, Robert Hale, 1981), *First World War* by Martin Gilbert (London, Weidenfeld & Nicolson, 1994), and *World War One A Chronological Narrative* by Philip Warner (London, Arms & Armour, 1995). Details of the 47th Division and its Order of Battle are from *Order of Battle of Divisions: part 2A: the Territorial Force Mounted Divisions and the 1st-Line Territorial Force Divisions (42-56)* compiled by A F Becke (London, HMSO, 1936).

After her husband's death, with only the pittance of an army pension to replace his earnings and support her family, May Frances scraped through life in a South London slum. Her young son's earliest memories were, he once described, "of depressing sights, nauseating smells and disagreeable sensations." They lived on the top floor of a tenement house: three flights of wooden stairs with a rickety banister led up to the landing and the flat's gas cooker; through one door was a single bedroom, through the other a kitchen with a shallow scrub-sink and a water tap. There was gas lighting and a coal fire for heating, but the toilet was an outhouse in the back yard, shared with the twenty or so other occupants of the building.

The roofs of these poverty row houses all communicated, and swarmed with vermin. May Frances stood the legs of their bed in discarded paint-pots filled with turpentine to keep it bug-free, but lying in bed, Steve could still stare up at the bugs crawling out from the cracked plaster ceiling. When rain began to pour through, timid complaints did result in some slates being replaced, but the plaster and lathe ceiling bowed ominously after its soaking and all appeals for it to be repaired were ignored for months. Eventually the ceiling came down in three great lumps that landed on the pillows where their heads would have been had it happened at night.

Stephen Frances grew up in the post-war world of disillusion and disenchantment, where the Victorian value of self-sacrifice had been pounded out of returning soldiers by a constant barrage of German guns. The veterans arrived home to pick up their civilian lives in a world that had changed beyond all recognition: Armistice was a brief holiday between the trenches and the depression.

"Everybody in my world was wretchedly poor," Frances later wrote [2]. "An unskilled workman's wage condemned him to live in acute poverty. Our houses were in a terrible state of disrepair, but nobody dared to complain for fear that when we next got into rent arrears we would be turned out into the

---

[2] Except where otherwise noted, quotes from Stephen Frances used in this book are derived from personal correspondence or from Frances's unpublished autobiography, *The Obscenity of Hank Janson*.

street. Whenever my mother was hard up, she hid with me in the basement coal-cellar until the rent collector went away.

"As I grew older, unemployment increased and living conditions became worse. Two men in our street committed suicide and neighbours were often arrested for stealing from market stalls. Bread and jam was the staff of life, eaten in large quantities to keep bellies filled. A little girl who was very ill became the talk of the street because the doctor had ordered she should be fed chicken. Chicken was then a luxury and the family had to pawn to buy it. Everybody speculated upon how chicken tasted."

* * *

Because his mother would work late, Frances spent a great deal of his time during his youth with his maternal grandmother, born May Read but known in the family as "the Old Girl". Steve remembered the Old Girl with wry affection: "She taught me some of life's lessons." The first was how to get blind drunk at the age of six.

Grandma, the daughter of an opera singer, married Charles Abbott at sixteen, principally because she was pregnant. Grandpa told Steve: "All the other chaps were envious that I'd got it in. Little did they know!" They had eight children before Charles obtained a separation order and raced away to enjoy a belated bachelor's recklessness. Grandma was an alcoholic nymphomaniac, and the last straw, according to Charles, was when she and another young woman began to tour the pubs, searching for men and sharing them.

By the time Charles and the Old Girl separated, one daughter, Blanche, had escaped the family home and married a soldier from New Zealand; another, sweet and simple Emmy, was in a mental institution, where she lived without worries and eventually died peacefully; and their younger sister, May Isabel, had already married Southwark-born Stephen Frances, who had just been enlisted into the Army at Whitehall. Two sons, George – known to the family, with typical Cockney humour, as "Podge" because he was thin and hungry looking – and Charlie – "Long'air" because he was prematurely bald – agreed to live with Grandma, in her

19

bug-ridden, two-roomed tenement flat, and support her. Two other sons, Stanley and Arthur, were too young to look after themselves and were placed in the care of the local authorities.

Asking to visit her younger brothers, May Frances discovered they were living in a reformatory, sent there as a temporary measure while a home was being found for them. Arthur, only seven, told May that he had been obliged to clean out drains, and showed her his hands covered with infected sores. In defiance of all regulations and the outrage of the authorities, May seized Arthur and whisked him away to her humble home. There was an almost physical confrontation when the Mayor, accompanied by two policemen, called upon May with the intention of taking Arthur back into custody. May refused to hand him over, flaunting her obvious pregnancy as she held Arthur clutched to her and defying anyone to lay a finger upon her. She won the day, and foster parents were quickly found; Arthur and Stanley were adopted by a well-placed family and were later taken to Canada and a new way of life.

Hanging around outside pub doors waiting for Grandma later became a regular, youthful pursuit for Steve. From time to time, the Old Girl would stagger out to make sure her grandson hadn't been run over, got lost or been kidnapped, and would give him a dog-biscuit to nibble (they were available over the pub counter) or a glass of ginger beer to drink. A new sweet wine called Lisbon Port was introduced to the market, soon to be condemned by the medical profession. The Old Girl plied Steve with it too generously one evening, and he'd drunk at least three glasses before noticing that the world around him was behaving very strangely.

"I never once saw my Grandma sober; neither did I ever see her completely drunk," recalled Frances. "She lived at a staggery, boozy level that she maintained with a steady intake of whisky. She ruled her sons with an iron hand, exercising an octopus control that was a combination of sentiment and willpower. She sent them half-crazy with her tantrums, without losing her mastery of them. As a child, I saw Long'air so incensed he lashed out, an uppercut that lifted his mother up off the floor and hurled her back upon the bed. It was a shocking act. But having witnessed all the drunken screaming, accusations and abuse that preceded it, I wasn't sure she hadn't deliberately goaded Long'air into doing it. The Old Girl got up off the bed, seemingly none the worse, and started again. 'Ah my boy! You'll be sorry. Striking your mother! When I'm dead and gone, you'll remember this!' Long'air hung his head. She always had him beat."

Long'air was considered a very lucky man, because he had a steady job as a storeman. These were days of depression, and most of the neighbours were unemployed. Long'air had been wounded in the War. According to family fable, he'd hesitated to shoot a German who'd sunk down upon his knees and pleaded for his life, and the German had taken the opportunity to seize a gun and shoot him. That was how Long'air had become wounded in the buttock. He'd also been poisoned by mustard gas and was on a life-long diet of raw eggs, broken out on a plate and eaten with a spoon. As the depression deepened, Long'air lost his job, drew the dole and cycled around London learning to be a taxi driver. He had an attack of appendicitis, was operated upon and died soon after of a blood clot. There was no money to pay for a proper funeral, so Long'air was given a pauper's burial, which the Old Girl attended, so drunk that she fell into the grave.

This left Podge with the full responsibility of supporting the Old Girl, and he was no economic tower of strength. Having wrangled himself out of prison and the Army and possessing no references, he had no hope of finding regular employment, so he became self-employed in a business he invented to exploit his own, very special talents. With only a few pence in his pocket, he would visit a market-place and buy stock. This was anything that the street traders were about to throw away or would sell him for next-to-nothing.

"My earliest memories of him are as he trudged home, his unruly, thick, black hair curling out from under his battered cap, a Woodbine dangling from his lips, his hunched shoulders draped in a shabby raincoat and his arms looking abnormally long, dragged down by the weight of the two bags he carried," said Frances.

At home, he made his stock saleable. A few hot-water bottles salvaged from a fire he would wash, dust with talcum powder and repair by plugging any leaks with glue. Clocks that didn't work, he tinkered with until they ticked. He mended broken toys until they worked ... for a time. He bought fire-scorched velvet, which he cut up, stitched up, stuffed with newspaper and called Golliwogs. He gave them wool hair, shirt-button eyes and painted red mouths. He made teddy bears with large floppy ears and long tails.

Podge's true genius was his ability to sell this stock. From time to time, he invited Steve to go to the cinema with him. But before they could go, they had to obtain the price of the tickets. "We set off at midday, Podge trudging along with his two weighty bags and me following in his wake. Today we went north, entering the first pub on that route. I was too young to be allowed inside, but I could hold open the entrance door and watch Podge inside. He ordered a half-pint and then, surreptitiously, drew out from one of his bags a clock, a hot-water bottle, a toy or whatever. He placed it on a table where nobody was seated and then became detached from it. Little by little, the table would fill up with cracked cups, dented ash-trays, off-key mouth-organs or cracked hand-mirrors. Customers became interested, picked up the wares out of curiosity and bought them because they were dirt-cheap. Later, the hot-water bottle would leak when the glue melted, the clocks would stop ticking, the clockwork toys would have their limbs fall off, the mouth organs developed false notes and the Golliwogs leaked newspaper.

"Normally, regular pub-customers would be watching out for 'the bloke wot diddled me,' and landlords wouldn't allow such salesmen on their premises. But Podge had an angle. This was before television was thought of, and even radio was a novelty. Almost every pub had a piano. Podge would sit at the piano and play the sentimental tunes of the day. He was soon surrounded by happy, singing drinkers who urged him to play this or that. Whenever he got up to leave, they sweetened him by buying something. And there was always a couple of half-pints for him on the piano top that he had to drink before he trudged on to the next pub on this route. Customers were tolerant of Podge's damaged wares, landlords wanted somebody to play their piano and Podge made a bare living.

"He was a mild man, with an unusually sensitive face that always wore a soppy grin. His fingers too were sensitive and long. 'Draw me something,' I'd urge. 'Tell me what?' 'An elephant with wings,' I'd suggest. Then he'd open up an empty Woodbine packet and, with a few deft strokes of a stubby pencil outline, an acceptable representation of a flying elephant [would appear].

"His piano-playing was a mystery. He'd never had a lesson in his life and certainly couldn't read music. It was doubtful if he could read anything at all, except kids comics. But he played the piano.

"He couldn't tell me how he did it. He simply 'did it,' he explained. I often watched him play a new popular song for the first time. He'd pick at the notes with one or two fingers, seeming to find a key that suited him. Then he'd play a few notes, adding a few chords, then after a few minutes he'd be playing without sounding a false note. And ever after, the song pattern seemed impressed upon his fingers. I once got him to play very slowly so I could record the notes he played. When I compared them with the original music score, he'd chosen the same key and almost the same accompaniment. Playing the simple popular songs of the day could not be compared with playing Liszt's 'Hungarian Rhapsody', but I often wondered how Podge would have fared if he'd been encouraged to study music."

Podge also had a talent for dealing with creditors. When people needed something, they often paid a Tallyman a few pence every week, and the article was handed over against the last payment. In effect, the Tallyman was a bank. Sixpence put aside on Friday to buy a pair of boots usually vanished before Monday, having been spent on some other necessity. But cash paid to a Tallyman could not be recovered, and eventual delivery of the boots seemed assured. The Tallyman had to be flint-hearted to safeguard his own family. He had to listen unmoved to heart-rending stories. He knew that to hand over the goods before they'd been fully paid for was disastrous. He'd never receive the balance of the payment.

But even the toughest of men can have an Achilles heel, as Frances recalled:

"The Old Girl was an artist at softening up Tallymen. For weeks she'd keep them in suspense while almost deciding to put her name down for new sheets, an overcoat or cooking pans. Simultaneously, she'd wistfully plead to possess the article on order that she was still paying for. There is no denying she had a certain boozy charm and, when confronted with beautiful eyes brimming with tears, some Tallymen succumbed. The next time they came, they handed over the article she wanted, although it hadn't yet been fully paid for. That was fatal. They neither received a new order or final payments on the old one.

"Naturally, they tried to obtain payment. And since the Old Girl often looked after me while my mother was at work, I was often present when a persistent Tallyman called. Although she was almost permanently semi-sloshed, the Old Girl's senses seemed attuned to the approach of a Tallyman. When she heard his tread upon the stairs, she whipped into the other room and locked herself in before he reached the landing."

Podge, who was usually on his knees working, perhaps stuffing newspaper into a cloth bear, looked up as the Tallyman entered. "The Old Girl's out," he'd say.

The Tallyman knew Podge never had a penny. The Old Girl handled all the finance. "I'll wait," he'd say, grimly, and sit down on the bed.

"She might be a long time," Podge warned.

"Why? The pub's are shut, ain't they?"

Podge would shrug his shoulders and resume work. Presently he would look up, his curly black hair flopping over his forehead and his face set in its soppy grin. "Well. How d'yer feel?"

"All right."

"Good."

Then, after a few minutes: "Well. How d'yer feel?"

"I just told you. I'm all right."

"Got a fag then?"

"No. I ain't got a fag."

"How d'yer feel then?"

"How do *you* feel?"

"I'm all right. I just want to know how you feel."

"I've bloody well told you three times. Why d'yer keep asking!"

"Keep your 'air on mate. Don't get excited."

"All right then. Now forget it."

"All I wanted to know was how you feel."

"So now you know!"

"So if you feel all right, there's nothing to worry about."

"Yes there is! My bleeding money!"

Podge would ignore this and go back to his work. After a few minutes he would look up, his soppy grin even soppier. "Tell me," he'd ask. "How d'yer feel?"

That was when the Tallyman usually decided he would come back another day.

* * *

Podge worked long hours, seven days a week, but earned very little. Often he hadn't even the price of a packet of Woodbines. But overriding all demands upon his pocket was the Old Girl's quota of whisky. Podge's first obligation when he arrived home at night was to hand the Old Girl a half-bottle. When he set off on his round of the pubs, he didn't breathe freely until he had earned the whisky money that was his priority; on occasions, he would stay out all night because he hadn't earned enough and was afraid to face his mother. On other occasions, he'd be so desperate that he'd even try to borrow money from his sister Maud, which he must have known was a sheer waste of time.

Maud, the eldest of the Abbott children, was for some unknown reason called "Dob", and the family believed she never removed her hat, not even when she went to bed. It was always clamped firmly on her head, secured there with long and dangerously-pointed hat-pins. Dob went to live with a married man who already had a wife and two children. Together they had six children in quick succession. Like all the Abbott family, Dob knew the extreme poverty of the post-war depression. Harry, the father of her children, was at his wits-end to feed so many hungry mouths, and when he was offered a handyman's job, a small wage and accommodation in the country, he accepted with alacrity. Life in the country was rumoured to be healthy, and somehow the idea got around to May Frances that a few weeks in the country would do her son some good.

"I hadn't much say in the matter, because I was only six or seven years of age," recalled Steve, "and my memories of it all are very dim. But a few memories do stand out very sharply. The accommodation was a simple, one-room wooden shack. I remember being tucked up in a wooden bunk with three little-boy cousins, two heads one end and two heads the other end of the bunk. There was a pail in which everyone urinated, and this pail was tucked away under my end of the bunk. The stench of that pail lingers in my memory even today.

"I suppose the life there was healthy. I vaguely remember living on bread, marge and jam and mugs of tea. After some weeks, I returned home, apparently intact. But I soon sent my mother berserk. I idly scratched my head, and a large louse fell onto the table-cloth.

"My mother, and her sister Dob, unwisely decided that the Old Girl could take me and my cousin Lily to Southend to enjoy a day at the seaside. It was the nearest to a summer holiday that poverty would permit us to have. Return tickets were bought, and the Old Girl was given enough cash to pay for lunch and a few extras. As was usual with the Old Girl, we were late in getting away, and the train out from Fenchurch Street arrived in Southend at midday, just as the pubs opened. So Lily and I played in front of the station pub until it closed at three o'clock. The Old Girl took us to a café for a ham sandwich and a cup of tea and then fell asleep on the beach while we kids dangled our bare feet in muddy pools. The tide was out and the sea was a mile away, so we weren't even able to paddle.

"When the Old Girl awoke, we had another sandwich and cup of tea, and as soon as the pubs opened, Lily and I resumed our ritual waiting outside.

"The pubs finally closed, and as the Old Girl staggered through the late-night streets with us, our plight slowly dawned upon me. The last train home had long since departed, and the Old Girl hadn't a penny left in her purse.

"A kindly taxi-driver allowed us to sleep in a taxi-drivers' wooden shelter, using overcoats as blankets. Luckily, the Old Girl hadn't lost the return tickets, and when we arrived home the following day, we found the family so distraught and desperate that they were even considering asking the police to help them find us."

May Frances worked late over the Christmas period because she could earn double rates, and one Christmas Eve used her wages to pay for a chicken, which was to be collected by the Old Girl. This was to be a really grand Christmas; chicken was a luxury. Steve was sleeping overnight with the Old Girl while May worked Christmas morning, and the plan was that when she got home at midday, the family would have Christmas dinner together.

The Old Girl took Steve with her to collect the chicken from the butcher, as arranged, but on the way home popped in to a pub have a drink. She didn't stagger out until closing time, and by then the bag containing the chicken had gone. All the Old Girl could remember was putting it down somewhere. Somebody else must have picked it up.

* * *

"When I was fourteen and able to go out to work myself, I saw less and less of the Old Girl," Frances recalled. "I was eagerly discovering new interests and becoming increasingly disenchanted by a boozy woman who embraced me like an octopus, huffed whisky fumes into my face and whined: 'Little Stevie doesn't love his Grandma any more now he's got his other friends.'"

One of his interests was chess, a game he was to enjoy playing all his life. In his semi-autobiographical first novel, *One Man In His Time*, Frances wrote: "When I was ten, I used to go up 'rag alley' and pinch books off the second-hand bookstalls. My Ma had to work late some nights, sometimes as late as eleven o'clock, and I'd be at home by myself. It was in those days that I first began to love books. One of those books I stole was a big volume entitled *Illustrated Parlour Games*, and it was full of pictures of people dressed in old-fashioned clothes playing all sorts of games. There were a

27

dozen or more chapters on 'The Art of Chess Playing'. I read these chapters over and over again and made myself some chess-men from pieces of firewood.

"Later on, when I managed to buy a chess set for myself, I taught other boys how to play." [3]

Another growing interest was politics. Within three days of his fourteenth birthday, he had left elementary school and was working on an apprenticeship. Exposed to life beyond poverty row tenements and pubs, he quickly formed a juvenile impression of what was wrong with society:

"A few rich people lived extravagantly while the rest of the world existed miserably in poverty. Wars were fought to maintain these unsatisfactory conditions.

"I could see that in a natural state, a man could be a man and live like a man. He could break down trees to fashion a shelter, hunt animals for food and to fashion skin coverings, forage for berries and nuts and plant crops.

"But a man born poor into a civilised community finds that everything is 'owned'. He is denied the material to build a shelter and a place to build it upon. All meat, fish and fowl are 'owned,' and his only way to keep alive is to stand in line, cap in hand, pleading to be allowed to work hard for less pay than the labour is worth."

Some older boys Frances knew joined the Labour Party League of Youth. "I questioned them excitedly, because I sensed they may have discovered a way to put right all that I saw was wrong. Every answer they gave me confirmed this impression. I asked the question that was a clincher: 'What do you intend to do with the Royal Family?'

"To my immature mind, royalty symbolised the inequality of society. I hung upon their answer, hoping, but fearing it would not satisfy me.

"'They'll have to go' I was told. 'We'll probably put them on the dole.'

"How do I join?" asked fourteen-year-old Steve Frances eagerly.

---

[3] Stephen Frances, *One Man in His Time*, p 43.

CHAPTER TWO

LOOKING FOR MILLER'S FARM

The 1930s were a time of upheaval in the UK. Politically, it seemed nothing was united, with parties divided and subdivided into warring factions.

1931, the year in which Frances joined the Labour Party League of Youth, crucially saw the formation of the New Party, led by Oswald Mosely, a former Labour MP, with the backing of John Strachey, another disaffected Labour and Independent Labour Party (ILP) member, and C E M Joad. The ILP split from the Labour Party following the 1931 General Election (a landslide victory for the Conservatives) because of a standing order that prohibited the nineteen ILP MPs from voting against the decisions of the Labour Party Executive.

Unemployment at this time stood at a record 2.7 million people, nearly one in five of whom had been out of work for over six months. Unemployment insurance benefit was 17s a week for an adult man, 9s for his dependent wife and 2s for each child. Even Prime Minister Ramsey MacDonald acknowledged that: "Unemployment benefit is not a living wage; it was never meant to be that." Many were not eligible for benefits and had to fall back on the Poor Law Authority for relief, and things were about to get worse still with the lowering of benefits and the introduction of the means test, carried out by Public Assistance Committees, in November 1931.

By January 1932, nearly half a million people had been struck off from receiving benefits and twice that number were under investigation and receiving a maximum transitional benefit of 15s 3d per adult man and 8s per dependent woman. Violent demonstrations broke out in boroughs that operated a policy of even lower payments. At the same time, those of

29

the Public Assistance Committees that were disallowing fewer people were being warned by the Government against making "illegal" payments. [4]

The Public Assistance Committees gave way in the mid-1930s to the Unemployment Assistance Board, eventually scrapped under the Determination of Needs Act 1941. The unemployment count steadily fell – although partly through changes in the way the total figure was reached – and in mid-1939 was below 1.4 million; but poverty and malnutrition were still rife.

Unemployment and changes in the law had reduced the power of the trade unions since the days of the General Strike, but the economic security of the middle classes had also been seriously weakened, giving rise to middle class radicalism. The Communist Party of Great Britain had been founded in 1920, growing out of the Third International adopted in Moscow in 1919, and for years had sought to affiliate itself to the Labour Party, only to be rebuffed; things had come to a head when Shapurji Saklatvala, voted in as a Labour Party MP in 1922 despite also being a member of the Communist Party, had stood in the 1924 General Election as a Communist. Labour had then adopted a policy that no member of the Labour Party should also be a member of the Communist Party. This ruling was still in force in 1933 when Stephen Frances, at sixteen and already a member of the Labour Party League of Youth, became an undercover member of the Communist Party.

By 1933, the League of Youth had been heavily infiltrated by the Young Communist League, and Frances was exploring different political ideologies. He had left school at fourteen and started an apprenticeship as an office boy for a trade paper publisher in Fleet Street, but within a few months the publication had been wound up and Frances had found himself unemployed again. "I had many jobs after that," he later commented. "My grandfather accurately surmised that

---

[4] In 1935, R Seebohm Rowntree estimated in "Human Needs of Labour" that a family of two adults and three children required a minimum income of 53s to survive. At that time – when only one in six women worked – nearly half the adult male workers earned under 55s a week and nearly a quarter under 45s a week.

I got the jobs on the strength of the interview but the sack on the strength of my ability."

At sixteen he was employed as a shipping clerk with an import and export agency, and starting to find his voice as a minor political spokesperson, first with letters written to the *Daily Worker* and later with longer features, the earliest of which was a double-page spread with the bold headline "The Victimisation Of Shipping Clerks".

"I received a summons to go to the boss's office," recalled Frances. The boss was a hard man who never seemed to be aware that other people existed unless he had to address them about business. Scowling over his glasses he pointed to a chair.

"I sat down uneasily and then watched with increasing dismay as he opened a desk drawer and took out that day's issue of the *Daily Worker*. He opened it out and smoothed it down flat on his desk."

Underneath the headline was the name of the author. "Did you write this?"

Frances owned up, wondering whether he'd be asked to leave immediately or given a week's notice. The boss stroked his jaw thoughtfully. "Not bad," he eventually conceded, "but don't you think you're overstating it a little ...?"

"He kept me discussing politics for more than an hour, seemed to thoroughly enjoy the discussion," the relieved author later wrote. "Afterwards, whenever he wasn't very busy, he called me into his office for a political argument."

One of the leading lights of the ILP was Fenner Brockway, a dedicated socialist and pacifist who had enrolled in the Progressive League as a teenager and in the ILP in 1907, speaking out and agitating against unemployment at Regent's Park before heading to Manchester to become the editor of the *Labour Leader* at the age of 24. He had been co-founder of the No-Conscription Fellowship in early 1914, and had been jailed for distributing leaflets attacking the Conscription Act. Soon after the completion of his sentence, he had been arrested again, under the Military Service Act, and this time had not been released until four months after Armistice. In 1929, he had been elected to Parliament.

In the 1930s, Brockway was the reason for Stephen Frances's first public speech. Climbing up onto a soap-box at Camberwell Green, Frances introduced him as the main speaker to a crowd of fewer than twenty people, of whom at least half were ILP supporters. "I suffered a bad attack of stage fright when I heard my own tiny voice lost in the vast emptiness of the open air," Frances recalled. "I only once spoke again in the open air, and that was at Speakers' Corner in Hyde Park. I managed to keep talking then for more than an hour, but I was all the time acutely conscious that I am no orator."

In their early days, the ILP had formed a brief alliance with the Communist Party to campaign against the rise of fascism in Germany, but had pulled out when two thirds of the membership objected. Like the ILP, Frances was favourably disposed toward the idea of the changes brought about by the Soviet Revolution, although he had reservations, especially after a trade agreement was reached between Hitler's Germany and Stalin's Russia.

Frances's desire for change meant that he approached new political philosophies with an eagerness that made him stand out. Summoned to the Communist Party headquarters in King Street, he was asked if he would be willing to go beyond being merely an underground member and undergo special training. "Where [the training would take place] was not stated, but I wondered about the Marx-Lenin Institute in Moscow."

In July 1936 in Spain, the Nationalists under General Francisco Franco launched a rebellion against the Popular Front government and the Spanish Republicans. Franco had sought aid from Germany and Italy, and they backed his struggle with men and arms. The government of the Spanish Republic meanwhile sought help from France, where socialist leader Léon Blum had recently led the Popular Front to election victory. Unlike their European neighbours, the French government decided that it was a war in which they should not be involved; Blum initially agreed to send aircraft and artillery, but changed his mind when he was persuaded that the Spanish government was likely to lose, and that French involvement would lead to greater tensions with other

European nations and possibly outright war. The British government had a similar stance: since British interests weren't at risk, why not let the war remain an internal conflict?

A total of twenty-seven nations, including Germany and Italy, signed a non-intervention agreement, although the Non-intervention Committee set up in London to make sure that the embargo of arms and men to Spain was observed by all, was looked upon as little more than a joke. The German and Italian aid continued to pour in to Franco.

Joaquim Maurin, leader of the CNT trade union in Catalonia, became head of the POUM (the Workers Party of Marxist Unification), which fought in support of the Popular Front, aided by nearly 60,000 volunteers from foreign countries who formed the International Brigades, organised by the Comintern (formerly the Communist International). Internal conflict began to make itself felt in the loyalist ranks, the Communists attacking POUM and eventually outlawing them in order to take control of what was left of the government- and loyalist-held areas. This coup was short-lived; Franco's forces soon overwhelmed the Communist forces.

It was in these latter days that Stephen Frances was expelled from the Communist Party. Following the conflict closely, he was in correspondence with Constancia de la Mora, the granddaughter of prime minister Antonio Maura y Montaner and wife of Ignacio Hidalgo de Cisneros, the chief of the Republican air force. Both men were prominent members of the PCE (the Communist Party of Spain), and Constancia herself was a power in the Popular Front press service, through which she supplied information to Frances and others to be distributed in Britain.

Along with his distribution of anti-Franco propaganda, Frances was helping to organise meetings throughout Britain to raise money to aid the Spanish Republicans. At the same time, a man named Alexander Orlov, sent to Spain as a military adviser to the Popular Front and in charge of a large number of NKVD (later KGB) agents who formed a secret police suppressing any anti-Communist sentiment, was ordered by Stalin to ship the gold reserves of the Republic to Moscow where they would be safe from Franco's advancing forces. Six hundred million dollars' worth of gold was shipped from the port of Cartagena via the Black Sea and Odessa.

This caused Frances much consternation: "When I began to enquire why, with so much available wealth, the Spanish Republicans needed the Communist Party to take up collections, I was denounced as a Trotskyite and ejected from the Party."

It was not a bitter departure. "The Communist Party then was composed of many very fine and altruistic people who sincerely wanted to improve social conditions. The Party was a natural home for idealistic youth ... until [they] learned that the Party was not communistic. To be a Party member for a few months is an excellent experience for anyone who [then] breaks free from the Party and does not become a fanatical Party member."

Being dumped by the Communists in 1938 did not relieve Frances of his political ambitions. Since "the Labour Party didn't move fast enough" for him, he became a member of the Socialist League, a group founded in 1932 a day ahead of that year's Labour Party Conference (at which the ILP had finally split from the Labour Party) under the chairmanship of Frank Wise and later (following Wise's death) of Stafford Cripps. Their policies – of protest against the formation of the Unemployment Assistance Boards in place of the Public Assistance Committees to means test the unemployed, and of resistance to capitalist wars – had Frances's enthusiastic support, even if the Socialist League was being condemned by the Communist Party. Nonetheless, in 1936, the ILP, the Communist Party and the Socialist League were in talks about a joint national campaign for unity in the labour movement. This campaign was eventually launched in January 1937. The Labour Party immediately disaffiliated the Socialist League. Rather than face mass expulsion of its members from the Party, the Socialist League folded in 1937.

In 1938, Frances then became a member of the Federal Union, founded on the principle of decentralised government and the devolution of control to local authorities, who should be in a better position to deal with local problems. Frances, with his distaste for Authority (whether it be the government, the police or any other body that was, in his eyes, motivated

34

by a desire for power), would probably have gone further and dismantled the whole power structure of Britain brick by brick. In *One Man In His Time*, to all intents and purposes the autobiography that Frances wished he could write, the unnamed protagonist grows up in the slums of London and struggles to find constant work; he is a fine orator and speaks from the platform at a strike meeting when it is broken up by the police; when the Spanish Civil War commences, our hero heads out immediately to fight with the International Brigade. Amongst all this action, Frances records that the happiest moments in the life of this man surrounded by political turmoil are spent on a farm. Happening upon the farm while he is out of work and hungry, he is invited in to eat; his host, a rough-looking farmer, proves to be pleasant and cheerful company, and our hero is invited to stay to work on the farm: "You can stop here if you like. I can't pay you much, just a few shillings. But you'll get your food and somewhere to sleep," says Mr. Miller, the farmer. "I jumped at the chance," replies author Frances [5], and for the next few months spends his days working hard in the fields and his evenings talking, playing chess, reading books and writing stories, encouraged in his literary efforts by the farmer's beautiful daughter.

Years later, Frances was to find his own "Miller's Farm" in Spain. But that was in the future, at a time when Frances had grown disillusioned with politics. In the 1930s, he worked tirelessly:

"In my search for answers to the world's problems, I attended lectures given by John Strachey [6] at Marx House, Clerkenwell Green, when we used *Das Kapital* as our text-book study. For a time, I was editor of the *Wall Newspaper* there. At Morley College, I learned some German and Spanish and completed a philosophy course under Professor C E M Joad [7]. I was secretary of a Left Book Club group and I joined

---

[5] *One Man in His Time*, p 42.

[6] Evelyn John St Loe Strachey (1901-1963), Labour MP for Aston, 1929-31, who resigned his seat and contested it as an Independent; later became Minister of Food, 1946-50.

[7] Cyril Edwin Mitchison Joad (1891-1953), head of the Department of Philosophy at Birbeck College, University of London. Joad wrote a number of books popularising philosophy and was a regular broadcaster on radio.

the Peace Pledge Union. I spent most of my teens trying to find a way to make the world a better place. I even felt guilty if I took an evening off to go to the cinema instead of doing party work."

Frustration finally took its toll after eight years of intense activity. "After attending hundreds of meetings listening to windbags indulging their egos, and distributing thousands of leaflets, I finally realised I was wasting my time. The mass of the population simply wasn't interested in idealistic dreams. I decided to let the rest of the world go hang and get along the best it could without my help. I abandoned all political activity and decided the best I could do was to bring about as much good as possible in my own limited circle."

* * *

Frances had been arrested for the first time in 1932, at the age of fifteen, in the aftermath of an anti-fascist demonstration.

This was in the early days of Mosely's Blackshirts. John Strachan and C E M Joad, who had been supporters of Mosely's New Party when it was formed in 1931, had soon noticed that Mosely's intentions were not in line with their own ideas for a socialist Britain. Mosely showed his true colours when the New Party became the British Union of Fascists in 1932. Until 1934, the BUF enjoyed the respect of many and was supported by the British press, notably Lord Rothermere's *Daily Mail*, which ran headlines like "Hurrah for the Blackshirts" [8] whilst explaining to its two and a half million readers that Germany and Italy were the best-governed nations in Europe and that the BUF was a safeguard against the real enemy: communism.

It was this acceptance of the fascists that created a partiality in the police force, although Frances's claim that "it was general knowledge that there was a very strong pro-Mosely element within the police force," may be simplifying the case. Sylvia Scaffardi notes: "Police inspectors were also said to be favourably impressed by the show of discipline,

---

[8] *Daily Mail*, 8 January 1934.

the uniformed ranks, the patriotic displays of Union Jacks carried by fascists. But the bias or prejudice of individual policemen would probably count for little in a disciplined force, where the line laid down at the top passed on by their superiors, was the only expedient way for maintaining solidarity and for moving towards promotion." [9]

Whatever the truth of the matter, to the anti-fascists demonstrating against the large fascist public meetings held in 1933 and 1934 – by the summer of 1934, the ranks of the BUF had swelled to as many as 40,000 members – it seemed that the only actions being taken by the police were one-sided, against them. This criticism came to a head at Mosely's infamous meeting at Olympia in 1934, where the police had been ordered not to enter the building unless they believed that something contrary to the law was taking place. Mosely used his own Blackshirt "Defence Force" as stewards at the meeting, and hecklers were singled out in the spotlight and dealt with severely.

Even as the streets outside the gates began to fill with the beaten and bleeding, some kicked into unconsciousness, the police did nothing but try to quell the increasingly angry crowd shouting for the Blackshirts to be arrested.

The use by Police Commissioner Lord Trenchard of *agents-provocateurs* and undercover officers was known to the National Council for Civil Liberties (NCCL, now known as Liberty). The NCCL had been founded by Ronald Kidd [10] in 1934. This followed the Hunger March on London in 1932, during which Kidd had observed two disguised policemen trying to incite the crowds and then arresting two men. On more than one occasion, the police had used strong-arm tactics to break up demonstrations.

It was precisely one such demonstration that ended in arrest for Stephen Frances. A traffic jam in Piccadilly Circus had been seized upon by a number of anti-fascists, departing

[9] Sylvia Scaffardi, *Fire Under the Carpet*, p 97.
[10] Ronald H(ubert) Kidd (1889-1942). Editor of *Civil Liberty*, the journal of the National Council for Civil Liberties, April 1937-January 1942; author of *For Freedom's Cause: An appeal to working men* (London, Woman's Press, 1913), *British Liberty in Danger* (London, Lawrence & Wishart, 1940), and *The Fight for a Free Press* (London, National Council for Civil Liberties, 1942).

from a demonstration in Trafalgar Square, who were using the top decks of buses as makeshift platforms to shout slogans to their gridlocked audience. "I suppose they were breaking the law and could have been arrested, but policemen went up to the top decks and punched the demonstrators, pushed and kicked them downstairs, where they ran the gauntlet of other policemen. No attempt was made to arrest the demonstrators who, when they could, broke free and fled."

Standing in a shop doorway, Frances began taking notes of policemen's numbers. Tucking his notebook away in his pocket, he stepped out of the doorway and began walking away, only to have a heavy hand land on his shoulder. His arm twisted up behind his back, Frances was marched through staring crowds and into narrow side streets. "I braced myself for the beating-up I was going to get." But ahead of him was Vine Street Police Station.

Inside he was charged with "insulting words and behaviour."

"The arresting policeman plunged his hand into my pocket, pulled out my notebook, leafed through it and showed my list of policemen's numbers to the Desk Sergeant. The list was torn up. I had a book issued by the Polish Consulate about the Polish Corridor. This was described on the charge sheet as possession of communist propaganda.

"I was locked in a cell, and the next morning in court the policeman described how I'd shouted, jumped up and down and caused great offence to many people. My word against the policeman's. I was warned I'd be sent away if I did it again and bound over to keep the peace.

"One [later] fascist open-air meeting in Battersea was so closely protected by policemen that anybody venturing to heckle the speaker was very roughly treated. Mounted police patrolled surrounding streets, eagle-eyed for demonstrators. I caught sight of friends coming towards me, talking naturally. Without justification, a mounted policeman charged them, slashing with his baton. They scattered, but one girl went down. When we got to her, she was covered in blood; we carried her to a doorway and phoned for an ambulance.

"When I began to describe this incident to Ronald Kidd next day at the National Council for Civil Liberties office, he broke in: 'Do you know this girl? Two Members of Parliament saw the assault and want to give evidence.'

"Some months later, when the police admitted full liability and paid the injured girl substantial compensation, I felt I'd evened up the score a little for my night in a cell."

* * *

At Morley College, Frances learned Spanish and German, attending evening classes once a week for two hours, during which time students practised pronunciation and were taught a little grammar. "Many friends wondered how I knew Spanish so well that even upon my first visit to Spain, I was able to make many friends. The answer is that I didn't know Spanish very well. But unlike most Britons, I'm not over-concerned about making a fool of myself and betraying my ignorance.

"The purpose of learning a language is to communicate, and for this it was not essential to understand genitive and dative. So I memorised about thirty useful nouns such as water, table, chair, car, and about twenty verbs such as want, eat, buy and so on. That was all."

With this limited vocabulary, and "talking like Tarzan of the Apes", Frances went to Germany in 1939. While his companions consulted pocket language guides and tried to compose their sentences – "Can you please direct me to the nearest restaurant?" – Frances would boldly approach the nearest pedestrian and ask: "Please. Me hungry. Where eat?"

"My method got results. Germans answered me in the same, simple way, and I conducted Tarzan-style conversations while my companions were still struggling to pronounce one correctly composed sentence. Communicating increased my vocabulary, and I learned more German in a day this way than in a month at evening classes.

"I made friends with Germans, and one young man invited me to dine at his home. His family's warm hospitality was marred only when I saw a photograph propped up on the mantelpiece. I'd accepted Helmut as a fine fellow, and it was a blow to see him wearing the SS uniform. He saw me off at Cologne station, which was thronged with soldiers waiting to board troop trains. Overhead, there was the thunder of warplanes flying in formation. 'Come again next year,' invited Helmut. 'Or perhaps I'll visit you in London.'

"I didn't share his optimism. Back in London, I was asked what conclusions I'd drawn from my trip. I reported that all the Germans I'd met were totally convinced that Hitler would invade Poland. But all were equally convinced that Britain would not go to war because of it.

"The next day, Hitler did invade Poland, and England declared war. If it had happened a week earlier, I'd have been in Germany and would have probably been interned."

Instead, Frances was nearly interned in England. "It would have been strange if I had not been a conscientious objector. All my conditioning had bred within me powerful anti-war sentiments," he later said.

"I thought, and still do, that war is madness. Whatever the problems, mass killings organised by opposing governments will not solve them. It was not known in 1939 that fascism would send millions of Jews to the gas chambers, but even had I known it, I am not sure it would have changed my attitude. I am anti-fascist. I would never have raised my arm in the Hitler salute, or shouted *Seig Heil*. If I had been lined up against the execution wall, I would still have refused to acknowledge fascism. I had the same attitude towards the British government that ordered me to take part in the madness of war."

Frances was not the first family member to make a stand against forced conscription. "Just before the First World War, my uncle George ('Podge') was employed as a postman. He was ambitious, and eagerly cooperated with a colleague in an enterprise that required a sack of registered letters to fall out of the back of a Post Office van. The operation was a success, but unwisely was not regarded as a strictly one-off deal. It was repeated. Subsequently a search warrant was issued, and when the police reached Podge's home, they discovered the lavatory blocked by Postal Orders my Grandma had been stuffing down it ever since she'd heard of Podge's arrest.

"Podge didn't like jail, but because there was a war on he got out of prison by offering to join the Army. But Podge didn't like the Army either, and soon his mother was sent for. She found Podge in a detention cell under medical supervision. He gibbered at his mother like a monkey, as he had at everyone for many days.

"Everybody knew he was malingering. But he acted loony so persistently that Authority was non-plussed. What could be done with him? The family had divided opinions. Some said he was half-potty to start with and that's why he could maintain his act so stubbornly; others thought he'd acted potty so long that now he couldn't break the habit. The Army eventually caved in, decided Podge was too much trouble for them and got rid of him. Podge once proudly showed me his Army discharge papers. In the space for comments under Conduct was written, 'Very Bad'.

"There was no family criticism about Podge's lack of patriotism. There was even a slight hint of approval because he'd got the better of the Army. There was no verbal criticism of me either during the Second World War, when the family learned I was a conscientious objector. But I detected the family's disapproval, and even my mother, I sensed, was slightly ashamed of me. I hadn't used my gumption and boxed clever. Instead, I'd declared openly that I wouldn't join the Army, which was a public admission that I was a coward. I was a stain upon the family's escutcheon.

"My first intention was to ignore my call-up papers and, when imprisoned, to hunger-strike until death or release. At twenty-two, I was fanatical in my beliefs. However, others argued that it was much more valuable and more practical to make a public stand against conscription and state a case.

"So it was that I appeared before a Tribunal composed of five judges whose duty it was to examine my conscience as though it was pinned down on a specimen board and decide if I was a genuine objector. Objectors were required to submit their case in writing, and the procedure was for this to be read aloud by one of the judges before cross-examination began. I had written pages and pages, and when it was my turn, the judge gave one weary glance at just one more lengthy screed and suggested that I might like to read it aloud myself.

"I'd been handed a propaganda opportunity on a plate. In a very loud and ringing voice directed at the public gallery, I was able to read out all my anti-war arguments.

"My statement probably surprised the judges. They were accustomed to listening to young men pleading that they shouldn't be forced to join the Army because God directed that they should not kill. In contrast, my statement was a strong, political attack on a government that was compelling the workers to fight against the workers of another nation. I finished: 'I deny the right of the State to use force upon me and others, to impose upon us moral concepts which we believe to be evil.'

"Dr C E M Joad, who was enjoying popularity then as a member of the Brains Trust [on the radio], had written a letter to the Tribunal stating that he believed me to be sincere. I had on occasions been his chairman at anti-war meetings. I'd persuaded him to attend. This letter was read aloud. There followed a long cross-examination, which gave me the chance to praise the ideals of International Socialism, and the Tribunal concluded that I should be exempted from military service. It ordered that I should remain in my present employment as costings clerk. One judge had it recorded that he considered me the best conscientious objector to have ever appeared before them.

"I did not remain in my job as costings clerk, and throughout the War I had many jobs in many different trades. I refused to be 'ordered'. I never notified Officialdom when I left an employment, and when Authority caught up with me and issued me with an order to remain in my new occupation, I promptly gave notice and moved on."

All non-conscripted men were legally obliged to sign a form applying to voluntarily take up fire-watching, and whilst Frances had no objection to sharing the duties of the neighbourhood fire-watch, he did have an objection to signing the form. The penalty was imprisonment. "It violated civil liberty," he said. "I was lucky. I knew many who went to jail for not signing the form, but I was never summoned. Perhaps my neighbours helpfully lost the form I should have signed."

CHAPTER THREE

A GLIMPSE OF BLUE SKY [11]

Frances had first seen his name in print at the age of seven. Blanche, the second eldest daughter of Charles and May Abbott, had married a soldier from New Zealand during the Great War and escaped the "octopus grip" of the Old Girl by moving to the other side of the world. Although it took six weeks for a letter to pass between New Zealand and England, Blanche corresponded regularly with Frances's mother and occasionally sent over a newspaper. In one, young Steve spotted a notice that a descriptive booklet about the South Sea Islands would be sent to anyone who applied. "I wrote my childish application and, months later, Blanche sent on a copy of the newspaper that had printed my letter in full, with my name at the foot of it." It didn't really make up for the fact that they never sent him his South Sea Islands booklet.

"As far back as I can remember, I have always wanted to express ideas on paper. Around the age of nine or ten, I spent pleasurable hours summarising the plots of films in rhyming verse. Writing letters to editors was another pastime."

By the time Frances was fourteen, the *Daily Worker* had started to publish some of these letters; and, as noted in the previous chapter, he was only sixteen when his first full-length article was accepted.

"What is surprising," Frances later admitted, "is that I could write anything an editor considered worthy of publication. I'm a terrible scholar. I hated school so much that I made great efforts to avoid being taught anything. English grammar was a mystery I had no wish to unravel. I enjoyed reading immensely, but I had no enthusiasm for

---

[11] "We, who knew only squalor and poverty, sought also for our glimpse of the blue sky." *One Man In His Time*, pp 11-12.

learning the rules and regulations governing the use of language.

"My early ventures in writing were stimulated by my resentment of the poverty in which I and so many others lived. I wrote articles that were political arguments. Then I discovered I also liked to write fiction. In my spare moments, in the office, on the tram going to work, or even waiting for a bus, I scribbled ideas, or character sketches on the backs of envelopes or scraps of paper. At the back of my mind hovered the dream that one day I might be paid for what I wrote and be able to earn my living at writing. I invented story plots, and they lived in my mind as vividly as though I was watching them on a cinema screen. Then I described what I had seen in words."

Frances's articles soon began to appear in *Peace News*, *The New Leader* and other non-paying publications. When the Second World War broke out, Frances and a friend named George Smith began publishing *Free Expression*, which declared its intention to publish any freely expressed opinion. Frances contributed articles himself: "Is True Pacifism Practical Pacifism?", "Stephen Frances sees Fascism", "The Irish Easter – 25 years ago" and others. *Free Expression* was poorly produced from stencilled pages and priced at a penny a copy, although from the ninth issue the cover announced an "optional" price of 2d. The following month, Frances and Smith added an assistant editor, A R Maddocks, to the roster, and the three launched another magazine, *The Nose*, subtitled "The organ of the unwashed Bolshie". *The Nose* folded seven issues later; *Free Expression* had a reasonably creditable run of twenty-one issues before it too folded with the issue for August 1941.

Both magazines were intended to challenge the censorship imposed by the Government. "We printed any sincere, although unpopular, point of view: that of pacifists, communists, and, of course, fascists." The production was a labour of love. "Our circulation was negligible, which was probably why Authority didn't clamp down upon us, although the police did raid my home in my absence and comb through all my papers and possessions."

Frances was living in Ipswich Road, Tooting, in South London. He changed jobs with regularity, but worked for a time as an estimating clerk for a building contractor with offices in Holborn. During the War, all traffic usually ceased as soon as the nightly air raids began, and travel by underground trains was unreliable. Frances consequently cycled to meetings, pedalling through deserted, blacked-out streets. Cycling and camping were his favourite weekend pastimes, too, but Britain's changeable weather often made it impossible for him to indulge his enjoyment of the open air, and inspired him to buy, for five pounds, a discarded, engineless, single-decker bus from a breaker's yard. For a further ten pounds a year, he rented a plot of land on the banks of the River Thames at Shepperton. He then spent his weekends converting the bus into a habitable caravan that he could use as a weekend retreat.

One weekend, an Austin Seven towed a caravan into the neighbouring plot. Frances helped the owner to position his trailer, and thus met Harry and Pam Whitby. The Whitbys were in their mid-thirties but had a "youthful vigour and outlook", and they and Frances became good friends. Harry was a doctor but had a private income, which meant that he worked only when he was low on cash. He owned a small plane, and a field with a wooden hut that served as his personal aerodrome. The *Evening Standard* dubbed him "The Flying Doctor" when he crashed and published a photograph of his plane, its prop buried in a hedge and its tail pointing skywards.

Harry was fascinated by gambling, and was well-known at horse- and dog-racing tracks. On weekends, he would fly to France to play roulette, carefully recording and analysing the results of every spin until he had developed a "Science of Gambling" – which became the title of a book that he wrote in 1945. His major theory was that on a crooked table, the player could win by playing "corpse" – backing small amounts against the play of bets [12]. Of course, it worked only on crooked tables. And sometimes it didn't work even then. Harry

---

[12] See *The Science of Gambling* by A K K (Pendulum Publications, 1945), p 63.

certainly hedged his bets when it came to writing about them. Harry had also invented a cigarette box that served the owner a cigarette; had played chess against Grand Masters; and was interested in philosophy, although he was not in sympathy with any particular political party.

"Harry and Pam used their trailer as an occasional weekend retreat," recalled Frances, "and I also had a key to it. In London, they lived a nomad life. They would rent a flat, buy furniture for it at an auction and move in. When they wished to move on, they would have the furniture collected and auctioned and use their trailer as a base while deciding where else to live."

Some months after the outbreak of war, Harry and Pam moved their trailer away from Shepperton. Frances then saw nothing of them until 1944, when, walking down Chancery Lane, he came face to face with Harry. Pam Whitby was living in the country and Harry was in London in rented chambers in Lincoln's Inn [13], studying to become a lawyer. At his chambers, he showed Frances some of the furniture he had picked up at auction, including a roulette table that could be converted into an innocent-looking card table in seconds and a billiards table that revolved over to become a plain-topped table.

Whitby, ever on the move, was off again within weeks, but offered Frances the Lincoln's Inn Chambers flat, if he liked. "I certainly did like," said Frances. "I was able to live rent-free in a very comfortable flat and could save fares, because I worked in Holborn and could walk to work in minutes."

Harry and Pam Whitby's gypsy life now included a genuine gypsy caravan, which they'd exchanged for their motor trailer. This they kept on a farm in the Barnet area, where they had also acquired a house. When they returned to London, they rented a small flat in Shaftesbury Avenue, which allowed Frances to remain at Lincoln's Inn.

"Harry and I spent a lot of time playing billiards in his chambers or studying doggy form at White City," noted Frances.

---

[13] 3rd Floor East, 10 Old Square, Lincoln's Inn, London WC2

Frances had walked out of his job and was facing a bleak and moneyless future when Harry asked: "Why don't you go into business?"

"No capital," was Frances's response.

"You're interested in writing," said Harry. "Why not publishing? We'll share half and half. I'll supply the cash and you'll supply the work.

"All I ask," added Harry, "is that you don't lose my money."

* * *

In the November 1944 issue of *The Writer*, Frances placed an advert for contributors to an anthology that was to be the first book from the newly founded Pendulum Publications. *Stories for All Moods* appeared in July 1945, containing thirty short stories and two poems, mostly written by young authors, who, at that time, had few markets when it came to selling short stories. The majority of the contributors to that first volume are little known today, with perhaps only J E Morpurgo, Victor Holdstock (the novelist) and Denys Val Baker (short story writer and anthologist) still being recognised literary names. Jack Morpurgo, later an editor for Penguin Books and Director-General of the National Book League, was then serving as a Captain in the Royal Artillery, and had no idea that his story had appeared: "My patient sister typed from my pencilled manuscripts, with one finger on an old portable, and then tried them on editors of periodicals about whom she knew nothing beyond the names of the journals." [14] Other authors went on excel in other fields ("My real abilities came to life when I became a factory owner, churning out plastic watering cans – the first in the world. How's that for a change in direction!" [15]). Some of the stories came from closer to home: Pamela Whitby contributed a story, as did George Watkins, who had been a writer for *Free Expression*. "No Lady!" was Stephen Frances's own contribution – and his first fiction.

---

[14] J E Morpurgo, private communication, 3 March 1999.
[15] Leonard Shibko (who contributed to *Stories For All Moods No.2*), private communication, 12 January 1999.

Over the next few months, Frances published as diverse a range of titles as could be found from any publisher. They included books of verse (*Cobwebs of Dreamland* by W H Hornibrook, *The City in the Sun* by Peter Noble [16]), a play (*Happy and Glorious* by actor Wilfred Walter), collections of stories by Donald Shoubridge, fairy tales by A C Bailey, a short novel for children by Edmund Burton, and Harry Whitby's *Science of Gambling*. "I didn't know he'd written this book until after I'd started publishing," said Frances. "Harry used no pressure upon me; I published his book because I thought it was worthy of publication. So did Richard Dimbleby, who praised it on the BBC. It sold out."

Arthur Peacock [17], the secretary of the Trade Union Club, wrote *Yours Fraternally*, his reminiscences about such working-class stalwarts as Tom Mann and Ben Tillett, his days working on the staff of the *Clarion* and of the inspired work of the Medical Mission in Spain during the Spanish Civil War.

The illustrator who provided pen and ink portraits of Peacock and others for this title was Philip Mendoza [18], introduced to Frances by the editor of *Russia Today*. Mendoza had exhibited at the Royal Academy and gained some fame before the war as an illustrator of the *Evening Standard*'s Damon Runyon stories. Ebullient and popular, he had dark, swarthy looks and drove around in a big, old-fashioned, racing green Bentley coupe. Later, in the early 1950s, he would go on to provide "good girl art" covers for many of Frances's paperbacks and become a popular comic strip artist. "Phil came on a bit like Oliver Reed, but without the evil temper," recalls Jenny Butterworth, who worked with him in those later years. In 1948, it was Mendoza who drew the silhouette motif that became famous on the Hank Janson book jackets.

---

[16] Peter Noble (1917-1997), noted film writer and critic, presenter of the BBC's *Movie-Go-Round*, editor of *The British Film Yearbook* and *Screen International* and author of many film-related books.

[17] Rev William Arthur Peacock (1905-), editor of *Clarion*, 1927-30, *New Nation*, 1932-34. Secretary-Manager, National Trade Union Club, 1931-48. Became an ordained minister in 1937, serving at Wandsworth Unitarian Church.

[18] Montague Philip Mendoza (1898-1973).

The D-Day invasion of France in June 1944 had involved the use of a series of unique floating docks named Mulberry Harbours. These Harbours had been, in essence, floating blocks of concrete that could be towed across the Channel to create an artificial harbour used to assist the landing of troops and transport. "The BBC broadcast a [radio] programme about the Harbours," recalled Frances, "which was written and produced by Cecil McGivern [19]. I knew Cecil and bought the script from him. I intended to publish it together with photographs of the landing. This was in the early days of Pendulum, and I'd gone out on a limb. If anything went wrong, I'd be in financial trouble. And things did go wrong."

Frances had successfully approached Ernest Bevin MP to write an introduction for the book. While he was still searching for photographs to use as illustrations, however, a General Election took place that displaced the Conservative wartime administration under Winston Churchill. As a result, Frances received a phone call to visit the Houses of Parliament, where he was told by an apologetic secretary that, as Bevin was now an appointed Cabinet Minister, he would be unable to write the introduction as promised.

"I stormed back to the office and asked Muriel [20] to get Mr Churchill on the phone. I doubted that he'd be willing to write the introduction [himself], but the issue never arose, because we couldn't contact him."

Frances was then informed that he could not print the photographs he had obtained unless they were authorised. "I was tenacious. Finally, I had an interview with an officer whose chest couldn't be seen for medals and ribbons, deep down in the basement of that mysterious, stone-built block that had appeared alongside Admiralty Arch in the early stages of the War. He authorised publication."

After all these problems, the book was finally published, under the title *The Harbour Called Mulberry*, in November

---

[19] Cecil McGivern (1907-1963). Worked for the BBC in various capacities as a producer and as Head of Programming, 1930-45; later worked for BBC Television, 1947-56. Awarded the CBE, 1954.
[20] Muriel, Frances's secretary – possibly Muriel Harris (1922-), who had contributed to *Stories For All Moods*.

1945. To add insult to injury, Frances had only been able to obtain enough glossy paper to print a break-even edition.

Finding paper was the curse of all the small wartime publishers. Strict controls on paper supply had been put in place in 1940, as supplies of the raw materials for paper making – esparto grass from Africa and wood pulp from Norway – were cut off. As the War progressed, the ration became even tighter. The Allied victory in Europe in 1945 did not immediately bring an end to the shortage, as the British Government was then faced with the economic problem of keeping imports to a minimum. Newcomers like Pendulum Publications were allowed only the minimum quota, whereas already-established publishers were allowed a percentage of the amount they had used before the War.

"It was a good time and a bad time to start publishing," reflected Frances. "Due to paper rationing and shortage, the bookstalls had little reading matter to display and eagerly snapped up anything on offer. Sales were assured. But it was difficult to obtain paper. I spent almost all my time running around to find printers who had paper to spare, and rarely having success. Most printers hadn't any paper to spare, and those that did gave quotations that included not only their printer's profit but a publishing profit too. Take it or leave it. I left it."

There were a few small printers, however, who had spare paper and whose quotations were not too outrageously high. "So, slowly, Pendulum Publications Ltd began to publish, and, while visiting printers and book distributors, I kept my ears open, asked questions and learned the rudiments of the publishing business.

"All this took place during the last months of the War and into the uneasy peace. The problems and frustrations of publishing were enormous. Everything was in short supply, and delay was a way of life. Bombs fell, disrupted deliveries and destroyed premises. Day-long electricity cuts during one of the worst winters on record stopped printers working and had us sitting at our desks in overcoats, trying to correct galley-proofs with numbed fingers. We were a staunch group of companions all trying to put Pendulum on the map.

"A circle of working friends developed, and on many evenings the offices of Pendulum Publications was a conversational meeting place with billiard balls clicking and the roulette wheel spinning in the background."

* * *

Frances was now employing some twenty people and running a business with a sizeable, albeit irregular, turnover. But he still found himself working for less than he would have earned as a costings clerk. "In practice, it was always touch and go if the business could pay the overheads and wages. It was the 'incidentals' that provided a little economic reserve against rainy days. Some people didn't use their paper quota and instead sold it at a profit. On occasions I was offered Bible paper, or thick paper I couldn't use, while I knew a publisher who had need of it. I bought and resold the paper by telephone, making a considerable profit for a few minutes' work. This 'profit' went into the business.

"A few years earlier, all this activity would have seemed to me to be totally immoral. I could never have imagined myself striving to become a capitalist. All my background and instincts had been opposed to profit-making. When Harry first proposed I should start my own business, I never had a moment's qualm about my ability to run a business; but I seriously considered if I could conscientiously make a profit. All my searching had modified but not changed my conviction that the profit-making of capitalism is immoral and anti-social.

"At the back of my mind was the ridiculous assumption that even with a very limited capital, I could quickly make profits. I soon discovered, as have countless others, that making a profit is more an illusory dream than an attainable objective."

Because of paper rationing, printing costs were very high and publishing profit margins extremely slender. "My first task on Monday was to consult the list of distributors owing us money and chase after them until I'd brought in enough cash to pay the next Friday's wage bill. I often failed and had to rely upon Harry for a temporary loan. We both drew for

51

ourselves the same pay as one of our typists, but Harry never received his and it figured in the books as owing to him."

Harry eventually wanted to occupy his Lincoln's Inn chambers, and Pendulum Publications had to find new offices at a shop in Chancery Lane [21] and rent a stockroom in Southampton Row [22]. "This increased our overheads," noted Frances. "But our staff liked their work and accepted low wages, while editors worked on a royalty basis. If it had been otherwise, we couldn't have stayed in business."

Frances quickly learned some of the many dodges used to obtain paper. A friend phoned: "Remember I told you I'm an election agent? How about writing a Party propaganda pamphlet for me?"

Frances refused: "Why should I? I don't even like your politics."

"Because," his friend pointed out, "as a political agent, I'm granted an allocation of paper for electioneering. Once you've got the paper, you can decide to print or not! Understand? I can let you have half a ton. Pay me in cash at market price but put five percent on for me!"

Frances understood.

Not all deals were without risk. Frances found a source for a certain type of paper, a printer found a buyer in Scotland, and the two pooled their resources and scraped up the cash to buy the paper and send it off. "That night there were very heavy air-raids. I rang my printer friend in the morning: 'Tell me. Did you insure that paper?' There was a long, strained silence. 'No,' he admitted huskily. We both thought of a falling bomb and a truck veering off the road in flames.

"For eight days, neither of us had a good night's sleep. We'd both borrowed money right and left, and were in debt well over our heads. Then the good news came: the paper had got through safely. 'Never again,' vowed the printer, as

---

[21] 81 Chancery Lane, London WC2. This address appeared on publications by November 1946, but the previous address continued to appear around that period as well.

[22] 104 Southampton Row, London WC1; Pendulum shared the building with Nobbs (Cleaners) Ltd, the Woman's International League, and (at 104A) C Charles & Co., opticians.

he counted pound notes of profit into my hand. But the wages bill for that week was ensured."

Pendulum's output was ambitious. As well as novels, a series of poetry collections ("The Pendulum Poets"), anthologies and non-fiction, they published a number of magazines. A quarterly movie magazine was edited by Peter Noble. It staggered through four issues under a variety of titles (*Film Quarterly, Film, Film Miscellany*) but was successful enough when it appeared to warrant a companion title, *Stage and Screen*. *Carnival* was a quarterly ballet magazine edited by Pauline Vigo. Pendulum also launched a science-fiction magazine, *New Worlds*, under the editorship of John Carnell.

Carnell was on demob leave when he met Frank Edward Arnold, a journalist who was also a long-standing science-fiction fan and occasional writer, well known in science-fiction circles. Arnold had just sold a collection of stories to Pendulum [23] and informed Carnell that Frances was interested in launching a science-fiction magazine with Arnold as editor. Arnold, however, insisted that here was an opportunity for Carnell to relaunch his pre-war fan magazine (*Nova Terrae*) on a professional basis.

"At a meeting two weeks later," recalled Carnell, "I spent an entire afternoon telling [Pendulum] how impossible it would be for them to produce a regular science-fiction magazine – shortage of paper, shortage of authors, difficulties of distribution, lack of artists – and, in short, that they were raving mad! The outcome of this meeting was that I was given one hundred per cent control in producing the first professional issue of *New Worlds*! If successful, further issues would follow." [24]

The first issue appeared in April 1946 and was a flop, selling only 3,000 of its 15,000 print run. Still, Frances was convinced that it could be a success, and went ahead with a second issue. Carnell took control of the cover illustration this time, and when the issue appeared in October it sold

---

[23] *Wings Across Time* (London, Pendulum "Popular" Science Series no. 1, 1946).

[24] John Carnell, 'A History of New Worlds', in *A History and Checklist of New Worlds* (London, BSFA Publications, 1959).

out. The first issue was then stripped of its original, uninspiring cover by Bob Wilkin and reissued with a new one reusing the illustration from the second issue. It too sold out.

"When I discovered that bookmakers had no trade magazine," Frances later recalled, "we launched *The Penciller* to fill this gap." Professor A M Low [25] meanwhile worked on producing a monthly science magazine, as well as a volume of essays entitled *Nobody Cares*. Quiz books and crossword books were extremely popular at the time. Pendulum published both.

Frances also wrote his first novel, which appeared under the Pendulum imprint in October 1946. This was the aforementioned *One Man in His Time*, a fictional autobiography of an adventurous young man whose life mirrored Frances's own – growing up in poverty in South London, struggling to find a career that suited him – but whose experiences diverged markedly. The unnamed protagonist was able to join the International Brigade in Spain, had mixed blessings gambling at Monte Carlo (using a system devised by Harry Whitby) and ran a factory manufacturing and selling an ointment called "Rubway". A reviewer for the *Statesman and Nation* commented: "Given such a life, few could have failed to succeed. The real test for this author will come when he tries to write fiction."

Under a second imprint, Ward & Hitchon, Frances launched a Film Book Club with the intention of publishing four books a year under the editorship of Peter Noble. Ward & Hitchon became the first publishers of Hank Janson.

A printer phoned one Friday afternoon to tell Frances that he had purchased enough paper to print 20,000 copies of a twenty-four page demi-octavo book. The problem was that the printer had a machine sitting idle and wanted to have it running on Monday. Frances jumped at the chance. "Leave it to me. I'll deliver copy to you on Monday morning."

---

[25] Archibald Montgomery Low (1888-1956), inventor of the first guided missile in 1917, amongst some 200 inventions. Low also penned a number of other fiction and non-fiction books.

Phoning around, it began to dawn on Frances that nobody had a manuscript of the right length. Peter Noble, Frances's most prolific editor and author, was in the middle of a Film Book Club book; other writers were happy to write something but could not meet the tight deadline.

A distributor phoned wanting 2,000 copies of one of Ward & Hitchon's glossy film star books. "We can't deliver until the end of next week," Frances told him. "These electricity cuts are disrupting everything." To console him, Frances mentioned that he'd soon have a twenty-four pager on offer.

"What category?" asked the distributor.

"I don't know yet. I'm selecting a manuscript," said Frances, only half lying.

"Avoid Romance," warned the distributor. "Too much on the market. Crime, Westerns or Gangster are preferable."

Still unable to find a manuscript, Frances was about to give up and phone the printer. Instead, he turned to Muriel, his secretary, and asked if she was willing to work over the weekend.

At the flat in Lincoln's Inn chambers, Frances dictated while Muriel typed. "We worked all Saturday and until after midnight on Sunday," recalled Frances many years later. "But by then we had the exact number of typed pages the printer needed. I was hoarse from dictating, while Muriel's shoulders ached from hunching over the typewriter."

Frances had already decided on a title for his 15,000 word thriller: *When Dames Get Tough*. The dialogue tried to mimic the first person narrative that Peter Cheyney used for his hugely popular Lemmy Caution novels.

Half way through the book, Frances found that he couldn't escape naming his lead character. In the text, the hero is a commission agent, selling beauty products across America, whose boss is known by the initials S D (not a stretch for S D Frances). The name needed to have an American slant. "Hank" he chose because it rhymed with Yank, and "Janson" because it carried over the "Yank" sound, although few readers would pronounce it correctly, preferring a hard "J". "I'm Janson. Hank Janson. Remember, you sound the Jay like it's a Y," says Hank in the later novel *Skirts Bring Me Sorrow*.

"Hank Janson," said Muriel. "I like it. It rolls off the tongue. Do I put your name on it as author?"

But the first person narrator dictated that the book was another fictional autobiography. Frances put "by Hank Janson" on the cover.

* * *

In 1947, Harry and Pam Whitby decided to go to Australia, and Harry asked if Frances could return his capital investment in Pendulum Publications and buy out his half-share of the business. At the same time, the two received an offer from a third party to buy the company outright.

The winter had been the snowiest in 130 years, and one of the coldest on record. Snow fell somewhere in the UK every day between 22 January and 17 March 1947, and the temperature barely rose above freezing. Drifts of snow over twenty feet high blocked roads and railways, and the army had to be called in to drop supplies to people who had been cut off for days. The sun was rarely seen. When the temperatures did begin to edge up in the second week of March, the thaw was rapid. Melt-water floods broke the banks of rivers, eventually lasting well into the spring, and severe gales whipped across southern England. The country was brought to a standstill. Four million workers were idle because of power cuts; transportation ground to a halt because even rationed fuel supplies could not be moved.

Pendulum Publications also ground to a halt. As the floodwaters slowly receded, the first books finally began to arrive off the printing presses for distribution, but the writing was on the wall. Frances accepted the third party offer made for the company. Harry was repaid his initial investment and went off to Australia, signing over the residency of his flat in Grape Street to Frances, who received a small advance payment for his shares in the company and began planning his future.

Shortly before this, Frances had accepted for publication by Pendulum a boxing-themed book, *White Hope*, written by a former serviceman named Oswald Snelling while he was still in the armed forces. Snelling had recently been

56

demobilised and was sharing a flat with Peter Noble, through whom he had met Frances.

"Pendulum was doomed," recalled Snelling [26]. "Pendulum published *too much*. They went bankrupt about a fortnight after they brought out my *White Hope*. It got into the bookshops, and onto the bookstalls, and actually sold very well, but I never received a penny."

"The new owners of Pendulum Publications almost immediately overreached themselves," explained Frances, "and the company went into the hands of the Official Receiver. The promissory notes that Harry and I had accepted so trustingly [in return for our shares] were never honoured.

"My venture into capitalist profit-making had been instructive, exciting, but not lucrative. On the credit side of my personal account, I occupied a rent-controlled flat and had £250, the nominal payment I'd received in advance for my Pendulum shares. On the debit side, I had no business, many disgruntled business friends who accused me of selling out to unreliable buyers, and no plans for the future.

"It looked as though I'd have to become a disillusioned capitalist, find a job, climb back on the treadmill and once again become a wage-slave."

---

[26] O F Snelling, private communication, 19 March 1985.

CHAPTER FOUR

A HOLIDAY IN SPAIN

Becoming a wage-slave again was not a real option to Frances. He had tasted economic freedom and enjoyed it. "I had no wish to return to working at the dictates of an employer. I'd rather work sixteen hours a day for myself than work a forty hour week for double the pay under a boss.

"I decided to gamble all to maintain my independence. I could have lived a year on my £250. But I put aside enough to live on for three months and regarded the balance as my capital. This capital I had to invest, and recoup with profit, within three months. The profit I made would have to be sufficient for me to live on for another three months while I repeated the operation.

"I couldn't afford to employ anybody but, having had some business experience, I didn't want to do so. I had enough know-how and energy to run a small publishing business single-handed.

"Pendulum Publications had published my first novel, which as far as I knew hadn't earned general condemnation, and I felt confident that if I studied the background, I could write a reasonably acceptable Western."

Frances hammered away at his typewriter, and fifteen days later had the manuscript for a Western. An artist was commissioned to draw the cover, and a printer lined up with enough paper to print 10,000 paperback copies to sell at one shilling and sixpence each.

At that time, the distributor was normally allowed a 40% discount on the cover price; in turn, the shopkeeper was given a 25% discount, from which he made his profit on sales. Frances visited Julius Reiter, the Director of Kosmos International Distributors, and made him a proposition: "This is the dust-jacket drawing and this is the manuscript. I am willing to print and publish an edition of 10,000 and sell you the entire edition for 50% discount."

It was an attractive proposition, almost doubling the usual distributor's gross profit (25% rather than 15%). The only risk was that the books would not sell well enough to cover the purchase cost of the whole print run; but in those days it wasn't very difficult to sell 10,000 Westerns, and Julius gave Frances a written order.

Born in 1907, Julius Reiter was one of five brothers raised in Hof, Bavaria. Trained as a lawyer, he had defended communists in Hitler's fascist Germany and eventually been forced to leave, along with his younger brother, Eric, to join two other brothers, Bruno and Kurt, who had already escaped to Britain.

Arriving in Britain in 1938, the brothers had set up a business, known as the Kosmos International Agency, importing German newspapers and delivering them to other Jewish refugees from a tricycle, building the business up until they could take an office in the Elephant and Castle.

With the outbreak of war, Julius, who had been in the country only briefly, had been abruptly arrested and taken to the Isle of Wight, where he had been stripped of his possessions and interned. Later he had been sent to a concentration camp in Canada. "Luckily for him, he had a manager who kept the business running with scrupulous honesty and handed it back intact when Reiter returned to the UK," Frances wrote.

In September 1947, Reiter created and incorporated Gaywood Press Ltd to put his business on a sounder footing. His co-directors included his younger brother Kurt and his General Manager, Fred Shoubridge.

The economics of Frances's publishing venture were simple. An artist's drawing for the cover of a book cost £10 and the printing blocks for it another £30. A manuscript could be bought for £50 (sometimes less) and printing would cost £250. The total cost for 10,000 paperbacks was thus £340.

At a cover price of 1/6, the gross receipts from the book would be £750, of which Frances would receive 50%, or £375 – a profit of £35, or £85 if he wrote the book himself.

Since the average working man's wage was about £6 a week, Frances would be earning a living wage as long as he could continue to write a new novel and have it published every three months. By shaving down his profits to give Julius Reiter a 50% discount and selling the whole print run, he no longer needed to employ salesmen or packers to get the books into the hands of newsagents. It was a no-risk deal, as long as the deal lasted.

His only problem was actually delivering the books within three months. Power cuts and printing failures dragged out delivery of the first book, and Frances found himself with time on his hands between correcting the galley proofs and waiting for delivery of the finished books. "So I thought up another scheme to earn cash," said Frances. "At Pendulum Publications, I'd spent a great deal of time correcting manuscripts. From the flood of manuscripts that swamped into our office, I knew that the writing bug afflicts a great many untalented as well as talented authors, so I advertised, offering to assist would-be writers to get into print.

"To these hopefuls who applied, I sent a four-page leaflet I'd written, offering to read, correct and give marketing advice about a manuscript for a fee appropriate to its length. I pictured myself profitably time-filling while waiting for the printer to deliver the books to Julius. But only four hopefuls applied. I sent them leaflets and one was sent back within days.

"It was a beauty!

"The man who returned it was probably a university professor. In bold, very red ink, he'd corrected all my grammatical and spelling mistakes, modified my faulty punctuation and underscored clumsy sentences. My leaflet looked like a backward schoolboy's exam essay savagely corrected by a teacher who detested him.

"I hung my head in shame."

* * *

While waiting for the return of his Western, Frances settled down to write another. Reiter, though, was lukewarm. He would give Frances an order this time, but the Western market

60

was swamped, and selling the whole edition quickly was chancy. "Try something else," suggested Reiter.

"Gangsters?" suggested Frances, remembering the escapades of Hank Janson, who had starred in *When Dames Get Tough* and in two other novelettes, *Scarred Faces* and *Kitty Takes the Rap*, published in a single volume under the former title by Pendulum's Ward & Hitchon imprint at 1/6.

"I'll take a chance on one," said Reiter.

Over the next few weeks, Frances wrote *This Woman Is Death* by Hank Janson, the title almost certainly inspired by Peter Cheyney's best-selling gangster novel *This Man Is Dangerous* (1936), which had introduced the wise-cracking Lemmy Caution and launched Cheyney on an enormously successful career as a novelist.

"It flowed so easily from my mind and typewriter," said Francis, "that I wrote a second book, *Lady, Mind That Corpse*. I was optimistic and hoped that Reiter would accept it." He did.

While *This Woman Is Death* was being delivered to Gaywood, Frances was already working on a third title, *Gun Moll For Hire*. He approached Reiter with the same deal as usual, but Reiter had been keeping his eye on the market. For two years, Modern Fiction had been publishing a series of Gangster yarns written by F Dubrez Fawcett under the pen-name Ben Sarto, and these had been selling well at the inflated price of 2/6. Ben Sarto could sell 40,000 copies of a novel, and Reiter realised that Hank Janson could be a creditable rival. He asked for 15,000 copies of *Gun Moll For Hire* rather than 10,000, and added that he would take a further 5,000 copies of each of the first two books. Frances's reaction wasn't the one he expected. Reiter eyed him anxiously as Frances admitted that he had only enough money to print 10,000 books. "You're asking for an additional 15,000. It can't be done."

"How much would you need?" asked Reiter. Frances calculated quickly. It was about £400.

Reiter took out his cheque-book and began to write. "This is a personal loan," he said, handing over the cheque.

"I couldn't believe it," said Frances. "In almost all my dealings in business, everybody was obsessed with getting their hands on money and never letting go of it. Julius trusted me and asked for no guarantees. I never forgot this and, later on, when powerful book distributors made me extremely tempting offers, I never for a moment considered taking the distribution of Hank Janson away from him."

Gun Moll For Hire and the reprints were delivered to Reiter, who said he wanted 20,000 copies of Frances's next Hank Janson title, *No Regrets For Clara*.

One of the luxuries that Frances had inherited from Pendulum Publications was a car. With Hank Janson being successfully distributed by Julius Reiter and sales (and profits) now heading towards twice his original estimate, Frances decided to take a holiday.

* * *

In France, Frances had to apply for petrol coupons to get fuel. He topped up his car at a town close to the Spanish border, as he had read that petrol was hard to come by in Spain. He mailed a postcard to a friend, writing the date and the time on the back. It was a precaution, just in case he should disappear.

The road that wound up to the frontier was broken and pot-holed, like most of the roads in France. It had taken Frances four days to drive down to the Mediterranean, with long detours and countless delays. Some of the villages he had passed through had been reduced to rubble.

At the border, two customs officers, who had been lounging in the shade of a wooden shed, strolled over to the car as it came to a halt before the red-and-white-striped pole of the frontier post.

"You want to go to Spain?" asked one officer, studying his passport. Not many people passed through the post, and then only when it was absolutely necessary. Border peasants and traders. Never tourists.

The Spanish Civil War had dovetailed into the Second World War. Little was known in Britain about the conditions in Spain – only what one read in British newspapers from journalists who had passed through. There were stories of extreme poverty and hunger. No meat, no eggs and only black bread. Spanish guerrillas still made raids across the border from France in this area; and further south, in the heart of Spain, anti-Franco militants still fought on. Tanks and military vehicles could not be used in the mountains, and Franco's military were no match for born and bred mountainsmen.

The officer lifted the barrier, and Frances edged his car forward. There was still some considerable distance of mountainous terrain before he reached the Spanish frontier. Armed Civil Guards watched as he approached and braked. They aimed sub-machine guns at him while they peered into the car, ignoring the passport he proffered.

Eventually they lifted the barrier and let him pass. In his driving mirror, Frances watched one of the Civil Guards stride over to the customs shed – perhaps, Frances thought, to telephone an official about his arrival.

Spain had been isolated from Europe since 1936, and the roads around the border allowed to deteriorate. Frances must have driven a mile, the queasiness slowly leaving his stomach, before he turned a blind corner only to find himself having to stamp hard on the brakes to stop before another frontier barrier.

Four Civil Guards watched stonily as a Sergeant walked over to the car. "You speak Spanish?" he asked.

"If you speak slowly," replied Frances.

"Everything," he said, pointing to the car, and then at the shed. "Inside!"

"Everything" meant just that. Suitcases, some books, tins of food, camping equipment, the tools and cans of oil from the boot of the car. All lined up on the trestle table of the customs shed.

"Why do you come to Spain?" asked the officer, studying his passport. "Nobody comes here on holiday," he stated flatly when Frances gave his reply.

A customs officer stood up and for twenty minutes inspected everything minutely; outside, the Guards were checking the car, one lying half under it, another with the bonnet up. Eventually, Frances's passport was stamped. He packed everything back into his car.

The mountainside road snaked down through volcanic rock and blended into hills through which Frances drove, past olive trees and black-garbed people who paused in their work in the vineyards to watch him drive past. The road was sun-baked, and cart wheels had dug two deep ruts along its centre. There was virtually no motor traffic. He hadn't seen another vehicle for twenty miles. The road snaked on, now lined with tall trees. Barcelona was another two hundred kilometres away, and he had no idea how far he would need to travel before he could get food and petrol. A rusted sign pointed towards a village a few kilometres away. Rosas.

Frances turned the car in the direction of the village.

As he entered Rosas, the road ran along the beach towards a bomb-damaged building with "Hotel" painted drably on its façade. A small crowd gathered, eyeing Frances and his car with unashamed curiosity as he rapped on the door and received no answer.

"Bang hard," they encouraged. "Bang loudly!"

One man stepped forward and hammered on the door mightily.

"Are you open?" asked Frances, when the sleepy-eyed proprietor appeared.

"No. But I can be if you want."

* * *

"I dropped in casually at Rosas to have lunch, and stayed for weeks," said Frances. "I was enchanted by this small village nestling under mountain foothills. On one side of Rosas, a wide, unspoiled beach swept for sixteen kilometres around the bay to the next village, Escala. Not a building marred its beauty. On the other side of Rosas, a broken, asphalt road led up to the lighthouse and ended there. From there on, a footpath followed the coast to Cadaques. This rugged, volcanic rock coast was surely one of the most lovely parts of the Costa Brava! Its savage beauty was breathtaking. Its many bays and coves could be reached only on foot or by boat, and as I followed the footpaths, I often found myself thinking that contemporaries of Christ might have trodden this same track

2,000 years earlier, and it would have looked the same to them then, as it looked to me now."

Spain was a revelation. At the Mar y Sol hotel, where Frances had found himself the centre of attention, he could not resist requesting the impossible for lunch: a nice, thick steak! In Britain in 1948, food was still rationed. Thirteen ounces of meat, one egg, one and a half ounces of cheese and two pints of milk were the weekly allowance.

"Large or small?" asked the hotel proprietor.

"A very large steak, well-done," replied Frances. "A green salad, wine and white bread, not black."

"White, of course," agreed the proprietor, imperturbably. "Will you have an aperitif while you wait?"

"I sat at the bar on a high stool, and after he'd poured my drink, he drifted away," recalled Frances. "I sipped my drink and wondered what I'd be served. I guessed at a garlic-flavoured fried egg, swimming in grease. I'd read a report by a journalist who claimed to have travelled from Irun to Madrid. He'd had to cope with petrol shortage and had lived on meagre rations of black bread, fried eggs swimming in rancid oil, potatoes and beans."

At a table, the maid brought in an excellent green salad on a silver platter. She came back a second time with a silver tureen and removed the lid. "I couldn't believe it. I stared at a lusciously-thick, beautifully-cooked steak. I tested it with my knife. It was as tender as butter."

Later, over coffee and brandy, the hotel proprietor said: "You British have no food. Many starve."

"Not exactly," replied Frances. "But steaks like you serve are unobtainable."

The proprietor was surprised. "Not on the black market?" The black market was illegal in Britain, explained Frances. "Here too. Here everything is black market," said the proprietor with a shrug. "Without it, we'd starve."

The door was flung open and three men with cartridge belts around their waists and guns slung over their shoulders strode in, talking excitedly. They stopped talking when they noticed a stranger, eyeing Frances suspiciously before crossing to the bar and speaking to the proprietor in whispers.

One of the men turned to Frances. "Senor, I invite you to a drink."

"Thank you," Frances replied, nervously crossing to the bar, prepared to be interrogated.

"Senor, you are visiting Spain?"

"I'm on holiday," said Frances.

"Senor, why did you look so startled when we entered?"

"Are you guerrillas?" asked Frances bluntly.

They stared at him for long, shocked seconds. "Amigo," said one of them chuckling. "We've been out shooting rabbits." He slapped Frances on the back, breaking the tension in the atmosphere. "You will enjoy your holiday here. Tomorrow you will go out with us in my boat."

"My 'guerrilla' friends organised an excursion of which I was made the guest of honour," Frances later wrote. "We set off in two boats, the sea was like a millpond and the air so clear that the mountains, stark against the pure blue of the sky, looked as though cut out from cardboard. We landed in a cove, bottles of wine and melons were cached in the sea to keep them cool, and one of the boats circled around dropping lobster-pots overboard. We swam, we lazed in the sun, and when we pulled up the lobster-pots, they yielded a rich haul of brilliantly-coloured little fish, which we cleaned and cooked over a pine-wood fire. The fish were delicious, the wine was rich and, after we'd eaten our fill of melon and grapes, we dozed in the shade of olive trees. In the cool of the evening, we swam again and then sailed back to Rosas.

"It had been a perfect day. Most of my life, I'd known only the background of slum houses and grimy streets. Now, merely to look at the sea, the sky and the rocky coast filled me with joy.

"Every day I made more friends. The overseer of Perelada Castle invited me to see its treasures, and afterwards asked me to sign the visitor's book. I turned back the pages and was impressed by the names I saw. With a flourish, I too signed: Hank Janson. Antonio invited me to lunch at his Manor, a large mansion some miles inland with look-out towers and arrow-slits to repel attackers. During the French invasion of Spain, it had been briefly occupied and lived in by Napoleon. I visited many other homes and farms, met

66

Salvador Dali, took part in a clay-pigeon shooting competition, rode horse-back up into the mountains and spear-fished at night from a boat with a petromax lamp.

"Sadly, however, I had to fix the day of my departure. It was taken for granted there would be a farewell party, and extra tables were borrowed to cater for all of us in the hotel dining-room. We ate, we drank, we made speeches and we drank wine and champagne. It was hot and we took off our shirts. The tables were taken away, we drank, somebody played the piano, we danced ... and we drank!"

In the early hours of the morning, one of the revellers decided it was time to set off some fireworks. "It didn't occur to him, or anyone else, that rockets fly better in the open air. One of the rockets badly scorched the leg of his pants before it zoomed up, hit the ceiling and then ricocheted from wall to wall, hissing sparks while everybody dodged and dived for cover."

One female guest who had drunk far too much, ran out into the night screaming hysterically, chased by Frances and two others, although Frances, with champagne-inspired unsteadiness, tripped over a tree-root and landed on his nose. The Civil Guards, whose barracks overlooked the village square, saw a distressed young girl being chased by two drunken, half-naked men and assumed the worst.

Frances found them in the barracks room and plunged inside, his impetus brought to a skidding halt as a guard levelled a rifle at him. Seconds later, he joined his friends with his shoulders against the wall and his hands on his head.

"There is nothing so sobering as the hard eyes and grim face of a uniformed man who is pointing a gun at you," wrote Frances. The Civil Guards sent for their Captain, who listened patiently to the semi-drunken, hazy stories his prisoners told, before suggesting that everyone should try making a statement the following day.

Frances could not leave, as his passport was being held by the Civil Guard. It was only a few days later that he and his new friends were advised that no official action would be taken and the passport returned. He could now go home.

"Some months later, during my second visit to Rosas, I decided to establish a base here," Frances later said. "As a life-long city dweller, I found village life very enjoyable. Everybody knew everybody, and there was the friendly, helpful atmosphere of a large family. I was a novelty and was talked about. All that was known about me was known to everyone. Everybody greeted me by name and with a smile.

"The villagers possessed a natural independence, which I liked. They had little money, but they were rich. Almost all owned their own cottages. These were picturesque, many at least a hundred years old with walls a metre thick made from big rocks roughly cemented together. Most of the villagers owned small vineyards, olive groves and kitchen gardens; they also had small fishing boats drawn up on the beach. They worked hard, but only for themselves; and when and how they chose. They were not obliged to stand in line to seek employment, and each man felt the equal of all others. These conditions of social equality bred an atmosphere of pure anarchism that was much to my liking."

Frances had found the Miller's Farm that he had written about with such passion only three years earlier. Now he was in a position to live what seemed to him the perfect existence. "Most people have to live where they can earn a living, but I was free of such restrictions. I could do my work wherever I happened to be. Here in Rosas, I could swim and sunbathe from Spring to Autumn and sit out at nights beneath the stars in shirt sleeves without shivering. Where better to walk while wrestling with a plot of a book than along the lonely, limitless beach? Where better to write than in the cool shade of a room overlooking the Mediterranean?"

Rosas had been bombed from the air and shelled from the sea during the War. The hotel was still patched up after being bomb damaged. Since Franco's victory, living conditions had steadily deteriorated; industry was steadily running down, unemployment was high and wages scandalously low. Roads were allowed to crumble away, bomb damage was merely tidied up and not repaired, and public works and services were neglected.

However, a war-wealthy man in Barcelona had decided to rebuild his bomb-destroyed summer residence in Rosas. He planned to build three flats, one of which he would occupy himself. "I met him, he showed me the architectural plans, and I contracted to rent the top flat when it was built. It was in front of the sea, so close to it that I could toss a pebble into it from my veranda. I like spaciousness, and I offered to pay for the two front rooms to be merged into one large salon. I wasn't being extravagant. By British standards, the cost of alterations was negligible, and the rent of the flat was laughable."

With arrangements made, Frances returned to England to take care of his business.

CHAPTER FIVE

THE HANK JANSON TREADMILL

Stephen Frances wrote the Hank Janson books in the first person, describing experiences as if he had actually lived through them, a form of fictional realism that had proven so successful in *One Man In His Time* [27]. Frances had the conviction from the beginning that Hank Janson was going to be a winner. Of course, he was helped in that self-belief by the very nature of paperback publishing as it existed in 1948. If a publisher could get the books distributed into the newsagents, they would sell. The trick was to get the books distributed, and Frances had solved that problem through his agreement with Julius Reiter and Reiter's Gaywood Press.

The Janson titles were selling well, and Reiter wanted Frances to up the print-run to 30,000 copies and deliver them at the rate of one every few weeks rather than one every three or four months. Frances was filled with confidence.

The shortage of reading material had existed since the

---

[27] *One Man in his Time* (London, Pendulum, October 1946). The title comes from Shakespeare's *As You Like It* (Act II vii 139): "All the world's a stage / And all the men and women merely players: / They have their exits and their entrances; / And one man in his time plays many parts." The book was later reprinted as by Hank Janson (London, New Fiction Press, 1953), to which Frances added an introduction in which he said:

"As a child of the slums, I recall vividly the pre-war poverty and hunger. As street urchin, I saw street battles between the unemployed and the police and the misery of impoverished families whose breadwinners were unable to find work.

"I have listened to stories older people have told me, and at a tender age I saw much of this misery. To hard facts I have added the experiences of myself and my friends, combined fact and fiction together in *One Man In His Time.*

"While this book is fiction and does not reflect the life of one man, it may reflect the composite lives of maybe a dozen men who lived in those bitter years between the wars."

early months of the War. The Control of Paper order had come into effect in April 1940, limiting every established publisher to a set percentage of the paper they had consumed in the year ending August 1939. The allocation of paper for new publishers was barely enough to survive on, and many folded after only one or two publications. Others, like Pendulum Publications, survived longer only by seeking out paper on the grey-market – legal supplies that were illicitly diverted for use in printing books.

As we have seen, even this did not give any publisher a guarantee of survival. Pendulum had played the game and ultimately lost.

It was another wartime measure that helped create a niche market for paperback publishers in the post-war years and helped Hank Janson survive. In 1942, Britain had signed the Lend-Lease agreement with America, which allowed the British Commonwealth and other allied nations to draw on American resources; supplies of food and weapons were shipped across the Atlantic in the face of a determined blockade by German U-Boats. In 1945, however, following VE Day, this agreement had been abruptly terminated by President Truman, plunging Britain – still fighting in the Far East – into a financial crisis. A bill for $31 billion was presented just when Britain needed all her resources to repair or rebuild 5 million bombed houses, so that demobilised soldiers would have a home to return to, and replace the 18 million tons of shipping that had been lost during the War; this on top of the economic liabilities that the Government already faced, which had soared by nearly $12 billion.

The only solution to meet repayments was to take out a further loan (of $3.75 billion) from America and maintain a strict grip on the economy. The Government set a target of increasing British exports by 175%, which would help level off the financial crisis by bringing money into the country. The lack (and thus expense) of raw materials, and the fact that factories were still being reconverted from war work back to their previous functions, meant that the target was an impossible goal and the loan ran out far quicker than expected.

71

A condition of the 1945 loan meant that Britain was obliged to restore the convertibility of sterling (which allowed sterling to be exchanged for gold), which it did in 1947. This precipitated another financial crisis, and a quick U-turn as convertibility was again abandoned. The Labour Government's Chancellor of the Exchequer, Stafford Cripps, then had to bring in very strict controls to cut down on dollar imports.

One of the areas to suffer restriction was the import of books and magazines. Prior to the War, American pulp magazines had been widely available in Britain. They had been sent over originally as ballast on empty cargo ships, but had quickly found their way into the hands of hawkers and market stall holders. As their popularity had grown, a number of British distributors had arranged for unsold copies to be sent over and sold cheaply. Woolworth's, for instance, had sold bundles of remaindered "Yank Mags" for tuppence each.

American Crime, Western and Science-Fiction magazines had found a ready market. Especially popular had been the Crime magazines, in which "hardboiled" detectives had begun plying their trade in the 1920s, exemplified by the "Continental Op" stories of Dashiell Hammett and the slang-ridden works of Carroll John Daly, who had more novels published in the UK than in his native America. W R Burnett's *Little Caesar* was a perennial favourite, boosted by the regular appearances of Jimmy Cagney and Edward G Robinson in cinemas.

In the wake of the 1947 economic crisis, rules were passed that set a minimum price of 3/6 (70¢) for imported paperbacks and magazines at a time when the average price was 1/6 (30¢). Importing cheap American fiction became economically unviable.

To fill the vacuum, a number of British publishers launched British reprint editions of American magazines. Others shunned the formality of deals with American publishers for reprint rights and produced their own original magazines and paperbacks written in the "hardboiled" style of American pulp magazines.

An insatiable market for these tough, no-punches-pulled Americanised crime novels had made best-sellers of James Hadley Chase and Peter Cheyney during the War, and returning soldiers looking for more of the same fell upon their successors: Darcy Glinto (Harold Kelly), Ben Sarto (F Dubrez Fawcett) and Hank Janson.

Thus Janson was advertised on the covers of his early novels as "Author of Best Selling Tough Gangster Yarns" and "Best of Tough Gangster Story Authors", and when Frances fabricated the following background for "Hank Janson", many initially believed him to be a real person:

> Hank Janson tells us that he was born in England during the Great War. There is very little of interest about his early school life except, perhaps, when at the age of fifteen, in order to win a wager with his school friends, he borrowed his brother's motor-bike, which he had never previously driven, and entered himself for a cross-country endurance race. He smashed his brother's bike and wore his arm in a sling for months afterwards.
>
> When he was nineteen, he stowed away on a fishing trawler and started on an adventure which was to last until 1945. Not once during the intervening years did he come back to England. He dived for pearls in the Pacific, spent two years in the Arctic with a whaling fleet and worked his way through most of the American States. He obtained his American nationality some years ago, worked in New York as truck driver, news reporter and as assistant to a Private Detective Agency. During the War he served in Burma.
>
> Two years ago he returned to England and is now living in Surrey with his wife and children, spending his time gardening and writing about his personal experiences in a fictional form.
>
> His life has been rich, exciting and dangerous – and almost, it may be said, as true to life as his stories.

"So many readers believed Hank Janson was flesh and blood that Hank Janson fan clubs were formed around Britain that appealed for Hank to pay them a visit," Frances was able to boast.

Certainly in the turmoil of the British paperback publishing industry, Janson was reaping the benefits of import restrictions, but the credit for his continued success in the face of growing competition from other publishers and their *faux* American Gangster writers must go both to his author and to his cover artist.

From the very first, the covers to the Hank Janson novels were superb. When Frances went looking for a cover artist for *This Woman Is Death*, he had the good fortune to discover Reginald Cyril Webb, better known under the name he adopted to sign his artwork – Heade.

Webb, born in Forest Gate, London, in 1901, was the son of a young barmaid, but his upbringing was entrusted to an aunt, who encouraged the artistic talents that became evident in him at an early age. Webb was working professionally before the age of twenty, and by the mid-1930s was providing dust-wrapper art to established publishers Faber, Collins and Hodder & Stoughton, and illustrations for annuals and fashionable magazines such as *Britannia* and *Eve*. Poor eyesight made it necessary for Webb permanently to wear a pair of wire-framed spectacles, and, coupled with his age (38) at the outbreak of War, this meant that he was not required for military service. His cover artwork continued to appear throughout the conflict, on everything from Barbara Cartland Romances and Zane Grey Westerns to W E Johns's stories of the juvenile adventuress "Worrals". His style varied with its subject matter, but was probably at its best on Romances. Webb was adept at drawing beautiful women – often using his young wife, Lily, as a model – and endowing them with grace and allure; his attention to the folds of soft fabric gowns and lingerie and to details of coiffure was matched by his ability to charge the atmosphere around the subject of his painting.

Although vulnerable "dames" dominated the Hank Janson covers, they were never isolated completely. They looked askew at some threat just out of sight of the reader, shocked at a sudden intrusion or fearful of some continuing torment: Although bondage played a part on some of the Janson covers (e.g. *Blonde On The Spot, Torment For Trixy*), and seems to have a particular fascination for collectors, the Heade "dame" was often in control of the situation: the titular *Gun Moll For Hire* or the aggressive blonde of *Honey, Take My Gun* being two good examples. Heade's covers were erotic and never static; they always conveyed a feeling that something was about to happen.

Frances endeavoured to ensure that the text of the Janson novels lived up to the sensuality of their covers. He was a novice writer when he launched the series, but his talent had a raw vitality. The early Janson novels depicted their hero as a drifter making his way across the United States, and each (with the exception of *Gunsmoke In Her Eyes*) was set in a different State. Although patchy in terms of quality, they did give some indication of the strength of their author. The use of different locations for each book was more than a gimmick to provide some variation between the texts. Although Frances never travelled to the USA in his life, he studied tourist guide books so as to his make his locations as authentic as possible; and his text often digressed from the main story to discuss some geographic or economic detail relating to the place where the story was set, ranging from a description of the statue of Elijah Parish Lovejoy at Alton, Illinois (in *Smart Girls Don't Talk*), to the poverty statistics of Iowa (in *Lilies For My Lovely*). In seeking out these details, Frances was able to create complex plots where the setting had some reasonable significance – certainly a step up from the non-specific settings of most gangster stories, which trusted in sex and violence to move the plot along so fast that it didn't matter where the action was located, just that there was plenty of it.

As he progressed, Frances became more confident in using parallel plotting, with two strands of a story taking place concurrently, although he was not always successful in resolving all the threads; in some cases, he had to introduce a completely new character in the closing chapters of a novel to explain away some part of the plot.

Events in the Janson novels generally unfolded for the reader as they did for their hero; it was not until the sixth, *Lilies For My Lovely*, that Hank told a story with the perspective of hindsight. Using Hank as the eyes through which the readers perceived events as they happened was a conscious – and triumphant – choice by Frances, who knew that, through providing realistic detail in his novels, he could make Janson himself seem all the more real. The light-hearted, friendly tone that Frances used to open the books would lull readers into the story. Then, and as the various elements of the plot began to fall into place, they would find themselves emotionally caught up in what was happening. The first person narrative and generally unsophisticated language helped bond the reader with the character as much as it helped Frances identify fully with his creation. "When writing, I completely identified myself with Hank Janson," Frances later wrote. "If a girl slapped his face, my cheek stung. If he smelled rotting fish, I felt nauseated, and if he was exhausted, I had to gulp whisky to revive myself. Because I could identify myself so thoroughly with Hank Janson, my readers were probably also helped to identify with the book's hero, which is what many readers like to do."

Because of his author's total immersion in the character, Janson was prone to run off at the mouth about political issues in a way that other characters in this genre would not – the dialogue and action were not solely there to drive the plot forward. The identification between author and character was particularly noticeable in the emotional depth of Janson's narrative, especially in the later books where Frances was not only immersed in but totally comfortable with his alter ego. Even in the early novels, Janson was able to articulate his emotions in a far more genuine way than his fictional rivals, perhaps nowhere better than in *Angel Shoot To Kill*, where Frances contrasted the sexual chemistry of Janson's attraction to Linda Dargale with the more affectionate relationship he developed with Viola Robins.

The early novels were not without their flaws. *This Woman Is Death*, *Blonde On The Spot* and *Gunsmoke In Her Eyes* were not especially good Janson novels. The latter – a rewrite of *Kitty Takes The Rap* and *Scarred Faces*, two of the Pendulum-era novelettes – certainly seemed out of place in the new series. But for the most part, they were ahead of their rivals in both complexity and variation of plotting and quality of writing.

* * *

The request by Julius Reiter that Frances deliver his Janson novels on a more regular basis coincided with the making by Frances of a deal with Bernard Kaye of Kaye's Rotaprint Agency to write novels for them. Around March 1949, Frances had published a novelette-length story, *Dead Men Don't Love*, under the pen-name Link Shelton, and he was exploring ways of increasing his output. His desire to move to Spain required that he spread his wings, and the money earned from writing for others allowed him to pay for the increased print runs of new Janson novels and reprints of earlier titles without borrowing against future earnings.

Frances's first title under the Bernard Kaye Agency imprint was *Get Me Headquarters* – a piece of hack work that had little of the Janson gloss about it – for which he used the pseudonym Ace Capelli. Over the next few months, Frances continued to pen novels for Kaye, his "Capelli" titles including *This Man Is Death* (echoes of the debut Hank Janson novel), *Chicago Payoff* and *Death At Every Door*. The Capelli titles were typical of the growing tradition of British Gangster novels, involving mobsters, kidnapping and extortion. The best of the bunch was probably *Never Turn Your Back*, in which ace crime reporter Wayne Martin stumbles on a hot murder/suicide story and is forced to leave the *Kansas Chronicle* and the State. It had all the elements that made Hank Janson the "best of tough Gangster authors" – a strong emotional centre in Martin's relationship with Janie, the switchboard operator on the *Toscon Herald*, where Martin is later employed.

Adding the Ace Capelli novels to his workload at the same time as he increased his output of Hank Janson yarns would have been impossible had it not been for a discovery made by Frances. "I am a very slow and very bad typist," he admitted. The solution was to get others to type, as he'd found working on the very first Janson novelette for Pendulum. "In one of my previous jobs, I'd been supplied with a dictaphone to write up engineers' reports about malfunctioning diesel engines. I searched around and bought a second-hand dictaphone."

This was an Emidicta, made by English Musical Instruments; a fairly large machine, with a speaking trumpet, which recorded the voice by cutting tracks on a wax cylinder. Once Frances had dictated a number of cylinders' worth of text, they would be taken around the corner to Hilder's Secretarial Agency in Soho Street to be transcribed and typed up. The wax cylinder model was later replaced with a more compact Emidicta, which recorded on thin paper discs with a magnetic layer; it took about fifty discs for Frances to record a whole novel.

Frances developed a working and writing method that suited himself. "I don't think a sculptor buys a hunk of marble and begins chiselling out the little finger of his subject. I imagine he first hacks out a rough figure and then chips away steadily to obtain the form he wants. That's the way I work with a book. I dictate the book hot and fast. I put in everything that bubbles into my mind. Often the sentences don't make sense but the words conjure up an emotion. I can dictate so very much more quickly than I can type that I can quickly record a first 'rough' novel. Then, when I get back a mass of typed material from the typist, I cut drastically, eliminate ruthlessly, change, adapt, correct and edit until I feel I can send the amended copy for its final typing."

At the Secretarial Agency was an eighteen-year-old typist, Jean Fowler, whose job it became to type up Frances's dictation when it came in. The two got on well, and eventually Frances asked Jean if she would be willing to work for him directly. "Steve lived and worked in a flat at Grape Street. Here he would shut himself off for about a week and would work almost non-stop to dictate the next Hank Janson story, and I would type [it] up," she later recalled. "As typescript appeared, chapter by chapter, Steve would edit. I don't remember that he had to make all that many alterations, as he had a remarkable gift for just 'telling a story' and getting it right first time. It was a magical experience listening to Hank's exploits.

"In between stories, Steve would say 'Come on, sweetie, let's go and enjoy ourselves.' He would take me to the cinema, the theatre, out in his car (he had a lovely Daimler Coupe at the time). We lunched and dined at many famous London restaurants, and as he was in touch with a constant stream of people from the worlds of art, theatre, film and publishing, there was never a dull moment." [28]

The Hank Janson novels were by now appearing roughly once a month, and Frances still managed to find time to turn out an occasional extra novel. For Bernard Kaye he wrote *It's Not Easy To Die* by Steve Markham (published by Art Publicity) and *Lady Take The Chair* by Dave Steel (K Publications). He also penned a second Western, *A Grave For A Coyote*, under the Tex Ryland byline – his first book for Scion Ltd, who then asked him to create a new gangster series for them.

Shrouds Are Cheap appeared under the pen-name Duke Linton, and was the first of eight Linton novels with which Frances was involved for Scion. Binyimin Zeev Immanuel, who ran Scion, was building up a talent pool that already included John Russell Fearn (a talented writer for American science-fiction pulps who had turned to his sights closer to home) and Victor Joseph Hanson, both writing Westerns. During 1950, Scion debuted a whole mob of Gangster novel bylines, including Al Bocca, Sammy Coburn, Ross Angel, Brad Shannon and Danny Spade. The spearhead to this new line-up was Duke Linton.

Although the byline was created by Frances (he had earlier had a character named Chuck Linton in one of his novels), the stories were not. "Immanuel wanted me to write for him," recalled Frances. "I had no time. Instead, I got others to write for me, edited the manuscript and then sold it to Scion."

The "slashing and editing," as he described it, was done with extreme speed, the eight books Duke Linton appearing over just seven months, but with enough of the Janson flavour for Scion's editor Maurice Read to be convinced they were

---

[28] Jean Fowler, private communication, 9 August 1994.

79

Frances's own work: "Knowing Steve's style so well, I reckon he wrote the Duke Linton yarns." [29]

As Frances edited the books so heavily (although the original manuscript showed through occasionally where the editing was a little slipshod), it is impossible to say with absolute certainty who wrote the original drafts, but what evidence there is points to Geoffrey Pardoe, a friend who, according to Frances, was "a speed writer churning out Gangster novels at a great rate."

Pardoe remains one of the more mysterious figures connected with the Hank Janson saga – he was to play an important role during one of the later obscenity trials – and little is known about him. Born Richard Geoffrey Pardoe in 1890, he grew up the eldest of four children in Hanley, Staffordshire, where his father was a schoolmaster and later headmaster. Raised in "an excellent, kindly, nonconformist household," he later attended Birmingham University, where he collaborated on a short book of poetry, *Vacation Verses* by Two Undergrads (the other being Thomas A Baggs). Pardoe first came to London in 1912, and lived there during the Great War. Later he lived and worked for a while in Hastings, Sussex, by which time he had three children. He subsequently moved back to London, living in Kennington, where he had a fourth child around the beginning of the War. According to publisher Charles Skilton, "Pardoe was quite proud of a sudden little affair he had with a younger woman when I knew him, though I imagine she must have been seduced by his talk rather than his appearance." [30] His book, *This Is A Mystery*, was dedicated to "Kath" – Kathleen Read, the sister of Leonora Mackesy (better known as writer Leonora Eyles).

In 1945, Pardoe had written a social study of the declining birth rate entitled *The Baby Famine*, published by Skilton's Torchstream Books. In this, he predicted that, by 1960, the population of Britain would begin to tumble. Pardoe's solutions, which included the legalisation of polygamy and subsidies for people having children, earned him a full-page attack in the *Sunday Pictorial*. It began: "If Mr Geoffrey Pardoe

---

[29] Maurice Read, letter to Derek Thomson, 31 October 1968.
[30] Charles Skilton, private communication, 7 January 1985.

has any sense of decency, he will withdraw from public sale his book *The Baby Famine*."

"Geoffrey Pardoe was a small, elderly man who lived in poor circumstances in South Lambeth," Skilton recalled. "He was always indignant, and my only meetings with him were when he called at my Wimbledon offices. He had a certain writing ability, but my relationship with him was not financially successful. *The Baby Famine* was overtaken by events – with the return of many thousands of ex-servicemen!

"The attack in the *Sunday Pictorial* did nothing for sales, but Pardoe believed that it was my lack of salesmanship that stood between him and the public. So I fitted him up with a sandwich-board and he spent a couple of days in Oxford Street outside Selfridges before conceding defeat!"

A second book written for Skilton (although internal evidence points to it having been started before the War and updated some years later) was eventually published in a specially printed private edition, numbered and signed by the author, by S D Frances in the summer of 1949.

It seems probable that Pardoe was involved in plotting and writing first drafts of the Duke Linton novels, although editor Maurice Read said: "I don't think that Pardoe was really up to it." The evidence, including Frances's own admission that he did it, is against Read.

The Linton novels were a mixed bag. Like the Ace Capelli novels, they were written in the style then being adopted, under the influence of W R Burnett, by British hardboiled writers, who filled their books with gangsters and their floozies. Only one of the Linton novels featured a private eye (and then only briefly). In one instance, the W R Burnett influence showed through a little too closely: the centrepiece of *Bury Me Deep* – a hotel heist – was lifted almost word for word from Burnett's *High Sierra*, even down to the same setting. [31]

* * *

---

[31] See Duke Linton, *Bury Me Deep*, Chapter 4, and W R Burnett, *High Sierra*, Chapter 29.

During the latter half of 1949, Frances was dictating or editorially overhauling a book every fortnight. At the same time, he was dealing with the day to day business of being a publisher. Frances had taken over the stock room at 104 Southampton Row when Pendulum folded, and from there had run a small distribution business selling books by mail order. The offices comprised two rather gloomy rooms, reached by a passage inset between two shops, where Frances stocked such titles as *Compulsion and Doubt* (in two volumes) by Wilhelm Stekel MD, *Auto-Erotism*, also by Stekel, *Intimacy* by Jean-Paul Satre and novels by Charles Jackson (*The Outer Edges, The Sunnier Side*) and Leonhard Frank (*The Baroness*). Pardoe's *This Is A Mystery* was promoted in the price list as: "The most outspoken book we believe ever to have been written on the subject of SEX. To read this book will be an education."

Frances also published, as a limited edition (2,000 copies) numbered and signed by the author, *Sex and Sadism* by Val Vane, a comprehensive study of corporal punishment – including chapters on 'Some Instruments of Flagellation', 'Whipping in Public' and 'Corporal Punishment in Schools' – which asked the thorny question 'Can whipping be justified?'. It was intended to be the first of three books. The other, *Torture Terrific* and *The Story Of Prostitutes – From Babylon To Bayswater*, although advertised as in preparation, never appeared.

Another title that Frances did publish was written by a popular stage hypnotist and lecturer David Stewart. "Margaret [32] was very impressed by a demonstration of hypnotism and aroused my interest," recalled Frances. "I was always alert for interesting activities, learned that David Stewart lived in Woking and asked him to visit me next time he was in London. When I suggested he might write a book, he was eager to start on it immediately. He instantly hit upon a title, *Hypnotism And How To Do It*. I hadn't enough cash to offer him an advance against royalties. Instead, I offered to split any net profits with him. He accepted, raced away, slaved at his typewriter non-stop and presented

---

[32] Margaret ("Madge") was Frances's then girlfriend.

me with a finished manuscript within a few weeks. He didn't quibble with my editing and the book was published under the imprint S D Frances in hard covers and sold for seven shillings and sixpence."

All this extra-curricular publishing only added to the workload. There was still the chore of finding paper and chasing up printers, who were still struggling to get the 30,000 copy first editions of each Hank Janson novel and variously sized reprint editions off the presses and into the hands of the distributor, Julius Reiter. Frances had spread the printing over a half dozen firms in London, including Furnack Press in Friern Barnet, Progressive Press Co in Fleet Street, D J Canty & Co. (aka Bandon Press) in Barons Place, and the Middlesex & Herts Printing & Publishing Co.

"I had a new manuscript ready for printing, but my present printer was still delivering in dribs and drabs the order for 30,000 that he'd been engaged upon for four months," recalled Frances. "If I used the same printer, he might take five months to produce this next book. I was still looking around for another printer when Reg Carter telephoned."

Reg Carter – Reginald Herbert Carter, to give him his full name – was born in Walthamstow in 1919, and had worked as a compositor before the War. Married, he now worked as a sales rep for The Racecourse Press, a print works founded to publish the *Dziennik Polski* (Polish Daily), a newspaper for Polish refugees.

Unlike many paperback publishers, who used flatbed machines (on which a large sheet of paper is picked up and pressed against inked type, removed and replaced by another sheet), The Racecourse Press, being a newspaper printer, had a rotary press (on which paper is fed from a reel and printed both sides simultaneously at high speed). A paperback could be printed in a matter of hours.

The Racecourse Press was looking for work. The paper ration imposed in 1940 was about to be lifted. Although it would not solve all the problems of supply, from March 1950, publishers would no longer be limited to a quota. The paperback publishers were preparing to swamp the market, but only a few had the kind of print runs that made it feasible to print on a rotary press. Modern Fiction, whose Ben Sarto and "Griff" Gangster novels were selling up to 50,000 copies per title, owned their own printing press; most other publishers had print runs of 25,000 and below. The profit in printing on a rotary press lay in keeping the machine rolling and not having to keep breaking it down and setting it up for short runs. Hank Janson had the kind of print runs that made rotary printing possible, although Carter wanted to push the editions up to 40,000. Frances compromised and ordered 35,000 of his next book, *Torment For Trixy*. Carter wanted to print more than one book at a time – the ideal number was five books on the press simultaneously – and, to keep up with his commitments, Frances shut himself away, dictating at breathless speed. The flat in Grape Street was upstairs in a small block, reached by lift, and comprised a living room, bedroom, kitchen and bathroom. Although it couldn't be described as luxurious, it was quite spacious, and was close to the centre of London. Not that Frances had much time to benefit from the attractions of London. "While my corrected copy of one book was being typed for the printer, I was already well into the next book, the early chapters of which were already being typed and being passed back to me for editing. Incredibly, juggling with reprints, we did achieve the target of printing five titles simultaneously.

"I felt more like a factory than an author."

CHAPTER SIX

SUCCESS STORY

Business-wise, Frances had never been in a better position. His paper and printing worries were over; Carter collected the finished manuscripts, then printed and delivered without delay. He and Frances began to develop a strong bond of friendship. Julius Reiter assumed all responsibility for the distribution, and as sales became stronger, asked for larger print runs. Editions of Janson rose from 35,000 to 40,000 to 50,000. The earlier books, long out of print and much in demand, were also being reprinted.

Frances was able to stop writing for Bernard Kaye and Scion; the last of the Duke Linton novels by Frances appeared in September 1950, a few months after his last Ace Capelli, and the names were then assumed by other authors. In early 1951, Frances wrote and published *No Flowers For The Dead* under the name Max Clinten, perhaps to test the market for a new series of novels not featuring Hank Janson; the results were, presumably, not too good, as future novels, even those without Janson as the main character, appeared under the Janson byline.

Another experiment had a similar outcome: in the spring of 1951, Frances tried publishing a magazine, *Underworld*, edited by Hank Janson. The stories, by various hands, appeared under an assortment of Frances-created bylines: Ace Capelli, Max Clinten and Dave Steel; Brad Shannon, who was a regular contributor to Scion Ltd.'s Gangster line ("the best of the bunch," according to Frances) also contributed a story via a request by Frances to Scion editor Maurice Read. Shannon was the pen-name of Victor Joseph Hanson, who had taken over the writing of the Duke Linton novels.

Topping off the first issue was a novelette by Hank Janson written by Frances, who said, "The idea of *Underworld* was that bearing the Hank Janson name upon it would make it sell like Hank Janson novels. We would have a mag at just the expense of an occasional Hank Janson story." But the public didn't agree, and although it sold 30,000 copies, this was, by then, only half the number of a new Hank Janson novel.

In personal terms, things were less rosy for Frances, as his mother, May, was ill. Having half-convinced her that she might like to live in Spain, he made another trip to Rosas to see what progress was being made on his flat.

The flat was nearly complete. The wall between the two front rooms, which Frances had paid the owner of the flats to have knocked down and then rebuilt when he ceased to live there, had not actually been built. "Despite my protests at the stupidity of it, the builder insisted he must build the wall in accordance with his contract. When the last brick was being cemented into position, the builder called me in to see the completed wall. The next minute, picks were swinging and the wall was being knocked down again."

To Frances, the whole village seemed to be painted the same depressing, battleship grey colour. The owner of the flats allowed him to make his own arrangements about decorating, although with only one decorator and house-painter in the village, his choice was limited. Frances had the decorator mix up different blues until he achieved the colour he wanted – a vivid sky-blue – and had him paint a piece of wood as a sample. All the doors were to be painted that colour.

The new portable Emidicta with the paper discs could be used in Spain, which had a 110 volt power supply, so Frances was able to keep up his busy schedule even at the Mar y Sol hotel. Lowering the blinds against the hot morning sun, he stripped down to his underwear and settled back on the bed and began dictating. Every now and then, he would check the recording by pressing the playback button.

After about an hour, there was a thunderous hammering, and the door flew back on its hinges. Two Civil Guards burst into the room, levelling their sub-machine guns.

A commercial traveller had arrived late the previous night and been given the room next door. He had overslept and awakened to the sound, he thought, of his foreign neighbour operating a radio. Dressing quickly, he had hurried down to the barracks to report a foreign spy. The Guards had reached the same conclusion listening outside his door, although the sight of Frances and his dictaphone soon had them laughing.

The next day, the painter sought out Frances at breakfast, wanting his approval of the newly painted doors. "Beautiful," he promised enthusiastically. "Beautiful."

They were the same battleship grey that made the rest of the village look dull and depressing. "Lovely," said the decorator.

Frances pointed to the sample they had prepared. "Why haven't you painted it this colour?" he demanded.

"I put in a dab of green to bring out the colour more, make it sharper," said the decorator. "This is an even better blue than yours!"

"Paint this all again," instructed Frances. "But this time with *my* blue."

* * *

Frances was needed in England, and returned with a new set of discs for the next Hank Janson novel. "Whilst driving up to London from the coast, I passed through the Elephant and Castle cross-roads and, while halted at a traffic light, saw a news placard outside a newsagent's shop that read 'Read Hank Janson. South London's Best-selling Author'.

"It was the first time it occurred to me that Hank Janson had become an established best-seller."

Until this point, S D Frances, Frances's own publishing imprint, had handled all the Janson books. Reg Carter, however, had taken the advice of an accountant, and proposed that they should buy a bankrupt company with a large trading loss to publish Hank Janson, which would yield them quite considerable tax concessions.

Carter also knew where he could buy another rotary press, and, with Julius Reiter distributing the books, the whole company could be self sufficient. It would be a perfect case of vertical integration, with the three of them enjoying not only the publisher's profits but the printer's profits as well. It would mean hiring type-setters, stock controllers, typists, account clerks and dozens of others – precisely the situation that Frances had been avoiding since setting up his own one-man fiction writing factory – but the ambitious Carter insisted that was just the kind of business he could deal with.

"The decision was mine," recalled Frances. "The proposition could only be realised with the money in the kitty, and the kitty was mine, composed of stocks of paper, advance payments to printers, partially-printed books, money owed to me for books delivered, and some, but not much, cash in the bank. Hank Janson was a financial bonanza. My accountant told me that my little one-man business, operating from my small desk in Shaftesbury Avenue, showed a much higher profit than some of his other clients who employed two or three hundred workmen.

"On paper, I was financially well-off. There was some spare cash I could shake free that enabled me to live a little more extravagantly than previously. Now I could take a couple of girl-friends to dinner, pay by cheque, return to my flat by taxi and provide for my guests from a well-stocked drinks cabinet. But I'd been pulling myself up by my own bootstraps. From the beginning, all the money I'd earned I'd ploughed back into the business to pay for ever bigger editions of subsequent books.

"Hank Janson was the basic source of all profit, and as the author, it was commonsense that I should be relieved of all responsibilities so that I could concentrate on writing.

"I sold Carter all my interests in my Hank Janson business for £4,000. I suppose that I passed over to him about £30,000-worth of books and debts [owed to me], which made the sale nonsensical. But I trusted Carter implicitly."

Editions Poetry (London) Ltd had originally been the publishers of *Poetry* magazine, founded by Thurairajah Tambimuttu, a poet from Ceylon who had arrived almost penniless in London in 1938 but who had quickly established himself in the London literary scene around Soho and Fitzrovia. The magazine, first published in 1939, had changed hands after Tambimuttu left to concentrate on a new publishing venture, and by 1947, when Editions Poetry was incorporated, the business had been taken over by Richard

March and Nicholas Moore. Editions Poetry had maintained a reasonably heavy schedule of publishing books of verse and novels, including Lawrence Durrell's *Cefalu*, three books by Henry Miller (*The Cosmological Eye, Sunday After The War* and *The Wisdom Of The Heart*) and two by Vladimir Nabokov (*The Real Life Of Sebastian Knight* and *Nikolai Gogol*) as well as March's own novel, *The Mountain Of The Upas Tree*.

By 1951, they had amassed some considerable debts and, on 8 August 1951, Reg Carter (described on official returns as a merchant and director) took over the company. The next Janson book, *Frails Can Be So Tough*, was published under the imprint of New Fiction Press, which now operated out of the small offices at 104 Southampton Row.

The first hints of trouble were by this point beginning to make themselves heard. In 1950 and throughout 1951, newsagents were being raided and destruction orders were being issued against magazines and books seized by the police. A handful of prosecutions were successfully taken out against magazine publishers: Utopian Press, who dealt primarily with nude photos but also published a number of magazines in which to advertise them, were fined £100 in December 1950 over the content of their magazines *Fads And Fancies, Flip Flap* and *Sultry Stories*. A bookseller in London was fined £10 per title for selling the magazines *Abandon, Allure, Oomph, Sizzle* and *Slick Stories*, and £20 apiece for *Fluff, Jiggle, Surrender* and *Woof*. In the majority of cases, the magistrate simply issued a destruction order and the magazines were destroyed without any prosecutions taking place.

More important to the publishers of Hank Janson was the fact that a number of paperbacks with sexy "good girl art" covers were also being seized. Police officers uncertain as to what constituted an obscene book or magazine gathered up everything just to make sure. Indeed, the police were not there to make any judgments, just to gather evidence, and a destruction order put the onus on the newsagent to challenge the magistrate and defend the books – in other words, the newsagent was guilty until proven innocent. Most newsagents, weighing the possible costs of a court case against the costs of a few dozen magazines and books, usually chose the easier course and let their stock be destroyed.

In April 1951, Archer Press and its owner, Raymond Locker, were taken to court in Stoke-on-Trent and fined heavily for publishing *Make Mine A Corpse* by Michael Storme, *Spoiled Lives* by Pierre Flammeche and *You're Dead, My Lovely* by Gene Ross. This was the first time a publisher of Gangster novels had been specifically targeted, and two of the three books had covers by Heade. The following month, a bookseller in Blackburn was fined £5 for selling *Gunsmoke In Her Eyes* by Hank Janson.

When Reg Carter took over the publishing of Hank Janson, he approached lawyers in the hope of getting advice. Finding out what actually constituted an obscene publication proved difficult to pin down, so he asked his lawyers to vet the manuscripts ahead of publication, only to be told that they could not guarantee he would not be prosecuted.

Julius Reiter was also worried. He went to Scotland Yard to ask for advice on how to avoid buying books that might be seized, only to be told that Scotland Yard did not know what was obscene. "We don't have to know. Our job is simply to seize books if we are told to do so."

With no advice coming from the law, Carter decided to take no chances, and the first three Janson books he published under the New Fiction Press imprint – *Frails Can Be So Tough*, *Milady Took The Rap* and *Women Hate Till Death* – had their intended artwork covers stripped and replaced with plain coloured covers featuring just a Janson silhouette and the price. The covers of the next two books – *Broads Don't Scare Easy* and *Skirts Bring Me Sorrow* – were partially silvered over to obscure the artwork image.

In painting these ultimately "censored" covers, Heade had continued his mixture of eroticism and danger, and with *Broads Don't Scare Easy* had taken the ultimate step of showing a girl clad in only her underwear and high-heels, her breasts not quite covered by her hand. In the growing climate of police raids, Carter backed away from trouble. Although artwork covers returned for the next two books – *Sadie, Don't Cry Now* and *The Filly Wore A Rod* – Heade was asked to retouch his painting slightly for the first of these, to reduce the amount of flesh on show, and to produce a completely new, less erotic, painting for the latter. [33]

The "covering-up" of Heade's beautiful paintings continued for only a matter of months, although, because the practice of replacing artwork covers with plain ones was adopted for the reissues of older titles as well as the first editions of new ones, it meant that a great many books – in the hundreds of thousands – were appeared with only the Hank Janson silhouette.

And, as it turned out, this action was to no avail, because it was the artwork-less *Milady Took The Rap* that first landed Carter in court.

* * *

A phone call in the early hours of 28 November 1951 informed Frances that his mother had died at the Hostel of God at Clapham Common. She had been suffering from cancer for some time.

"All my life, my mother had known only poverty and hard work. She'd sacrificed most of her life to me. Yet in those last few years, when I began to repay her a little, it had been impossible. She was so inured to poverty it had become her strength, the only security she knew. If I hailed a taxi instead of waiting in the rain for a bus, she sat on the edge of her seat watching the ticking meter and clearly suffering. When she reluctantly let me buy her a new coat or dress, she rarely wore them, in case, one day, she was so hard up she would need to sell them. Almost her last words to me were to tell

---

[33] The original Heade cover for *Frails Can Be So Tough* was never used – the original cover stock was silvered over and used on reprints of *Death Wore A Petticoat* when it was reissued by New Fiction Press in 1951. The original cover artwork for *Milady Took The Rap* was used on a reprint of *Lilies For My Lovely* (and the original covers were silvered over for a reprint of *The Jane With Green Eyes*). The original cover artwork for *Women Hate Till Death* is possibly the alternate cover for *Sadie, Don't Cry Now* (the original covers being silvered over for reprints of *Don't Dare Me, Sugar* and *Lola Brought Her Wreath*). *Broads Don't Scare Easy* was later reissued with the unsilvered cover reinstated, but *Skirts Bring Me Sorrow* was never released at the time without the partial silvering. Many of these unused covers are finally seeing print on Telos Publishing's current editions of the books.

me where she'd hidden away the money I'd given her, in case one day I needed it.

"My misery was unbearable. I went out into the street. The sun was shining brightly but my mother had died. In Leicester Square, I bought an expensive ticket for a cinema seat and sat in dark isolation. The film being shown was *The Secret Life of Walter Mitty*. It was excruciatingly funny. That morning, my mother had died, but now I laughed and laughed. And laughed until I cried, and the tears that ran down my cheeks were for the irreplaceable love I'd lost."

A few months later, Frances applied for a divorce. He had married Gwyneth Mary Pratt, the twenty-three-year-old daughter of a retired railway clerk, at the Register Office, St Pancras, on 27 June 1947, but the two had soon separated. Obtaining a divorce in the late 1940s would have been no easy matter, especially as neither partner had committed adultery while they had been together, so instead Frances had had to wait some years before he could petition the High Court of Justice on the grounds of desertion. The divorce was eventually granted in July 1952.

Frances returned to Spain.

By then, his flat was ready for occupation. "All my needs had been anticipated, even to table napkins, cushions and toilet paper. I also had the services of a pretty eighteen-year-old girl who cleaned, cooked and served. She was the eldest daughter of a large, and poor, family." Frances protested ("I was quite capable of looking after myself"), but Pepita was installed to help the "wealthy Englishman" who had come to live in the village.

"I'd bought a small sailing boat with an inboard engine, and my friends now suggested I needed a sailor. [I took on someone called] Adrian [who] was content to work for me, became a close friend, and even occasionally allowed me to sail the boat or drop the anchor."

The lines of communication between Rosas and London were poor. The Spanish telephone network was worn-out through neglect. It was almost impossible to hear anyone phoning from London because of the static.

The Post Office was a tiny shop in the village main street and opened for only three hours a day. A group would gather in the doorway waiting for the bus from Figueras, which brought the daily mail sack. "The letters you send Express Post take even longer to reach me than a normal letter," wrote Reg Carter. "'Of course,' said the postman. 'Express letters always take longer. First I have to give it a number and enter it in this book. Then, when the day's mail is sent to Figueras, the Express letter is sent separately. The normal mail goes straight into the sack for Barcelona and goes out on the next train, but the Express letter has to be entered up in the book in Figueras. It misses the train. Then it has to be entered up in the book when it reaches Barcelona. There too it loses time. So if you want a letter to arrive quickly, never send it Express post.'"

Living in a tiny village meant enduring many inconveniences. The electricity was cut off a dozen times a day. It was supposed to be 110 volts, but never actually attained that level. There were only five or so radio sets in the village, all of them in cafés where villagers would gather, and even with stabilisers that boosted the flow of electricity, they would often fade to a whisper.

The bus to Figueras travelled the road twice a day. It was a single-decker and lacked the two front mudguards. On Thursday, market day in Figueras, the bus was always overloaded with passengers carrying chickens, rabbits and vegetables. Those riding on the roof clung grimly to the rails of the roof-rack and to each other as the bus wheezed, bumped and lurched along the broken road.

The train to Barcelona was straight out of a Western. It took five hours to cover the ninety mile journey, and during long, frequent stops, the passengers would dismount to stretch themselves, or pick grapes from adjacent vineyards. The cooperative driver always blew a warning whistle so that passengers could climb back on the train as it slowly gathered speed. It remained in Barcelona only an hour before it began the long journey back.

The laid-back Spanish attitude toward efficiency was nowhere more evident than when the authorities dealt with Frances's visa. The visa was rubber-stamped in his passport and had to be renewed after ninety days, and had now almost expired.

The Civil Guard in Rosas told him to come back in a week because the official who knew about passports was away. The official didn't return for three weeks, and then informed Frances: "This isn't us. The military should handle this."

The Commandant of the nearby garrison was on leave. Returning two weeks later he said: "I'll have to make enquiries. Give me a week or so." Two weeks later, Frances was told that headquarters had informed the Commandant that it was not a military matter. "Try the Town Hall," he suggested.

The secretary at the Town Hall said he would have to speak to the Mayor about it when he returned from Madrid, where his daughter was about to have a baby.

The Mayor was quite sure it had nothing to do with him. Frances should go to the top, he said, to the Civil Guard HQ in Barcelona. However, the Civil Guard HQ considered it a local matter that should be dealt with at a local level. Frances went back to the Civil Guard in Rosas, who then suggested that it was clearly a matter for the Harbour Master, who was in charge of imports and exports.

But not, it seemed, visa applications.

A friend of a friend introduced Frances to a Secret Service official, who explained why nobody knew how to prolong a visa: "It's because nobody ever wants to stay more than ninety days in Spain. Leave it to me."

More time passed. Eventually Frances was directed to an office in Gerona, where an official rubber-stamped his passport, prolonging it for a further ninety days. Frances looked at his visa and at the calendar on the wall and groaned. Because it had taken three months to obtain, the extension that had just been granted was due to run out the following day.

* * *

Reg Carter didn't like Spain. "He didn't even like holidays," recalled Frances. "Business and printing were his only joys. Wherever he was, he itched to get back to his office. Very, very unwillingly he paid me a couple of visits. He couldn't understand why I wanted to live in a remote village, and complained bitterly of the lack of modern conveniences.

"I persuaded him to come swimming. He stood with water lapping around his calves, eyeing it suspiciously. 'You're sure there's no dangerous fish? There's sharks in the Med, ain't there?'

"'Not around here. Don't worry, fish won't let you get near them. They run. Except for octopus. They're attracted by white. If you stand there much longer, your white feet might attract them.'"

"Doris!" Carter yelled at his wife. "Run upstairs and get my black socks."

However, Carter was in his element as a company director. Since he had taken over the publishing of Hank Janson, the sales had steadily increased, until by 1952 the initial print-run of each new book was 100,000 copies. On 31 March 1952, Julius Reiter and Reg Carter [34] registered Arc Press Ltd. Some months later, work was completed on installing a rotary press. In August 1952, *Whiplash* became the first Janson title to roll off the new production line.

Carter's faith that the boom in paperback publishing would continue was not diminished by the developments that seemed to be causing other publishers problems. Indeed, he was able to capitalise on the problems of one of his contemporaries: Scion Ltd was undergoing a period of instability and a management shake-up that left its authors unpaid, and Carter was able to tempt editor Maurice Read away from the company to edit a new line of Gangster fiction.

Comyns Ltd had published hardcover non-fiction and poetry books in the 1940s, but had vanished from sight by 1951. Carter bought up the company and, in March 1952, had issued a translation of Honoré de Balzac's famous *Contes Drolatiques*, followed by the *Memoirs of Casanova*. In August, four new Gangster titles appeared from some recognisable names: Dave Steel and Max Clinten, two Frances pseudonyms, were revived. Steel's *Beauty Found A Grave* and *Lovely But Deadly* show all the signs of being further Frances-edited Geoffrey Pardoe novels (similar in style and theme to those he had "hacked and slashed" as Duke Linton two years

---

[34] On paper, the company directors were listed as Julius Reiter and Carter's wife, Doris.

earlier); Max Clinten's *No Dame Wants To Die* was by Scion stalwart Michael Barnes; then the Clinten name was passed on to Victor Joseph Hanson (aka Brad Shannon). Dail Ambler, a close friend of Frances's, and one of the few female writers to establish herself in the testosterone world of Gangster fiction, brought her popular detective Danny Spade to Comyns, but as quickly departed to become involved in the setting up of a new rival company, Milestone Publications. Explorer and former Scion author Victor Norwood took the honours as Comyns's most prolific writer, under the pen-name Mark Shane.

But the jewel in Carter's new crown was still Hank Janson. Forty-five Hank Janson novels had been published, with sales approaching five million copies in under five years and increasing at the rate of 4,000 copies a day.

Frances was content. "Writing is hard work and very demanding, but I enjoy it, and those who are lucky and can enjoy their work are lucky indeed. I was content to work hard and have the advantages of a simple, natural life, far away from the hustle, bustle and greyness of city life.

"I had no dreams of attaining wealth and fame," he said, adding fatefully, "which was just as well."

The Author

▲ The masked Hank Janson interviewed at a Soho strip club.

▼ Frances at 50 on one of his infrequent visits to London.

▲ Stephen Frances at the time he created Hank Janson.

The first appearance of Hank Janson. *When Dames Get Tough* was
published by Ward & Hitchon in 1946.

The first full-length Janson novel, published in 1948.

Early novels by Stephen Frances including *One Man In His Time* (1946), which some reviewers thought was an autobiography, and various pseudonymous gangster and western novels.

Lost Heade Covers

In the wake of police activity, publisher Reg Carter attempted to minimise problems by replacing the usual Heade 'dame' with the famous Janson silhouette.

Censored Heade Covers

During the brief period of self-censorship, some covers which had already been printed were partially silvered over. The cover for *Skirts Bring Me Sorrow* did not appear in print until the Telos Publishing reissue in 2003.

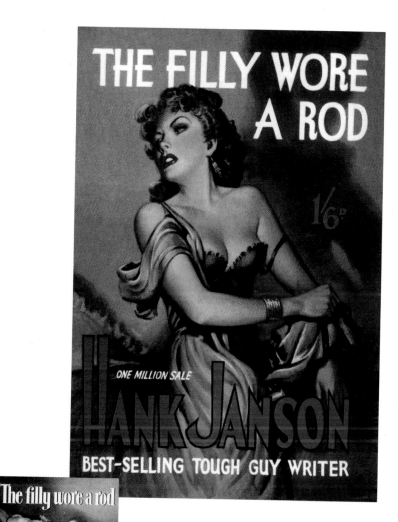

THE FILLY WORE A ROD

1/6D

ONE MILLION SALE

HANK JANSON

BEST-SELLING TOUGH GUY WRITER

The filly wore a rod

HANK JANSON

2/-

BEST of TOUGH GANGSTER AUTHORS

Lost Heade Covers

Heade was asked to paint a number of alternative covers to replace those that had yet to be printed. Note the price of 1/6, indicating that the artwork was painted before the decision was made to raise the price to 2/-.

The Banned Janson Novels

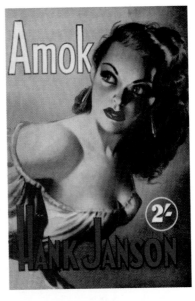

Four of the seven Janson novels condemned as 'obscene' at the Old Bailey.

Experimental Janson

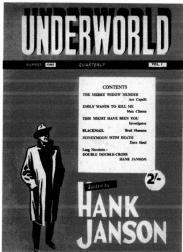

A number of attempts were made to capitalise on the Hank Janson name.
Frances experimented with science- and historical fiction and a Hank
Janson magazine. Carter even produced a Hank Janson comic strip.

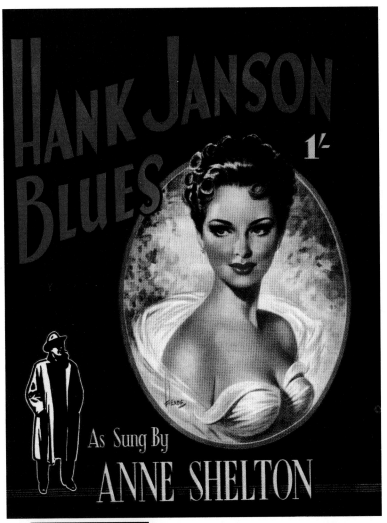

Such was Janson's fame that Britain's favourite singer, Anne Shelton, recorded 'The Hank Janson Blues'. The sheet music, with Heade's portrait of Anne, is a unique example of Janson memorabilia.

Alexander Moring

From the very first title, *Contraband*, the distinctive red and yellow striped title bands of the Alexander Moring titles were a conscious effort to move away from the style of earlier Janson covers. Heade was still involved (with *Cactus* and *Bewitched* being two of the best of his later covers). *Jack Spot* was the fictionalised biography of British gang boss Jack Comer.

Roberts & Vinter / Compact

The Roberts & Vinter titles were mostly illustrated by Spanish and Italian artists before switching, towards the end, to photographic covers. Hilary Brand was an attempt to create a female Janson by Hank's creator, Stephen Frances.

Foreign Editions

▲ Canadian

▲ German

▲ Dutch

▲ Norwegian

The Janson novels were successfully sold throughout Europe, reprints continuing to appear into the 1980s. *Orchids To You*, published in Canada in 1949, was a reprint of *Honey, Take My Gun* whilst the German, Dutch and Norwegian reprints seen here were translations of later Compact Books titles.

Frances, Later Novels

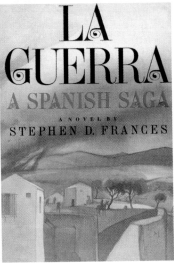

After the sale of the Hank Janson name to Roberts & Vinter, Stephen Frances continued writing for a variety of publishers and under a variety of names. With *La Guerra*, he hoped to escape the pulp market once and for all but excellent reviews failed to translate into sales.

Frances, Final Novels

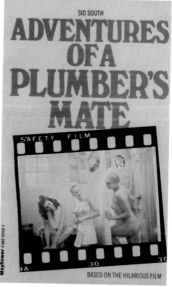

Towards the end of his writing career, Frances turned out a string of pornographic novels – quickly written for quick money. *Adventures Of A Plumber's Mate* was a film-script in the tradition of *Confessions Of A Window Cleaner*, but the results were, to quote Frances, a "balls-up."

The original Heade cover for the unpublished fifth series Hank Janson novel *Woman Trap*. The novel later saw print – with a different cover – as *Framed* in 1955. The cover was subsequently used on the Telos Publishing reissue of *Women Hate Till Death* in 2003.

PART TWO

THE TRIALS OF
HANK JANSON

CHAPTER SEVEN

FALLING TO TEMPTATION

The pin-up has had a long tradition, but was distilled in the 1930s by Hollywood glamour photographers who produced classic images of actresses that are popular even today. Betty Grable, with her fabled "million dollar legs," exemplified the classic pin-up shot on the cover of *Movie Story Magazine* (December 1942): Grable, in a yellow one-piece, figure-hugging bikini and red high heels, faces away from the camera, hands on her hips, her blonde hair pulled up onto her head in tresses. She smiles teasingly over one shoulder. Perhaps not the girl-next-door, but maybe the girl seen bathing down at the beach.

The photograph accompanied the announcement of Grable's next movie, to be called *Pin-Up Girl*, and the term was cemented firmly into the vocabulary of every movie fan who bought the magazine and every GI who ever had a space on his locker or barrack-room wall. 20,000 requests a week poured into Twentieth Century Fox for copies of the photo.

Rivalling Betty Grable as "Queen of the Pin-Ups" were Rita Hayworth and Jane Russell and, later, Ann Sheridan and Lana Turner. In post-war Britain, slim photo books of Hollywood (and British studio) stars brought a little glamour to an otherwise grey and depressing country. Everything was in short supply except sex appeal.

American artists George Petty and Alberto Vargas created the Petty and Vargas Girls for *Esquire*, and painted fold-outs of seductive girls became as popular in the UK as in the USA. Vargas's pin-ups were equally popular in the British magazine *Men Only*.

Although it was not encouraged openly by the military, having barracks turned into a picture galleries of beautiful girls was not discouraged either. There was, after all, a war on, and the morale of the troops was given greater emphasis than the potential moral decline that the sight of scantily-clad women might cause. *Reveille*, the popular forces magazine, printed photographs of girls in their bathing suits, and even "Jane", the *Daily Mirror* comic strip heroine, finally lost all modesty and appeared completely nude in a story printed during the Normandy landings in 1944. News that Jane was "giving her all" quickly spread along the front line, reputedly inspiring an Allied push that saw the 36th Division advance six miles in a single day.

In post-war Britain, the covers of Gangster paperbacks harked back to the cheesecake tradition of shapely females displaying much flesh. The term "cheesecake" is said to have come into use in 1915, when an American photographer named George Miller took a photograph of Russian diva Elvira Amazar. As Amazar was debarking from a ship, Miller asked her to hitch up her skirt a little for a photo, and his editor later commented that she was "better than cheesecake."

"The cheesecake image is based on the notions of teasing and allure," claims Mark Gabor [35], and nowhere was the allure better seen than in Heade's Hank Janson covers.

The relaxation of attitudes towards pin-ups encouraged more daring work from glamour photographers in the UK. There developed a thriving business of magazines and booklets, such as *Eves Without Leaves*, filled with nudes from leading glamour photographers such as Walter Bird, Roye and John Everard. Models became not only recognisable from repeat appearances but popular enough to support collections of photographs. Showgirl and model Desiree was, by 1942, perhaps Britain's best-known nude model.

The legitimacy of the nude as such was unquestionable – the Royal Academy would otherwise have been raided of its old masters – and naturism was a recognised form of public nudity practised since the 19th Century, with the English Gymnosophy Society having pioneered the first naturist site in 1922. Health and naturist magazines had been widely available since the 1930s, titles including the evergreen *Health & Efficiency*, *Sun Bathing Review* and *Naturist*.

---

[35] Mark Gabor, *The Pin-Up: A Modest History*, p 24.

Nude portrait photography, however, had previously been the province of expensive publications in hard covers. As the market for "art" photo magazines and magazines with pin-ups and cheesecake artwork increased, it was the volume available cheaply in newsagents that caused the first stirrings of concern among those in authority.

In the year ending 30 June 1939, only forty offences of obscene publications had been recorded in the UK, most having taken the form of destruction orders issued against magazines and photographs originating in the United States or France; in only nine cases had the offending material originated in the UK. In the eighteen month period from July 1939 to December 1940, the number of cases had fallen further, to forty-seven, and again, most – thirty-six – had involved publications from abroad. [36]

Gangster novels, deliberately sexy and violent and available widely, were an early target of the establishment. James Hadley Chase (Rene Raymond) and Darcy Glinto (Harold Kelly) were targeted in 1942; booksellers selling copies of *Miss Callaghan Comes to Grief* by Chase and *Road Floozie* by Glinto were successfully prosecuted, and Raymond, Kelly and their publishers all found themselves in the Old Bailey on 19 May 1942. Rene Raymond pleaded not guilty to charges of publishing an obscene novel, but was found guilty and fined £100. In the light of that verdict, Kelly changed his original not guilty plea to one of guilty and was fined £50.

However, apart from one or two more cases where booksellers continued to sell these titles, there were few major problems until 1950 when, with the restrictions lifted on paper supply, hundreds of new magazines and books began to flood the market. A number of booksellers and one or two companies were successfully prosecuted in the latter months of 1950 for carrying obscene material.

The standard sequence of events undertaken in a police investigation was laid out by Superintendent John G Gosling of the CID, New Scotland Yard, who stated:

---

[36] FO 371/30984 League of Nations Annual Report. Summary of annual reports for 1939-40 on obscene publications.

(1) When it is known or suspected that a person is dealing in pornographic literature, a test purchase is made and, should it be considered obscene, the purchase is laid before a Magistrate who then decides whether or not a warrant be granted under Section 1, Obscene Publications Act, 1857, to search the premises.

(2) In the event of the warrant being granted, the premises are searched by police and any material considered obscene is seized. [37]

In most cases, a destruction order would then be issued against the books and magazines seized, and it was the choice of the defendant whether he wanted to defend the items and have the case heard before a jury, or to not contest the destruction order. Where the newsagent pleaded no contest, the books were taken away and destroyed and the matter was at an end as far as he was concerned.

In April 1951, Mr F Thornton of the Home Office circulated a letter to all chief constables in which he said:

I am directed by the Secretary of State to draw your attention to an apparent increase in the number of indecent magazines and novels published in this country – reports of proceedings under the Obscene Publications Act, 1857 in respect of these publications, having been received during the year 1950 from Birkenhead, Birmingham, Blackpool, Bolton, Burnley, Canterbury, Eastbourne, Glasgow, London, Maidstone, Manchester, Middlesbrough, Newcastle, Nottingham, Oldham, Plymouth, Salford, Sheffield, South Shields, Southend-on-Sea, Stoke-on-Trent, Torquay, Warrington, West Hartlepool and Wigan. Large numbers of these publications have been ordered by the Courts to be destroyed.

I am to enclose lists of titles of these magazines and novels for your confidential information and to suggest that if you find any of these or similar publications being sold in your police district you should arrange for specimen copies to be

---

[37] Public Records Office, MEPO 2/9626.

purchased and, in accordance with Regulation 6(2)(d) of the Prosecution of Offences Regulations 1946, inform the Director of Public Prosecutions and send to him the specimen copies. The Director will advise you whether to make application for a search warrant and the steps to be taken thereafter, including the possible prosecution under the Common Law of the publisher and wholesaler.

It would appear that particulars of prosecutions in connection with indecent or obscene publications are not in all cases being reported to the Home Office as requested in the Home Office circular letter 678,544/9 dated 8th April 1938. The Drugs Branch of the Home Office is the British Central Authority under the International Agreement for the Suppression of Obscene Publications and a report on the traffic in Great Britain, including the details of all prosecutions, is sent to the United Nations each year. The Home Office also collaborates with the Customs and Postal Authorities in an endeavour to prevent, as far as possible, the introduction of indecent matter from abroad.

It is, therefore, desirable that the Secretary of State should be aware of all the ramifications of this traffic and he would be glad if you would forward reports of all prosecutions, and of all warnings where a prosecution was not found necessary, in connection with indecent or obscene publications, whether they have been published in this country or abroad. This includes offences under section 63 of the Post Office Act, 1908. If there have been any such prosecutions or warnings in your police district since the 1st January 1950, which have not yet been reported, it is requested that you will furnish information of these cases. It would be convenient if the following particulars were given:—

> Name and address of accused person.
> Particulars of charge (including Act under which charged)
> Date of hearing (or warning)
> Result of hearing (or warning).
> Particulars of articles, e.g. titles of books, magazines, etc. and the number of copies of each publication ordered to be destroyed.

103

Any information as to the source from which the indecent matter had been obtained.

Where orders have been made for the destruction of periodicals, magazines, books, photographs, postcards, etc. it would be useful for future reference if specimens could be sent with your report. Of those publications listed in the appendix it is however only necessary to send specimens of those marked with an asterisk, because specimens of the others have already been obtained.

If any case is brought to your notice in which an indecent publication or article has been imported from abroad, the report should embody all available information which may be of assistance to the Home Office in deciding whether the matter can usefully be taken up with the Central Authority of the country concerned. [38]

This letter had the effect of not just bringing the subject of "obscene books and magazines" to the attention of all the chief constables but implying that it was a problem that the Secretary of State, James Chuter Ede, was more than interested in seeing dealt with.

The effect was immediate. In 1950, sixty-seven destruction orders had been issued. In 1951, the figure increased fourfold to 271. Fifty-one people were found guilty of selling obscene books, magazines, photographs and postcards in 1951, compared with nineteen the year before.

"From all accounts, the 1950 lists were extremely useful and helped the police considerably in their efforts to stamp out the spate of pornographic novels and magazines which were being sold by the less reputable type of bookseller," wrote Mr G Williams (of Thornton's office) on 2 February 1952, in an introductory memo suggesting that an updated list should be compiled with the help of the Director of Public Prosecutions. The second list, which covered titles subject to

---

[38] F Thornton, letter to chief constables, 20 April 1951.

destruction orders up to 31 December 1951, was issued by the Publications Branch for distribution to chief constables on 26 June 1952. [39] Two further lists were issued on 2 July 1953, and a final one, which consolidated information for all proceedings taken between 1950 and 1953, on 28 May 1954. On this latter list, Hank Janson provided two of the top five books with destruction orders issued against them.

* * *

The problem with a destruction order was that it did not actually apply any test to prove or disprove the obscenity of the books it covered. What the destruction order tested was the tastes of the local chief constable, whose job it was to decide which of the titles gathered up by his officers during a raid were to be sent to the Home Office and which were to be returned. Books that appeared on the Home Office list as already having been successfully prosecuted were almost certainly doomed, as were any books that looked similar. It was not the job of the chief constable to read the books and decide if they were obscene, he simply had to submit the titles to the magistrate.

Guilty until proven innocent, it was down to the bookshop owner or newsvendor or market stall holder whose books had been taken, to prove that they were *not* obscene. This could be done only before a jury in a full trial, where the books could be tested under the then current laws governing obscenity. The test for obscenity dated back to 1868 and built on laws that had been established by Lord Campbell, the Lord Chief Justice, in 1857, the first Obscene Publications Act designed to stem the flow of Victorian pornography.

In 1868, a zealous Protestant metal broker by the name of Henry Scott had published a pamphlet entitled *The Confessional Unmasked*, in which he had attacked the morality of the Catholic priesthood. To aid his argument, he had quoted extracts alleged to be from Catholic manuals and theological publications, which detailed cases of priests seducing penitents and other moral and criminal outrages.

---

[39] Public Records Office, HO 45/24972

Scott's stock of 252 copies was seized, and Wolverhampton magistrates ordered their destruction under the Campbell Act, which gave magistrates the power to do so if, in their opinion, the publication involved amounted to a "misdemeanour proper to be prosecuted as such."

Scott appealed, and the case went before the Quarter Sessions, where the Recorder, Benjamin Hicklin, revoked the destruction order, claiming that Scott's purpose had been not to corrupt but to promote the objects of the Protestant Electoral Union and expose the misdemeanours of the Church of Rome.

This, of course, outraged the Roman Catholics, who appealed to the Queen's Bench, where Sir Alexander Cockburn was faced with the problematic question: if a pamphlet was obscene but the intentions of the publisher were permissible in law, did that make the book a lawful publication? Chief Justice Cockburn decided that it did not.

This case was important in the history of the law regarding obscene publications, because Chief Justice Cockburn, in setting out his decision, also tried to find a test for obscenity, which he defined thus:

> The test for obscenity is this, whether the tendency of the matter charged with obscenity is to deprave and corrupt those whose minds are open to such immoral influences and into whose hands a publication of this sort may fall. [40]

Cockburn's definition had no statutory basis, but was seized upon by others and was generally accepted by the legal profession as a proper test for obscenity – even if it simply shifted the problem of deciding what the word "obscenity" meant to deciding what "deprave and corrupt" meant. As it first appeared as part of the appeal *R -v- Hicklin*, it became commonly known as the Hicklin test.

The right for a magistrate to grant the police a warrant to search a premises if it was believed to contain obscene material for sale or distribution was defined in the Obscene

---

[40] L.R. 3 Q.B. 360. (1868)

Publications Act 1857. In practical terms, this meant that a book or magazine could be brought to the attention of the police by someone who had purchased a copy, or by a plain-clothes police officer who was sent in deliberately to purchase a copy. Once this proof of purchase was established, the search warrant could be acted upon.

A book or magazine charged with being obscene was usually prosecuted as an "obscene libel", the term dating back to a change of law that took place in 1727. Prior to that date, there were no laws on the statute books to outlaw pornography but many laws that could be used to suppress opinion. In the days of the Inquisition, these were the laws relating to blasphemy and heresy; as that age gave way to a new era of more local systems of government, books that attacked Parliament or royalty were dealt with through the laws of libel.

The first book to be prosecuted as an obscene libel was *Venus In The Cloister; or The Nun In Her Smock*, published by Edmund Curll in 1724. It was argued by the Attorney-General that, although there was no physical breach of the peace, the book tended to corrupt the morals of the King's subjects and was therefore "against the peace of the King." "I do not insist that every immoral act is indictable, such as telling a lie or the like," continued the Attorney-General, "but if it is destructive of morality in general, if it does or may affect all of the King's subjects, then it is an offence of a public nature." [41]

Publishing an obscene libel [42] thereafter became an offence.

* * *

Blackburn is the principal town of North East Lancashire, and a historic town that existed in Saxon and Viking times, its name derived from "blaec" and "burna", meaning "black brook", inspired by the peat-stained water that flowed off the surrounding moors and into the river now known as the

---

[41] 2 Stra. 788. (1727).
[42] Libel, in this instance, was not used in its popular sense but derived from "libellus", meaning "a little book".

Blakewater. The Industrial Revolution saw the town expand tenfold, from little more than a village into the cotton weaving capital of the world. The completion of the Leeds-Liverpool Canal in 1816 allowed the mills to bring in fuel cheaply by barge from the Wigan coalfields and export its textile goods to the port of Liverpool; and transport became even easier with the arrival of the railway network in 1846. The town's expansion was recognised in 1851 when it received its Charter of Incorporation.

The declines in the textile industry in the 20th Century have changed the town dramatically, although Blackburn and the neighbouring Darwen remain prominent in the brewing industry. Surrounded by some of the most visually stunning landscapes in England, Blackburn was the gateway to the West Pennines, the Ribble Valley and the Yorkshire Dales.

In 1951, Blackburn was also one of the districts most active in the prosecution of obscene books. In March, the local police carried out a series of raids on local booksellers and seized hundreds of titles; destruction orders were issued by local magistrates on 458 books, whilst others, according to Alderman R Sugden, were to be held by the police as evidence in the event of further prosecutions. [43]

Five booksellers were summonsed to show cause why the books should not be destroyed: Thomas Evans, a driver and bookseller; hairdresser Leslie Hunter; bookseller Edward Walter Potts [44]; James Callow Preston, a wholesale and retail bookseller; and Livingstone Preston, a professional picture-framer who also ran a bookselling business with his wife.

On 30 May 1951, a bookseller was fined £5 for selling a copy of *Gunsmoke In Her Eyes* by Hank Janson, but this was the thin end of the wedge. The following August, Blackburn magistrates sat on what was then one of the largest cases to be bought against "obscene" Gangster novels, involving sixteen charges against ten people.

The charges were brought in relation to five novels sold by James Callow Preston, whose bookshop was located close to

---

[43] *Northern Daily Telegraph*, 13 March 1951.
[44] A later report in the *Northern Daily Telegraph* gives his name as Walter Edward Potts.

the Technical High School and Technical College, "right under the noses of adolescents," as Mr Cunliffe, for the prosecution, told magistrates Woolley, Giles and Davies.

"That was where he got all his custom from," says Ian Holt, who was one of the lynch-pins of the prosecution. "Pin-up magazines ... the window was full of them. Nudes and goodness knows what. And when you went into the shop, they were even better ... or worse, whichever way you look at it. But it was right alongside the Technical College, which, presumably, was one of the reasons they decided to raid it. There was always a crowd of kids around the window.

"When I was at school, if anyone had a Hank Janson, everyone wanted to borrow it. He was hot! If anyone had a Hank Janson, it used to go around the class like wildfire. Everybody used to cough up thruppence here and fourpence there and somebody would go in and buy it."

Holt left the local grammar school in 1950 and joined the Blackburn Police Force as a police cadet messenger, only the second of the force. At the age of seventeen, he stood six feet tall but could still pass for a student because of his age.

"I was called into the office and they said, 'We've got a job for you. We want you to go into Preston's Bookshop,' which, I have to say, was notorious in the town, because it was the only shop that sold dirty books. I had to come in in civvies the following day, and was asked to go in and act normally as any youth would just coming from the College. I was escorted up to the end of the street by a plain-clothes man and went into the shop, and James Callow Preston, the proprietor, was there. I said 'I want something good' or 'something hot' – I think I said 'something good,' as far as I can remember – and he went to the back of the shop. He came back and said 'I think you'll find that's all right,' and I said 'Well, how much is it?' It was half a crown or something, which I paid out of police funds.

"I came out of the shop all agitated and hot under the collar and met this plain-clothes policeman, and he snatched this book off me. It was parcelled up in brown paper and snatched away from me immediately, so I never got to read a passage or anything. Then we were met by another plain-clothes policemen who escorted me back to the yard, and I had to make a statement for court purposes. But I was led through that by the experienced policemen."

The court case, which took place a few days after Holt's eighteenth birthday, was one of the first against multiple defendants, ten in all, including bookseller James Callow Preston (five summonses), John Pemberton and his company World Distributors (Manchester) Ltd (both on two summonses), Julius Reiter and his company Gaywood Press Ltd, Bernard Kaye, Harry Edmands and his wife Jenny, and Irene Lillian Turvey and her company Modern Fiction Ltd.

The importance of the case, which convened on 20 August, was emphasised by the style of the prosecution. "The prosecution was handled by a solicitor, which was extremely unusual in the Magistrate's Court in those days," recalls Holt. "The prosecution case used to be put forward by the chief constable or his deputy. In later years, when I was demobbed [after National Service] and went into the police force, I worked for a time in the Prosecution Department, which was responsible for typing the case histories up, and I had to hand these to the chief constable before he went into court. He never swatted up on anything; he was just handed these sheets of paper before he went up, and the magistrate would say 'Case number one, so-and-so and so-and-so' and he'd read out what I had written."

The case against Preston and his co-defendants was conducted by Mr Cunliffe under the instruction of Mr Henry Fazackerley of Preston, an agent for the Director of Public Prosecutions.

In an ironic twist, the book that young Ian Holt had purchased and that had led subsequently to the raid on Preston's Bookshop by the plain-clothes department – not the CID, but a four-man department that dealt with underage drinking, prostitution and obscene publications amongst other matters – was found not to be obscene. Irene Turvey, owner and managing director of publishers Modern Fiction Ltd, had been interviewed by an officer from Scotland Yard and said that she had received no complaints against the book in question – a Gangster thriller entitled *Come And Get Me* by "Griff". When asked to make a statement, she had stated categorically: "I do not think the book is obscene."

During his defence of Mrs Turvey and her company, barrister Mr Charles Lawson, who pleaded not guilty for his clients, said that some "so-called classics" contained passages far worse than anything suggested in the book in question. The prosecution countered by saying that throughout the whole story there was an atmosphere of violence and the use of drugs. The magistrates, however, agreed with Lawson.

The magistrates also agreed to drop the cases against World Distributors Ltd and John Pemberton after Mr Cunliffe accepted that the two books concerned were no worse than the one for which the case was dismissed.

Harry and Jenny Edmands ran a book library and booksellers in Sheffield and, in 1950, had picked up the reprint rights to two popular titles after their original publisher, Glasgow-based M C Publications, stopped publishing them. *The Web Of Desire* and *The Amours of Marie*, both by D L'Arnaud (a house name used to cover the work of at least two authors), were to be the only two books they published. *Web Of Desire*, the book under prosecution, concerned a village girl who ran away to London after winning a beauty contest. One phrase – "flaunting her physical charms" – summed up the book, said the prosecution. The two accused had pleaded guilty and were fined £40 and £10 respectively and ordered to pay five guineas advocates' fees.

Mr Christmas Humphreys, representing distributors Julius Reiter and Gaywood Press Ltd and publisher Bernard Kaye in respect of the novel *Temptation* by André Latour, made an effort to argue the innocence of his clients, even though they had also pleaded guilty. He claimed that *Temptation* had been written by a Frenchman and subsequently translated – although, in truth, all the "translated" novels published by Bernard Kaye were written in England. It was not, argued Humphreys, like the "anonymous filth" secretly printed in this country and abroad. In this book, the printers' and publishers' names and addresses were given, and the book had been on sale in London for nearly a year without being prosecuted.

Mr Cunliffe invited the magistrates to look at some "particularly lurid passages" in the novel, about a young English girl's first visit to Paris. Humphreys countered that there was only one page – "a description of the hero falling to temptation" – that might have gone too far.

The case against Julius Reiter was dismissed. Reiter could not be blamed because he had never read the book, said Humphreys: "Never before has one of the books they have published or distributed been impugned, and the same applies to Kaye."

However, the guilty plea had already pre-determined the outcome of the case for Bernard Kaye (absent through illness) and Gaywood Press Ltd, each of whom was fined £50 and told to pay advocates' fees of five guineas and £3 14s costs.

What the case emphasised was the state of confusion in which the law on obscene publications stood. The book purchased by Police Cadet Ian Holt had been considered "obscene" enough for one magistrate to issue a search warrant, but had been dismissed by three other magistrates from the same Borough. And when the case against that book had been dismissed, the charges against two other titles had been withdrawn by Mr. Cunliffe – representing the Director of Public Prosecutions – who admitted that they were "no worse" than the book against which the case had been dismissed.

Had they pleaded not guilty, it seems likely that the cases against Bernard Kaye and Gaywood Press Ltd would also have been dismissed.

CHAPTER EIGHT

"LIKE LIFE; MAYBE WITH A LITTLE EXTRA FLAVOURING"

The Home Office had circulated on 20 April 1951 their list of books against which destruction orders had been successfully issued. On 24 April, the *Sunday Pictorial* published an article under the headline "Drop sex, publishers tell authors as Vice Squad goes into action".

> Publishers of lurid Gangster magazines, worried by the clean-up campaign of Scotland Yard's "Vice Squad," have sent this confidential directive to their authors: cut out the sadism and sex.
>
> And the more reputable publishers who have tried to confine their paperbacked novels to straightforward "blood and thunder" are considering an approach to the Home Office.
>
> They may ask the Home Secretary to set up an advisory board of psychologists, magistrates and others to advise publishers on broad lines. [45]

As previously noted, Reg Carter and Julius Reiter were amongst the publishers who approached both Scotland Yard and legal advisers for guidance, only to find that none was forthcoming. There were no guidelines that could be issued, since obscenity could be tested only in the courtroom, and the verdicts coming out of the courts were contradictory. On 24 January 1951, a destruction order was issued by Coventry City magistrates against 2,259 books and 639 magazines picked up in raids on five book shops. The raids had been the result of complaints received by the police from "certain religious sections of the city and also from private persons."

---

[45] *Sunday Pictorial*, 24 April 1951.

Test purchases had been made and submitted to the Director of Public Prosecutions, on whose advice proceedings had then been brought. The raids had netted a further 1,253 books and 1,695 magazines that were subsequently returned to their owners. Each bookseller had approximately £200 of stock removed from his or her shop during the raids, which would have put many of them out of business. Over half the stock originally taken away was eventually returned.

One of the defendants in the case was Frank Collis of H E Porter & Co., who was also a director of the distributors and publishers Thorpe & Porter. Collis attempted to defend a book entitled *She Talked With A Gun*, published by Thorpe & Porter under the Beacon Publishing Co imprint in 1950, complaining that he knew the author and knew that his stories were founded on fact. Collis also argued that although the book could be banned one day, it could be bought out again the next under a different title such as *The Gun Talked With Her*. The magistrates perused passages marked by the prosecution, and the chairman, Councillor W H Malcolm, announced: "We have no hesitation whatever in condemning this book." [46]

In Willesden, North-West London, a destruction order was issued on 25 January against a variety of books, including a number published in Paris such as *The Fleshy Prelude* by Robert Sermaise, *I Shall Spit On Your Graves* by Vernon Sullivan, *The Love Orchid* by Eric Wensleydale, and, bizarrely, one copy of *The Collector's Digest*, a duplicated magazine published in Yorkshire for fans of children's story papers starring the boys of Greyfriars School, St. Frank's and Sexton Blake.

In Colchester, police raided the shop of Leslie Frank Harris and took away 421 books. Later, in court, Detective-Inspector Kemp of Colchester's CID admitted that there was no suggestion that all the books seized were of an obscene nature. Many of them had nothing wrong with them, said Kemp, adding that some of them were detective stories. [47] One has to wonder why Kemp, who led the raid on the shop,

---

[46] *Coventry Evening Telegraph*, 25 January 1951. The case concluded with the bizarre remark from W H Malcolm that "The magistrates would like to say a lot, but we shall say nothing."
[47] *Essex County Standard*, 2 March 1951.

felt it necessary to seize books that he himself felt were in no way obscene.

The Hank Janson novel *The Jane With Green Eyes*, published in July 1950, had twenty-two destruction orders issued against it during 1951, but was declared to be *not* obscene by magistrates in Stockton-on-Tees in July of that year. The same book was later successfully prosecuted and found to be obscene in Darwen eighteen months later.

It was shortly after the decision at Stockton-U-on-Tees that Reg Carter took over the publication of Hank Janson and temporarily removed the Heade covers. He, author Stephen Frances and distributor Julius Reiter then set up their own guidelines as a precaution to ensure that the books they published were not obscene. If the books were then seized, they could then at least make a legal issue of it and try to clarify the law.

"Any scene, action or words used in any of the books they published must be commonplace and generally accepted in society," said Frances, explaining the guidelines. "If a naked girl was mentioned in a book, it could be shown that widely-read magazines also featured a naked woman. If a woman was tied to a chair, it could be shown that a 'U' certificate film [48] also featured a woman tied to a chair. If strong dialogue was used, it could be demonstrated that national newspapers also printed similar scandalous words."

Carter and Reiter felt secure with these guidelines and continued to publish and distribute new titles.

* * *

To the collector, who may take years to amass even a reasonable collection of the early Hank Janson novels, it is sometimes difficult to appreciate how quickly the character developed. The books came out in such rapid succession that when Reg Carter took over their publishing in August 1951, it was with the twenty-ninth Janson novel.

---

[48] The "U" certificate was issued to films that were universally acceptable to viewers of all ages.

Frances had recognised early on that Janson was a character capable of sustaining a long run, and had deliberately set out to create a situation that would help the character remain fresh. One move in this direction had been to group the novels into series of twelve. Thus the first series had seen Hank on a journey across America, while the second series had established Hank in the role that was to be his most enduring, as a crime reporter for the *Chicago Chronicle* daily newspaper The early novels in the third series were notable as the first not to feature Janson as a character – although whether that was planned by Frances or simply a convenient and practical way for him to use plots for novels he had originally intended to issue under other bylines is unknown. Frances had stopped writing under his other bylines (Ace Capelli, Duke Linton) in 1950, but had experimented with a novel under the name Max Clinten in early 1951, shortly before he published *Underworld* magazine. As both had proved less successful than the novels appearing under the Hank Janson byline, it may have seemed pointless to Frances to issue them under any other name. The Janson name was, by then, selling books in sufficient numbers to sustain him in a lifestyle he had never previously enjoyed. Frances was also spending considerably more time in Spain and making plans for Carter to take over his business, so a reduction in his output was only to be expected.

With his final, permanent move to Spain, Frances no longer needed to maintain a flat in the relatively expensive Bloomsbury area of London. Reg Carter purchased a large house called "Restful", with about seven acres of grounds, in Pease Pottage, and this was available to Frances on his still-frequent visits to the UK.

As his publishing ventures expanded with the addition of his second publishing company, Comyns, in 1952, Carter found new premises for his businesses at 139 Borough High Street. These had a shop front and a yard as well as offices above. Maurice Read, formerly the editor for Scion Ltd, now worked from the new office as editor for Comyns and other lines that were being published by Julius Reiter under the imprints Gaywood Press and Paladin Press.

In early 1952, Carter began reprinting genuine American Gangster fiction under the New Fiction Press imprint. The first of these titles was *I, Mobster*, written anonymously by Joseph Hilton Smyth and promoted as the true confessions of an American crime czar. It was also promoted by way of a white band across the cover which had the familiar Hank Janson silhouette saying "Read This Book!"

Later that year, Carter increased the number of American novels he was producing, drawing them from the hugely popular Gold Medal paperback line published in the US by Fawcett Publications Inc. This was an innovative move, as Carter had the choice of authors and titles. He chose Gil Brewer and Edward Ronns and published Brewer's *13 French Street, So Rich, So Dead* and *Satan Is A Woman* and Ronns's *The Decoy, Passage To Terror, I Can't Stop Running, Don't Cry, Beloved* and *Catspaw Ordeal*. The Brewer titles in particular are now recognised as hardboiled classics.

As the line expanded, in November 1952 Carter incorporated New Fiction Press as a limited company, and under the Comyns imprint began reprinting from the American Phantom Books line.

Freed from the worries of finding paper, finding a reliable printer and finding the time between books to chase up debts, Stephen Frances settled down to writing at a more relaxed pace – a new book every six or so weeks rather than every fortnight.

His talent as a writer had developed rapidly over the course of the first series of Hank Janson novels, but even the most ardent Janson fan would have to admit that it had been patchy at best. The second series, on the other hand, contained only a handful of novels that did not come up to scratch.

To give some continuity to the first series, Frances had sometimes carried over a female companion from one book to the next, but this had invariably meant that the first chapters of the new book needed to deal with the affairs of Janson and his latest girlfriend. Sometimes Frances had played to his strengths, such as in the keenly-observed deteriorating relationships with Patricia Hale (*Gun Moll For Hire*) and Sally Taylor (*Blonde On The Spot*); at other times (such as with Muriel in *Smart Girls Don't Talk*) it had been obvious that Frances wanted to jettison the character as quickly as possible. With the background of the *Chronicle* offices offering continuity, the second series of Janson books could now launch each new adventure in a more measured way, either establishing a situation that would draw Janson rapidly in or lulling the reader with an abstract anecdote about some colleague or a description of the daily routine of newspaper publishing.

The *Chronicle* provided Janson not only with a social context but also with a useful supporting cast who could be called upon as the narrative demanded. Recurring characters included cigar-chomping Chief Healey, the *Chronicle*'s hard-working editor; Sheila Lang, the woman's page editor, who had a long-suffering relationship with Janson; and Inspectors Sharp and Blunt of the local police force. The arrival of these and other familiar characters in a novel added a soap-opera element to the Janson saga, and fostered a desire in his readers to find out how characters would interact at their next meeting.

The Hank Janson of the first series was a slippery character to pin down, because he was still evolving in the mind of his author; he became more consistent over time. There were fundamental traits and familiar plot devices that ran through many of the books: corruption in authority; the falsely accused man; the lone avenger seeking justice that the law cannot or will not provide; and a climax that sees the downfall of the enemy through "poetic justice". Janson usually chooses his actions based not on the word of the law but on what he feels is morally right. He will destroy evidence if he feels it will complicate a case that has been solved to his satisfaction (as he does by destroying the body of Tony Rogers in *Lady, Mind That Corpse*); engineer a group of individuals into facing an insane gunman because it is a more fitting end than any the law could devise (*Gun Moll For Hire*); or contrive a gunfight between the principal offenders because he believes the police are implicated in corruption (*Honey, Take My Gun*). With this "eye for an eye" attitude to justice, it is notable that that he never carries out any extreme punishments himself but manipulates a situation until a group of people or an

118

individual become the cause of their own destruction. Retribution is served, but Janson himself as absolved of the responsibility.

In the new setting of the *Chicago Chronicle*, Janson develops a more rounded attitude towards justice and those who had to enforce it, even to the point of allowing those charged with the duty to dispense it. Rather than systems being depicted as inherently and wholly corrupt, corruption now becomes centred on individuals. Thus we find Janson working closely with Detective Inspector Blunt (in *The Bride Wore Weeds*, *Skirts Bring Me Sorrow* and *The Filly Wore A Rod*), who may condemn Janson's actions but secretly supports them. Blunt's polar opposite, Detective Inspector Sharp, meanwhile remains to show that brutality and a willingness to achieve results by whatever means necessary (legal or illegal) still exists in the police force; but the corruption within the system is now contained in such individuals, meaning that Janson has less need to step completely outside the law to achieve justice.

Janson still lets his own sense of justice outweigh the law on some occasions, allowing the escape of bank robber Muriel Hanton in *No Regrets For Clara* and murderess Marion Langham in *Women Hate Till Death*. More frequently, though, lawbreakers agree to surrender themselves (the Blooms in *Don't Mourn Me Toots*, Thomas Carter in *The Lady Has A Scar*) or allow Janson to devise a ploy to reduce their sentence whilst still deferring to the judicial process (Virginia Leighton in *The Jane With Green Eyes*).

Janson's attitude to women is somewhat contradictory. He states on more than one occasion that he is opposed to violence against women, and complains bitterly at others who mistreat their female companions or relatives; this is implicit from the first novel, *This Woman Is Death*, where Janson objects strongly to Nat Garvin's cruelty towards his sister, Gwen. Yet his actions often contradict his statements, especially in the early novels where, admittedly, he is still evolving as a character. In *Slay-Ride For Cutie*, he releases Eve and Gloria semi-naked into the wilderness; in *Gun Moll For Hire*, he forces Patricia Hale into a position where there is a high chance she will be shot; in *Honey, Take My Gun*, he

119

savagely pinches Pam to make her divulge the location of a meeting; and in *Lilies For My Lovely*, he recommends "slapping around" June Miller for being contrary.

In the cases of Eve and of Gloria and Patricia Hale, Janson's actions are an extension of his Old Testament attitude towards retribution, leaving their survival in the hands of Fate.

For all the torment that he put his female characters through, author Frances never had Janson hit or kick a woman in the pages of his novels, even in his more questionable moments. Unrestrained cruelty towards women had disappeared by the second series of novels, although Janson still voiced the opinion that some women responded to a "slapping around," and stated that married women "sometimes ask for it." It could be argued that these sentiments were more prevalent at that time, and that these opinions were put into the mouth of Janson to reinforce his "tough guy" image. The very fact that Frances did not have Hank follow up such suggestions with actions perhaps adds weight to the latter theory; indeed, in one incident in *Don't Dare Me, Sugar*, Jessica Hardiman, a college graduate whom Janson is supposed to be shepherding through work experience, suggests that the reason why Janson has spanked her is that he is sexually frustrated:

> "You're not married, you have no normal outlets for your natural impulses. Since you're a healthy man, your natural impulses have to find sublimation channels. It seems fairly obvious your form of sublimation is sadism. That's why you spanked me." She smiled at me sweetly. "I hope you feel better now. It's relieved you, hasn't it?"
>
> I stared at her in amazement. "Do *I* feel better now?" I echoed. [49]

Janson is forever having the tables turned on him by the opposite sex, because he is vulnerable to them. His tough guy stance on "dames" is vocalised in phrases like "I'm a sucker for dames – cute looking dames"; but at the same

---

[49] *Don't Dare Me, Sugar*, p 22.

time he must admit (as in *Sister, Don't Hate Me*): "Maybe outwardly, I am hardboiled. But if you dig down beneath my crust, I'm soft, just like I said, like a baby."

Frances was often at his best when showing Janson's relationships with women. Hank's encounter with Jessica Hardiman mentioned above is atypical and meant as a brief, light hearted moment (although telling nonetheless). A cursory reading of the Hank Janson novels may make Janson appear to be a sexual predator, since Hank does have a habit of finding himself immediately sexually attracted to women, but this would be a vast oversimplification of his affairs with women. Janson has an identifiable although idiosyncratic code of conduct, suggesting, as in *Gunsmoke In Her Eyes*, that sex without romance holds little interest for him; nor does he enjoy playing the role of substitute, no matter what the benefits might be. Janson may flirt and encourage flirting constantly, but he still has the opinion that anyone capable of two-timing their fiancée is not to be trusted (*The Bride Wore Weeds*). Sex will sometimes win out, as in *Angel, Shoot To Kill* where Janson is faced simultaneously with the sexual charms of Linda Dargale and the far more complex attractions of Viola Robins. The guiding rule on two-timing, however, seems to be covered by the convenient caveats that cheating is okay if it is not "serious," and that if his partner is married or engaged, culpability lies squarely with her rather than with Janson.

Janson often finds himself racked with guilt over his relationships: in choosing Linda Dargale over Viola Robins, for instance, he feels he has betrayed the latter. Worse is his infatuation with Mindy Hiller in *This Dame Dies Soon*, which reduces him to abject pathos, accentuated by the amused, rather superior indulgence of Frank Carstairs, with whom Mindy is smitten. At other times, Janson is completely wrong-footed, as with Cora Reid's cool and unexpected rebuff in *The Jane With Green Eyes*; elsewhere he adopts an attitude of injured resignation, often a part of his relationship with fellow *Chronicle* employee Sheila Lang.

Janson's relationships with women are often a source of humour, notably in extended sequences involving Sheila Lang at the opening of *Some Look Better Dead* and rival reporter

Jenny Finton in *Women Hate Till Death*. Every cabbie or doorman in Chicago equates a scowl with problems at home: "Wife trouble, huh?" or "I'm a married man myself."

Humour pervades the Janson novels, but is usually expressed in brief, dry one-liners: "Did you see it? A yellow cab!" "Listed bud," I said grimly. "The cabs in this town ain't yella. They'll attack anybody." (*Torment*)

Certainly the humour is never overplayed: "Henry's all right in his place, I guess," says Sandra with an angry grimace in *Skirts Bring Me Sorrow*, "but it ain't dug yet."

Janson retains an abrasive tongue for many subjects. In the first series, he is used by author Frances to voice his opinions from a soap-box; from the second series onwards, with Janson in a more established social setting, there is less fire and brimstone and more discussion, with Hank playing the role of healthy sceptic.

Thankfully, having Hank settled in the role of newspaperman did not eliminate one of the series' great strengths: that of presenting him in a variety of locations. Chicago became a base from which Janson could travel, and from which Frances could examine problems such as racial hatred in the Deep South (*The Jane With Green Eyes*) and provincial prejudice in the small-town setting of Little Falls, Wisconsin (*Torment For Trixy*).

Torment For Trixy [50] in fact provides a good example of Frances using Janson's voice to discuss his own concerns – in this case, literary censorship. Published in March 1950, it was frighteningly prescient of the kind of legal action that had just begun to be brought against Gangster novels and was, perhaps, inspired by some early reports of newsagents having their stock destroyed.

The opening of the novel revolves around the publication of a sexy novel, *The Inconstant Lover*, by one Jane Grey, whom Janson tracks down, only to discover that she is really an inexperienced small-town girl called Trixy Pugh.

In Little Falls, Janson attends the local Church Literary Group meeting where *The Inconstant Lover* is condemned as

---

[50] Later editions give the title as *Torment For Trixie*.

a disgrace. To Janson, on the other hand, "the story doesn't say anything happened."

> I repeated slowly: "There's nothing wrong with that book. The only thing wrong is the way you folks look at it. You've got a suburban attitude. You see rottenness where no rottenness exists. This book isn't obscene. It's like life; maybe with a little extra flavouring. The only vice and obscenity in this book is what your own evil minds read into it." [51]

A unique aspect of the Janson novels, and another reason why his readers often thought of him as a real person, was that the character Hank Janson would occasionally incorporate his novel writing into the plot. This occurs most obviously in *Torment*, where Janson assists Betty Scott and she begrudgingly invites him into her apartment for drinks and sex, since she is under the impression from having read his novels that this is the kind of behaviour he expects. Turning her down, Hank says: "Either you don't read good or I don't write good."

Vengeance takes this notion a step further when Hank visits *The Horseshoe*, a club previously featured in *It's Always Eve That Weeps* – one of the Hank Janson novels that did not feature Janson as a character. The latter title had been set in the era of Prohibition and, on re-visiting *The Horseshoe*, Hank finds that the staff have aged in the interim. Fats, the owner, and Susan, one of the hostesses, remember him from years before, when he was researching his novel: "I read your book," she said. "The way you wrote about it made it all seem real." "A lot of things were," I said. "Exaggerated maybe, but basically real."

The notion of exaggerated realism was clearly what author Stephen Frances was trying for in the Hank Janson novels; and to do this he created, in Janson, a character of emotional depth who mirrored many of the concerns Frances himself felt about the world he lived in. Janson allowed him to explore

---

[51] *Torment For Trixy*, p 51.

areas that he could not in real life, but the attitudes and occasional polemics that sprung from Janson's mouth were all the more forceful for being something in which their author believed.

His vulnerability, particularly his emotional vulnerability, made Janson stand out in a genre that made a virtue out of lack of emotion. British Gangster fiction was filled with emotionally bereft killing machines whose only notable quality was an ability to store up beatings like a capacitor until it was time to unleash violence back upon their tormentors. When Frances turned to writing stories that did not feature the Janson character, as he did in the third series, they were often more bleak, since he was able to indulge in telling a story that was not filtered through the attitudes and interpreted by the already established world-view of Janson. In Hank's world, the story had to reach a reasonably safe conclusion, with the innocent protected from further misfortune and the wrongdoers receiving some form of just punishment.

In the novels without the Janson character, all bets were off. The male leads did not have the moral strength or ethical convictions of Janson, could be manipulated more easily or react more violently. Life for them often proved brutal: in *Baby, Don't Dare Squeal*, Amber Blake contemplates murder to win the object of his passion, only to be dumped penniless by the roadside when he finally proved to be no further use to her; in *Sadie, Don't Cry Now*, Harry Smith's stoic resolve in the closing pages cannot mask the fact that he now faces a life as a fugitive wanted for murder and robbery after becoming an unwilling pawn in his (female) partner's plans; in *Hotsy, You'll Be Chilled*, Hal Burgess, accidentally responsible for the deaths of four colleagues, descends into alcoholism and also loses the girl he loves; in *Amok*, Jimmy Martin sits on death row for a murder he commits by mistake; and in *Pursuit*, Jim Mason loses his freedom through happenstance and his wife through a combination of police negligence and his criminal past, and is now faced with losing his life through the rash actions of one of the gang he had hoped to use to claw himself back from the brink of oblivion.

For the most part, these Janson-less novels were chilling tales of suffering and betrayal. (Even the more "traditional" Gangster yarns were never allowed to slip into unoriginality of plot or character.) But while Frances seemed to revel in chronicling the misery of the human condition, depicting characters so alienated from society that they repel one another even in their shared bond of desperation, the world was not always so dark and pessimistic. Thus *Death Wore A Petticoat* remained optimistic despite the suffering of its central character Frank Hardwick, whose life has been tormented by a false accusation of blackmail. In the end, Hardwick is able to turn his back on civilisation and materialism and find a tranquil existence in the arms of those he loves.

Beyond the emotional content of the Janson novels, it is also worth noting that some of them are substantial thrillers with complex and intriguing plots that give them an appeal on a more entertaining level. *The Lady Has A Scar*, with its cast of finely observed characters, and a basic murder plot that, once moving, hurtles relentlessly towards a conclusion upon which Janson has staked his reputation (and the *Chronicle* has staked $200,000). And *Suspense* certainly lives up to its title. Both *Women Hate Till Death* and *Tension* have all the classic elements of a "police procedural" interwoven with other aspects to give two or more converging storylines. In the former, the additional aspect is the harrowing story-within-a-story of two cousins and their experiences in a Polish women's prison under the Nazis; in the latter, it is something decidedly more light-hearted.

Not that Frances was without his faults as a writer – too many stories rely on coincidence to jolt a plot forward, and the fourth series suffered from revisiting plots and themes that had been better handled in thirty-six earlier novels – yet the flaws in the diamond are sometimes what gives it its value. The Janson books were not murder mysteries in the traditional sense, and if the villain becomes obvious to the reader half-way through the story, so be it. The destination is unimportant compared with the emotional journey.

CHAPTER NINE

THE HANK JANSON BLUES

After the fourfold increase in legal actions against allegedly obscene books in 1951, the following year was relatively quiet. Only 115 destruction orders were issued against some 32,000 books – half the number destroyed in 1951.

In January and March, there took place in Sheffield three separate trials resulting in fines against booksellers. One of these, *Paget -v- Watson* [52], raised questions amongst the judiciary. The case involved the publication of a magazine filled with short stories; the stories themselves were not held to be obscene, but a photograph printed on the inside front cover was. Paget Publications offered to strip the covers from the magazine, leaving the bulk of it intact – it would be a relatively simple matter to print a new cover (or even overprint the photograph as Reg Carter had done with some of the Hank Janson covers). This offer was rejected, the argument (which became widely used in subsequent prosecutions) being that if a part of the magazine was considered obscene, the whole magazine had to be considered obscene. The dirty photograph somehow contaminated the benign fiction by its presence.

If booksellers were feeling besieged in Sheffield, Hank Janson was receiving the same treatment in Blackburn. On 30 May 1952, a bookseller was fined £5 for selling *Angel Shoot To Kill*, as was S D Frances for publishing it. The following August, Mr Christmas Humphreys QC was back in court, defending a case involving *Milady Took The Rap* in nearby Darwen. He found himself alongside Charles Lawson, the barrister who a year earlier in Blackburn had successfully defended Irene Turvey and her company Modern Fiction Ltd

---

[52] 1 All E. R. 1256 (1952).

over the publication of *Come And Get Me* by "Griff". Lawson was again defending Mrs Turvey and her company, this time over the title *Some Rats Have Two Legs*.

Copies of both *Milady Took The Rap* and *Some Rats Have Two Legs* had been seized during a police raid on the Crown Press in Darwen in August 1951, following the earlier prosecution in Blackburn. Christmas Humphreys, who pleaded guilty on behalf of Editions Poetry (London) Ltd, complained that it had taken the authorities twelve months to decide to prosecute *Milady Took The Rap*, adding that the book could not be considered to be very obscene. "We are now brought to the North of England to answer a summons regarding this book which, as far as we are concerned, has been out of our hands for twelve months."

Humphreys argued: "When it comes to deciding the obscenity of a book, there is no standard to say whether a book is or is not obscene. No two courts have ever dared to lay down what constitutes obscenity.

"The people I represent cannot tell when they publish a book whether or not it is going to be found obscene. There is no censorship and no-one to advise them. This book was published in 1951, and this is the only Borough out of 995 in England where a case has been bought against it." [53]

Editions Poetry was pleading guilty, said Humphreys, because it was the policy of the firm to try to keep within the law.

Irene Turvey, on the other hand, was in court to defend her book. The managing director and sole proprietor of Modern Fiction Ltd, she was the wife of Edwin Henry Turvey, who had been a bookseller in the 1930s. In 1938, Edwin Turvey had been found guilty of selling an obscene book and photographs and sentenced to two years imprisonment. Modern Fiction Ltd, based in Liverpool Road, Holloway, North London, had been established in 1943 and had gone on to become one of the leading paperback publishers of the late 1940s, due to the success of its Gangster novels. In 1946 it had published the first novel by Ben Sarto (F Dubrez Fawcett); and in 1948 it had expanded its line with a series of novels,

---

[53] *The Darwen News*, 29 August 1952.

written in some cases by Ernest L McKeag and in others by William S Newton, under the house name "Griff". In 1950-51, Ben Sarto was Hank Janson's most credible rival, outselling him by 20,000 copies per book, although their positions were soon to reverse as Reg Carter began to push up the print runs of Hank Janson titles in 1951-52.

Irene Turvey owned not only Modern Fiction Ltd but also the Fulton Publishing Co, a retail and wholesale booksellers based in Birmingham, and was in addition a director of E H T (Printers) Ltd. By 1952, she was no doubt feeling the same confusion as to what constituted an obscene book as those involved in the production of the Hank Janson titles. Books that had been openly on sale for up to six years were now being judged obscene, while others in the same genre that were as widely distributed and available remained in bookshops and on the shelves of libraries.

"What is the test for obscenity?" asked Charles Lawson, producing six books that could be picked up at most bookshops and railway station stalls. "Is the standard to be different in the case of books printed in stiff covers and in the reach of the pockets of the limited class, and in the case of the working man's literature in a paperback cover? Or is it to be a different standard in the case of the so-called classics?

"Who is to say what will be the classics of the future? In 200 years' time, this book might be a classic, and in that time we may use the kind of English in that book."

Lawson argued that obscenity had to be confined to pornography, and that mere descriptions of crimes could not be obscene as there were similar descriptions to be found in newspapers almost every day. The magistrates disagreed, and fined Modern Fiction Ltd and Editions Poetry (London) Ltd £100 each and ordered them to pay £4 17s. 11d. witnesses' fees and £5 5s. 6d. advocate's fee. Irene Turvey was fined 20 shillings.

* * *

On 16 April 1952, Detective Constable John Swain of the Metropolitan Police travelled from New Scotland Yard to 104 Southampton Row where he met Stephen Frances and Reg

Carter. "I knew Mr Carter as the general manager of Arc Press Ltd and as managing director of the New Fiction Press Ltd," said Swain in a later deposition.

"I showed both men the two books, *The Jane With Green Eyes* and *Milady Took The Rap*. Both books are shown as being written by Hank Janson.

"Having shown them both books, I asked them if they admitted publishing them. The defendant [Frances] said 'I wrote both books. The book *The Jane With Green Eyes* was published by me when I was trading in my own name about eighteen months ago.' *Milady Took The Rap* was published by New Fiction Press, which is an imprint of Editions Poetry (London) Ltd. Mr Carter is a director of that firm."

On 22 January 1953, Stephen Frances was in court before the Borough magistrates at Darwen to answer summonses against the two books. Mr R H Rowland, who had directed the case against *Milady Took The Rap* earlier, was again prosecuting.

Faced with the previous conviction, Frances pleaded guilty in the case of *Milady Took The Rap*, but felt he was on surer ground with *The Jane With Green Eyes* as it had been dismissed in a case before Stockton-on-Tees magistrates in July 1951. "The law is so vague on this subject that it is impossible for me to define [obscenity] myself. I have consulted several lawyers, but under no circumstances, due to the uncertainty of the law, will any of them give me a guarantee that a book is not obscene."[54]

The Borough magistrates added to the confusion by finding him guilty on both counts. Frances was fined £50 for each book and ordered to pay £7 7s advocate's fee and £5 witnesses' expenses.

Frances was the first author to appear in court for obscenity in Gangster novels since the prosecution of Rene Raymond (James Hadley Chase) and Harold Kelly (Darcy Glinto) in 1942. He'd travelled back from his home in Spain to attend to the case personally. Surprised and perturbed, Frances could not understand why his novels, which had been published for years without comment, were becoming

---

[54] *The Darwen News*, 23 January 1953.

increasingly prone to legal censure. Even worse was the idea that his novels were depraving and corrupting. To Frances, the books were "frank and outspoken" but certainly not obscene. He avoided language and words that were offensive to the vast majority, and in most of his books he even avoided the characters who made up the standard British Gangster novel – the stock 'gang' usually comprised an intelligent but sadistic boss, a plug-ugly, punch-drunk thug, and a trigger-happy "torpedo". Given their set of clichéd characters, few authors of Gangster novels tried to stretch their plots beyond a formula that would allow the narrative to include a regular dose of sex or violence or sexual violence.

Of the forty or so Janson novels published up to the time of these prosecutions, only a quarter could have been said to contain bona-fide Gangster characters. Specifically, these were *This Woman Is Death, No Regrets For Clara, Gunsmoke In Her Eyes, Slay-Ride For Cutie, Sweetie Hold Me Tight, Don't Dare Me Sugar, Lola Brought Her Wreath, It's Always Eve That Weeps, Broads Don't Scare Easy* and *The Filly Wore A Rod*. Gangsters featured obliquely in *Gun Moll For Hire* and briefly in *Angel, Shoot To Kill* and *Don't Mourn Me, Toots*. The vast majority of the Hank Janson novels involved corrupt officials, fifth columnists and a variety of other ne'er-do-wells. Even amongst the bona-fide Gangster novels, *Sweetie Hold Me Tight* and *It's Always Eve That Weeps* were studies of individuals who did not conform to a Gangster stereotype. Freed for the most part by avoiding the clichéd characters, Frances could explore a wider range of themes and social issues.

That he was writing "hot" novels, Frances was well aware; but they were in the tradition of erotica rather than that of pornography. Hank was forever hot under the collar in the presence of husky-voiced dames whose clothing clung to their curvaceous figures, showing the tops of creamy white breasts. At the same time, Frances was a master of deception and innuendo, using Janson's reactions to hint at things he was not actually describing:

> She didn't even give a damn about clothes either.
> Her short skirt, which finished three inches above
> her knees, was manufactured from squirrel skins

roughly stitched together. For a blouse, she wore one of her father's old worn shirts. Yeah, it was certainly worn. There was rents and tears in it, which left no doubt whatsoever that the girl's body was as bronzed as her face. [55]

Everything here is left to the imagination of the readers, who can see the rents and tears wherever they care to.

Frances's sleight-of-hand style meant that much could be implied between the lines. In *Women Hate Till Death*, Doris (a captive in a Nazi women's prison) is forced to stand with her arms outstretched until her shoulders begin to ache and her arms sag; one of the guards raps her knuckles with a steel ruler.

> The third time the ruler cracked across her knuckles she fainted. When she recovered consciousness, she was lying on the floor with her skirt around her waist. They were watching her, grinning expectantly. She moved, winced and discovered the revolting trick they'd played on her. They roared with laughter as she hurled the ruler at them blindly, shuddering with loathing. [56]

The implication is obvious, but all we know for sure from the printed page is that the steel ruler has passed from the hands of the guard to Doris.

* * *

Frances was still in London on 31 January 31 1953, when a storm hit the East coast of England, killing 307 people. Gale force winds coupled with a deep depression and a spring tide drove a surge tide southwards into the North Sea between England and the Netherlands. [57] Ten feet of water breached the sea walls all along the East coast, flooding more than 12,000 homes and 76 square miles of land. 21,000 people,

---

[55] *Angel, Shoot To Kill*, p 81.
[56] *Women Hate Till Death*, p 103.
[57] The death toll in the Netherlands was 1,700.

some still living in temporary housing following the War, were made homeless.

The Army was deployed to drop sandbags and even wheelbarrows from helicopters, and thousands of volunteers began the almost impossible task of cleaning up the flood damage and feeding and sheltering the people who had escaped the freezing water.

"Carter and I discussed how we could help," recalled Frances.

"Put it this way," said Carter. "You can serve in a relief kitchen, or row around flooded houses rescuing stranded people if you want, but there's hundreds of volunteers to do that. You can help much more in other ways."

So Hank Janson wrote *Britain's Great Flood Disaster*, a sixty-four-page glossy magazine containing dozens of photographs, which was published in April, priced 2/6. All the proceeds were to be donated to the relief of flood victims.

"We offered the entire edition to the Lord Mayor's Fund to send out to all the relief organisations to sell. We believed that people would pay much more than the selling price as a relief contribution. But the Lord Mayor's Fund refused to accept the books, because they had no machinery for disposing of them. Other organisations refused for the same reason. All they understood was receiving cash and paying it into the bank."

As official channels seemed to be barred, Frances and Carter made their own arrangements, and the magazines were hawked at football matches and greyhound tracks. "We passed on all the money we received from sales to various charity organisations, but we still believed that the charity organisations could have gained much more by selling the books themselves."

There was a sting in the tail. A year later, Carter's accountant told him that he would have to pay tax on the full cost of the flood book. It had been published and sold in the same was as every other book Carter published, and the fact that all proceeds had been donated to charity was no concern of the Inland Revenue. He still had to pay tax on them.

* * *

Anne Shelton was Britain's most popular singer in 1953. Born Patricia Sibley in 1928, she had shot to fame in the early 1940s as a singer with bandleader Bert Ambrose, who had recognised in her a mature talent, even though the thirteen-year-old had arrived at her audition in her Forest Hill convent school uniform and accompanied by her mum. She had become a huge hit with the armed forces, had toured Army, Navy and Air Force bases across the country, and had soon been broadcast widely by BBC radio. *Introducing Anne* had been broadcast to North Africa, and her signature tune, an anglicised version of 'Lili Marlene', had been a huge hit. Tours with Glenn Miller and Bing Crosby had helped seal her popularity, and heavy touring in America had spread her fame.

In 1953, Shelton was the star of the BBC's Saturday night programme, and it was the BBC Orchestra conductor Philip Cardeu, using the name Peter Cornish, who composed for her the music for a song entitled 'The Hank Janson Blues', released as a 78 rpm record by Decca Records (DR 17846) in the summer of that year. The lyrics were by George Korel, and the song was introduced on the record by a voice that was supposedly Hank's.

Shelton was accompanied on the piano by Johnny Franz, who was soon to become an A&R man for Phillips and would later be a producer of note in the 1960s, helping to develop the sound and success of Dusty Springfield and the Walker Brothers.

New Fiction Press published the sheet music to 'The Hank Janson Blues,' with a delightful portrait of Shelton by Heade. The list of titles on the back cover announced that Hank Janson had sold over eight million books.

* * *

On 24 July 1953, the High Bailiff of the Isle of Man, Mr Howard Lay, presided over the case of five booksellers who were in court on sixty-two charges of selling obscene books. A considerable number of Hank Janson titles appeared amongst the thirty-nine novels listed. These included: *Death Wore A Petticoat*; *Lady, Mind That Corpse*; *Skirts Bring Me Sorrow*;

Lola Brought Her Wreath; *Lilies For My Lovely*; *Some Look Better Dead*; *Baby, Don't Dare Squeal*; *Tension*; *Sister, Don't Hate Me*; *Conflict*; *Torment*; *Sadie Don't Cry Now*; *Killer, Suspense*; and *Accused*.

The Isle of Man is independent of UK law, and the prosecutions were brought under the island's own Obscene Publications and Indecent Advertisements Act 1907. The books were purchased by police constables who, it was admitted, had access to "a list of books which were in effect banned" before they went into the shops [58]. Inspector T A Cringle, who was prosecuting the case, responded to a plea from shopkeepers that they should be informed of the books on the list, so that they could avoid them, by saying: "The list is compiled from prosecutions in various parts of the country and is confidential. If the police made it available they would put themselves in the role of censors of literature, and we are not going to do that."

That, however, is precisely what was happening. "Police evidence was that constables bought the books, and when they read them, they marked passages which they considered to be obscene," records the *Isle of Man Examiner*.

The case, heard at the Douglas Police Court, highlighted the problems of booksellers. The police were armed with lists of books that had, at one time or another, had a destruction order issued against them and were therefore, *prima facie*, obscene books. Booksellers who asked to see these lists issued by the Home Office, so that they could avoid offering obscene books for sale, were rebuffed and told that the lists were confidential. They were confidential at the request of the office of the Director of Public Prosecutions.

The High Bailiff disagreed, and said that it would be helpful if the list in the possession of the police was made available to booksellers, prompting Inspector Cringle to respond: "Those shopkeepers who are members of the local Newsagents' Association should have a good idea, for the Association have a list of their own."

One of the booksellers, Granville Clague, had asked to see the police list, but was refused. Contacting his

---

[58] *Isle of Man Examiner*, 31 July 1953.

134

distributors, Pemberton's of Manchester, he was assured that, as far as they knew, none of the books they had sent had been banned. In this, Pemberton's were only partly correct: although none of the thirty-nine books had been individually named in a charge of obscenity, all appeared on the Home Office list as having been the subject of a successful prosecution. Another bookseller asked the officer buying books in his shop: "Are they on your list? Because they are not on mine." The constable understood the bookseller to mean the Newsagents' Association list.

One of the officers giving evidence was Detective-Constable W Cook, who remarked that the books were of a type that were "pure sex." "Have you read *The Cruel Sea*?" enquired the High Bailiff. "There's a passage in that which could hardly be more obscene." But, commented Inspector Cringle in response, a book like *The Cruel Sea* and others of a similar kind were not likely to fall into the hands of young holidaymakers. The High Bailiff concurred: "I suppose there is a distinction between good books and what are called 'literary tripe'."

At the end of the day, His Worship the High Bailiff made a decision to grant himself a fortnight to "generally look through" the books that he was being asked to condemn. A destruction order was subsequently granted on 7 August.

On 11 August, Julius Reiter was approached by Scotland Yard and asked to make a statement concerning the distribution of Hank Janson novels. Reg Carter was asked on 28 August about their publication.

In September, Carter's office at 139 Borough High Street was raided by police armed with a search warrant. All the books on the premises were seized and piled into a van.

Jumping into his car, Carter drove over to the Arc Press in Friern Barnet, where the latest Hank Janson was rolling off the presses. There he found more police officers already loading books they had seized into vans. They were even taking away the large, flat sheets that had just come off the press. When Carter realised this, he brought the rotary to a standstill.

On the same day and at around the same time, Julius Reiter watched as large vans drew up outside the premises of Gaywood Press. The police presented him with a warrant, and Reiter watched as all his stock was loaded into the vans and driven away.

Neither Reg Carter nor Julius Reiter was charged with any offence, but their businesses had been brought to a grinding halt. Carter, through the publishers New Fiction Press and Comyns, and his printers, Arc Press, employed around 100 people, who were now standing idle and wondering what the future held for them. Julius Reiter, who co-owned Arc Press, also employed dozens of people through his publishing and distribution businesses.

Carter quickly regrouped his resources, formed a new company, Top Fiction Press, and published *Corruption*, the last of the fourth series of Janson novels; *The Unseen Assassin*, a Hank Janson Special with a science-fiction plot, followed.

The Hank Janson Specials – an irregular series of books in different genres, none of them featuring the Janson character – had been instigated in mid-1952 with the publication of *Auctioned*. This was the first of a trilogy of stories about the adventures of a young Middle-Eastern girl captured by raiders and sold into slavery in the harem of the Caliph of Ripel. Valli, the girl, escapes to the desert city of Bey Turan. The sequel, *Persian Pride*, followed the story of Jan, a boy from the same tribe, whom Valli loved and who was also sold into slavery. The trilogy was then concluded in *Desert Fury*. In August 1953, New Fiction Press had also reissued Frances's first novel, *One Man In His Time*, as a Special under the Janson byline.

Science-fiction had always held a fascination for Frances. During his Pendulum Publications days, he had published *New Worlds* magazine; and, once the S D Frances imprint had been established, he had commissioned a science-fiction novel to appear under the name Astron Del Martia, hoping eventually to write novels under the byline himself. The first Del Martia, *The Trembling World*, had been penned by John Russell Fearn, and a second title, *Dawn Of Darkness* had been advertised to appear almost immediately.

However, the increased print runs of the Hank Janson titles had taken up all Frances's resources, and *Dawn Of*

Darkness had eventually been published by Gaywood Press in 1951. It had been followed by two more Del Martia novels of very poor quality, all by the same, unknown hand [59].

In 1953, Frances felt confident enough to try his own hand, and pushed the notion of a science-fiction novel through "A personal letter to his readers from Hank Janson" in the back of the contemporary Hank Janson novels. This invited readers' critiques of *The Unseen Assassin*, in what was a unique competition (comments on a postcard, top prize £20) for the Hank Janson range.

The advent of the Specials may have been an indication that both author and publisher had seen the writing on the wall for Gangster novels. At the very least, it showed that Frances wanted to expand his repertoire beyond crime thrillers. Even in the regular Janson novels, he was planning for the fifth series – dubbed the 'Continental' series – to take Hank away from the USA on special assignment to Europe. The first of these titles, *Silken Menace*, was set in Amsterdam, and the second, *Nyloned Avenger*, in Bonn. The third, *Woman Trap*, was to have taken place in Berlin, but an escalation of the legal problems besetting the range prevented it from ever being published.

On 19 October 1953, Reg Carter and Julius Reiter were both questioned again by police, this time specifically about the publication of three Hank Janson titles, *Amok*, *Vengeance* and *Killer*. On 23 November, the two men appeared at Guildhall Justice Room and were charged with publishing seven obscene libels in the form of seven Hank Janson novels.

---

[59] The same unknown author also wrote as Franz Harkon for Scion Ltd.

CHAPTER TEN

PROSECUTION

The Central Criminal Court in London, still widely known as the Old Bailey, was opened in 1907 and stands on the site of the old and infamous Newgate Prison. In the 18th Century, Newgate was the final home for murderers, highwaymen and cut-purses condemned at the Sessions House next door before they were taken by cart to Tyburn to be hanged. The building's baroque design is topped by a statue of Justice, blindfolded and carrying a set of scales and a sword in her outstretched arms.

The case officially designated *R. v. Reiter* opened on Thursday 14 January 1954 [60], before the Recorder of London. The position of Recorder was an ancient one, dating back to the 13th Century. The appointee, a High Court judge selected by the Court of Aldermen, was required to sit full-time at the Old Bailey, to take on administration duties for the efficient running of the Central Criminal Court, and to advise the Lord Mayor and the Court of Aldermen on questions of law and procedure.

The Recorder of London in 1953 was Gerald Dodson, who had been appointed to the post in October 1937. Born in 1884 and educated at Downing College, Cambridge, Dodson was the son of John Dodson, the Sheriff of Norwich and a Justice of the Peace. Armed with Bachelor of Arts and Bachelor of Law degrees from Cambridge, Dodson had been called to the Bar in 1907 and joined the South Eastern Circuit. Rejected on medical grounds (asthma) by the Army during the Great War, Dodson had served with the Royal Naval Volunteer Reserve and arranged concerts for the soldiers camped at Sandown Park racecourse awaiting mobilisation. These concerts had featured performances by well-known

---

[60] *R. v. Reiter*, 2 Q.B. 16 (1954).

music hall stars of the day, and occasionally by Goddard himself, humorously adapting popular songs and accompanied by his wife on piano. He had later served aboard a drifter in the North Sea – an observation post tracking the movements of enemy submarines and mine-layers. During this time, one of his commanding officers had been Montague Phillips, a composer and song-writer, and the two had worked together on a light opera set at the time of the Monmouth Rebellion. This had eventually been completed after the two were demobilised. Under the title *The Rebel Maid*, it had debuted at the Empire Theatre in Leicester Square, London in March 1921.

Returning to the Bar, Dodson had served as Treasury Counsel for nine years. He had then been Recorder of Tenderden from 1932, before being appointed a judge of the Mayor's and City of London Court in 1934. This had also made him a junior judge at the Old Bailey.

In his autobiography, Dodson recalled: "The first case I tried at the Old Bailey ended in the jury failing to agree, which somewhat troubled me, as I took it to be a reflection upon the clarity of my summing-up." [61] He added later:

> Since the occasion to which I have referred, I have often been obliged to discharge a jury from giving a verdict because its members were unable to agree, and to order that the case be tried all over again.
>
> This has sometimes happened under circumstances that have led one to form strong views as to the need for the legality of a majority verdict. Time and again I have been asked by the foreman of a jury, "Must the verdict be one in which we all agree?" showing at least some desire for avoiding such a course, and it is with regret that one is obliged to remind the jury that the present state of the law requires agreement in a verdict one way or the other of all their members.

[61] Sir Gerard Dodson, *Consider Your Verdict*, p 85.

A majority verdict would not endanger the liberty of anyone, provided the majority was reasonably large, say ten to one. But I have already dealt with this question in an earlier chapter, and it is only necessary to add that any disagreement about a verdict involves a waste of time and expense that could well be saved, and brings no resulting benefit to anyone except counsel, for at the Old Bailey, at least, an accused person is generally convicted upon a second trial, though, of course, there are exceptions to the rule. But if upon a second trial there is another disagreement by a fresh jury, it is customary in nearly all cases for the prosecution to proceed no further against the accused person, and the jury are instructed by the judge to return a formal verdict of "not guilty". [62]

Dodson certainly had some firm and entrenched attitudes by the time he tried the case against Julius Reiter and Reg Carter. Stephen Frances put it more strongly, and quoted Margharita Laski who, writing in the *New Statesman*, described the case as "a criminal miscarriage of justice."

"There were reasons why Carter and Reiter were (not 'found') 'made' guilty," Frances said many years later. "[Dodson] probably was in strong approval of the campaign being waged by the purity league against spicy foto-books. He wanted to give an example and wanted to handle the obscenity cases. But he was also such a cloistered religious fanatic he didn't know what was going on in the world around him, and when the defence, wishing to show what was the moral attitude of the day, read out extracts from books published by reputable publishers, he was deeply shocked. The extracts read were weighty and made Hank Janson read like a fairy story, and the judge refused to allow extracts [from the Jansons] to be read. All his venom against all of this was included in his summing up.

---

[62] *ibid*, p 86.

"The other factor was the importance of Hank Janson to business. The police were accustomed to picking up a few books from a newsagents. When they set off to raid Hank Janson, they probably had no conception of what was involved. At the warehouse address, they had to get vans to take away thousands of Hank Jansons ...

"If the prosecution *failed*, and immense claims were made for compensation, whose heads would roll?"

* * *

Before the Old Bailey proceedings began, the barristers defending Carter and Reiter offered a deal to the prosecution. Seven books – *Accused, Auctioned, Persian Pride, Pursuit, Amok, Killer* and *Vengeance* – were to be put before the jury, which would mean that the jury would be asked to read all seven books, a time-consuming business that would hold up the case. "Carter and Reiter wanted to make it easier for everyone, and proposed that the prosecution should select only one of the books to put to the jury," recalled Frances. "If the charge was proved against this one book, they would plead guilty to all. This would save the court's time, and the prosecution could present the book that was its strongest case."

The prosecution declined.

After the initial examination and cross-examination of various police officers regarding the sale of the seven novels, the prosecutor, Mervyn Griffith-Jones, outlined the case, saying that the books were on sale throughout the country at 2 shillings a copy. Five of the books dealt with murder, robbery and every other kind of crime. The other two had a background of slavery in some desert, with nomads and Arabs being enslaved by the local Caliph. The main theme running through all the books was, according to Griffith-Jones, sex. The second theme was cruelty, with descriptions of the hero being tortured and young girls being tied up. In the submission of the prosecution, the only effect of these books would be to corrupt and deprave.

Griffith-Jones also outlined two points of law that needed explanation to the jury: that whether or not the defendants *intended* to corrupt and deprave was not important; and that if part of the book was obscene, then the whole book was obscene [63].

Mr Griffith-Jones then suggested that, before the jury retired to read the books, he should first be allowed to give them a story outline of each of the seven, and to draw to their attention certain passages and provide page numbers of "particularly obscene passages." "I will then ask that you be allowed to go to your jury-room and look at the books; if not to read them in their entirety from beginning to end, certainly to look at them sufficiently."

This notion – that the books need not be read in their entirety – was challenged by defending counsel Gerald Howard QC [64], who eventually agreed to the arrangement begrudgingly and only "so long as the jury are given the opportunity of reading the books as a whole."

"Well, we can only do it by stages, I suppose," said the Recorder. "I think the first thing is to open the case and then we can look into it."

For the next hour and three-quarters, the prosecutor read out extracts from the Janson books, which he laced with his own running commentary, until eventually the Recorder brought him to a halt:

> MR GRIFFITH-JONES: I spare you in open court the description I had intended to read of the finding of the two on the kitchen floor by Freidman and the appalling scene as she lay across his knee, undressed, with a knife raised in his hands.
>
> THE RECORDER: At what page does that come?
>
> MR GRIFFITH-JONES: My Lord, it comes on page 88, it goes from page 88 to page 91.

---

[63] The precedents cited by Griffith-Jones were *R.* v. *De Montalk*, 23 Cr. App. Rep. 182 (1932) and the case against Paget Publications previously mentioned.

[64] Stephen Gerald Howard (1896-). Educated at Harrow (where he was Head of School) and Balliol College, Oxford. Called to the Bar in 1924. As well as his work as a barrister-at-law, Howard was also the Conservative MP for Cambridgeshire from 1950.

THE RECORDER: The jury can glance at it some time or other. I suggest, Mr Griffith-Jones, to save you the trouble of reading out passages after that one, when we take the other books you might indicate to the jury the page, and then give them two or three minutes to run their eyes over it, then it can all be done without you having to use your voice all the time.

After giving evidence for 105 minutes, Griffith-Jones suggested that the jury should then retire to their room to read the books as a whole. The Recorder, however, had a different idea:

THE RECORDER: I think that it is better that you should hear the evidence and some of the defence before they look at the books in detail ... if indeed they want to. I have looked at them and have been following them. And the jury have been following them and have looked at them; it may well be that, subject to what the defence have got to point out as being qualifying passages, or ameliorating passages, the jury will say, "We have seen enough of these books." I do not know.

MR HOWARD: My Lord, I should very much like to agree with that, but I am afraid, with respect, I cannot. These books are put in as being obscene libels as to the whole book, and are exhibited. They are exhibits, and in my respectful submission, whatever the view of the jury may be at this stage, it is right that they should read the books, and read them before any evidence is called in order that they may understand the course the defence propose to take.

THE RECORDER: What about adjourning this case until Monday, let the jury take the books with them and they can read them at their leisure.

143

MR HOWARD: With great respect, I should have thought that a convenient way of dealing with it. I am sure they could cover the contents of these seven books by then.

THE RECORDER: Well, I still think this is not the stage at which the jury should be asked to read the books. It may be that they may never have to, if we know what the defence is. I think it better, Mr Griffith-Jones, for you to prove your case after the adjournment, and then we will see what Mr Howard's attitude may be. I think it is very much better, Mr Howard, if you would indicate in your opening what your line of defence is, then when the jury comes to look at the books, if they have to, they will know what your contention is.

It was, by now, Thursday lunchtime, and had the case been adjourned, the jury would have had a reasonable opportunity to read the seven books, as Gerald Howard was requesting. Instead, the Recorder wanted the defence to indicate to the court what its defence would be, as if this might negate the need to read all the books.

Howard explained that it was his intention to introduce a number of other books into the case and it was necessary for the jury to have read all seven charged books if they were to have a full understanding of the defence.

MR HOWARD: It seems to me, with respect, that the defence is entitled to say: "We want these exhibits read."

RECORDER: Well, there may come a time when I shall have to decide whether the submission of other books is material to this issue and whether they are admissible. Members of the jury, I think that if you will come back at ten minutes past two and then take these things to your room, sit there quietly by yourselves, and then by four o'clock you can let me know whether you have been able to get the hang of the whole thing so as to be able to do the defence justice upon the line suggested by Mr Gerald Howard, so that you will be able to understand any submission that a passage here and there does not corrupt the whole book, which I take it is more or less the theme. I think we will go by stages and see what the position is at four o'clock. The jury have already seen a great deal. If they have not had time by four o'clock to get the real hang of the whole thing, they must say so. If that is the case, then it will be better to adjourn the whole matter till Monday morning, and then they can spend a grizzly weekend. I am speaking now from a literary point of view; these people do not utter or make a remark, but they always "grit" it out to somebody else; that is the sort of thing I am referring to, not the matter we are trying. If need be, members of the jury, you must take them, for these courts have tedious duties to perform from time to time, and if we have to wade through them, then we must. Come back at ten minutes past two, then take these books to your room and let me know how you are getting on by four o'clock. You may have completed your survey then. You may be quick readers.

Following lunch, the jury retired to their room at 2.12 pm. They returned to court at 4.00 pm.

THE RECORDER: Well, Mr Foreman. What is the position now?

FOREMAN: We have read enough of these books, my Lord.

THE RECORDER: You think you have been fairly able to assess the contents?

FOREMAN: That is so, my Lord.

THE RECORDER: All of them?

FOREMAN: Yes.

THE RECORDER: Very well. Thank you, Mr Foreman. Then, that being the case, we can adjourn until tomorrow.

In the absence of Gerald Howard, his colleague, Mr R P Moore, protested:

MR MOORE: I wonder whether discussion as to the next stage in the trial might be put off until when the court sits tomorrow morning, and that will give an opportunity for my learned friend to address your Lordship, if he thinks it right, as to whether he might ask the jury to take a little more time in looking at these books. Perhaps if the matter could be discussed when the court sits tomorrow, there would be no waste of time.

THE RECORDER: I do not think that the jury should be coerced into doing their duty. They are quite well able to assess what they think it is.

MR MOORE: Well, of course, My Lord, the defence has no desire to force the jury to read more than they want to.

THE RECORDER. No. They have said they have read enough and that they have been able to go through them. Why that statement should not be accepted, I do not know. For my part, I accept it. I have glanced through these books myself and I am quite well able to form an opinion, with no difficulty at all.

MR MOORE Yes, my Lord.

THE RECORDER: Nobody has suggested that the jury should go over every chapter and every bit.

MR MOORE: No, my Lord, of course not.

THE RECORDER: Well, the jury, conscientiously doing their duty, say that they have encompassed the whole of the subject matter of this indictment and say that they can deal with it as a book ... not as a paragraph but as a book. I do not see why any more discussion need take place.

* * *

The case resumed on Friday morning at about 10.30 am. From the Recorder's opening remarks, it would seem he had sent a note to the absent Mr. Howard, informing him that the jury had indicated that they had read "enough" of the books.

THE RECORDER: Perhaps I had better give Mr Howard an opportunity of saying anything he wants to say. Last night the jury said they had looked at these books, Mr Howard. I asked that a message be sent to you. I hope you got it?

MR HOWARD: I have a note here, my Lord.

THE RECORDER: I do not know if you would like to say anything about this?

MR HOWARD: No, my Lord, except this. I do not wish to repeat yesterday with regard to *that*. I did indicate what I felt – and it is what I still feel now, bearing in mind the task that is set before the jury here – that these books, being exhibited, all ought to be read, although I'm not saying every word, and it seemed to me a physical impossibility, and that even the extracts referred to by my learned friend yesterday took an hour

147

and three-quarters to read. Of course I, as everybody is, am bound by the jury's answer, and I do not for a moment question it, but I do repeat the observation I made yesterday, that it does seem to me a very difficult task, if not an impossible task, to have performed it in the way I, appearing for the defence, would have thought it ought to be done.

THE RECORDER: Well, if you are making any application that they should be given more time to read the books, I will ask them to do so if you think it necessary.

MR HOWARD: My Lord, why one thinks it necessary –and I am sure the jury will forgive me saying it – is that, in my submission, it is not sufficient merely to read an extract here and there; it is essential to read the books in the sense of being able to appreciate the characters, the story such as it is, the plot, and how these various extracts come into the whole thing. I, of course, give full credit to the jury for doing their utmost in the hour and three-quarters they have had, but I am bound to say that when I had to read the books, it took me roughly speaking and hour and half to read each one.

THE RECORDER: Well, do you want them to give more time to it? They will, of course, have a further opportunity of looking at them. Yesterday, the case was opened by extracts being read for an hour and a quarter; then they spent from two till four o'clock reading them.

MR HOWARD: I was supporting what I had to say upon a direction which the then Common Sergeant (I think it was) gave to a jury in a case of this kind a good many years ago, in which he indicated that they had to consider the extracts

148

in relation to the whole of the publication, and it seems very difficult for that to be done unless they have more or less mastered the whole of the publication.

THE RECORDER: I mentioned it so that the jury could hear again what you have to say about it. I think they do fully appreciate now that the charges here relate to the whole of the books and not to mere extracts; and, as I said yesterday, it is necessary to look at the whole book to see whether the rest of it qualified the selected passages – and that they have done. At the moment, it is very difficult to say how much time should be spent in that occupation.

MR. HOWARD: I did happen to notice that your Lordship mentioned that my learned friend should read a very few extracts; that he read only a tithe of those he is relying upon, and that he took a considerable time.

THE RECORDER: You see! The jury did have the advantage of that, and they had their two hours in the afternoon. Having heard what you have said and what I have said, I think they fully appreciate the position. Do you think, Mr Foreman, that at this stage you would like any more time to read these books?

FOREMAN: In the circumstances, perhaps that would be so, my Lord; although yesterday each member of the jury did feel satisfied that in the two hours they had been able to assess the general reading of each of the books. We feel that perhaps we should have a little more time, in view of what counsel has just said.

THE RECORDER: All right. It is essential, of course, that in every case, any reasonable request made on behalf of the defence should be met, and I cannot say that there is anything unreasonable in the application – so far as it is an application; perhaps it is more a suggestion of mind than anything else. Well, so be it. So far as the court is concerned, I have other business to go on with. The jury have the rest of the day and that ought to satisfy everybody, ought it not?

MR HOWARD: My Lord, with great respect, that was the original suggestion which I remember your Lordship making yesterday at one period – that if the jury read the books yesterday afternoon and today we could come back on Monday, and I think I said that would give them ample time and would be a very convenient way of doing it. As I say, nobody desires to put any undue burden upon the jury, who have enough to do in any event.

THE RECORDER: No, I am quite sure of that.

MR HOWARD: But one is bound to do one's duty as one sees it, and it did seem to me in a case of this kind that a mere, as it were, skipping through a book in a few minutes was not really doing what is required.

THE RECORDER: All right. Members of the jury, I think you are reasonably comfortable in your own room. I could send you up to a larger room, which is perhaps a little brighter, but it has not got the amenities which you have got in your own room, if you are comfortable there. I do not want you to feel you are locked up for the day, or anything of that kind. Of course, it is desirable that you should confer only with each other; that you appreciate, of course; these are very elementary things. If you go to your room, you have got an usher at your command and you have only to ring the bell. I think it would be a wise thing if you came back just before one o'clock and reported progress, so to speak, told me how you are getting on. Anyway, you will not feel quite so isolated and desolate; you can come back and have another look at us at one o'clock. Do that, then we will see about the afternoon. If you still feel that you would like further time in order to do justice to this case, which I am sure you are very anxious to do, then we will follow the same procedure this afternoon until about four o'clock, and let us hope that your troubles will be over; but we will see.

The jury retired at 10.48 am and was back in court at 12.45 pm.

THE RECORDER: Well, Mr Foreman, do you think that in order to satisfy the requirements of this case, you would like to have a little more time this afternoon, say from two to four or thereabouts?

FOREMAN: No, my Lord. Each member of the jury feels he has had sufficient time to assess the reading of these books, and that no useful purpose would be served in us devoting any more time to reading.

THE RECORDER: Very well. Then we will adjourn this case till Monday morning at half-past ten.

The jury had devoted less than four hours to reading seven books.

CHAPTER ELEVEN

ACCUSED

John Mervyn Guthrie Griffith-Jones, the prosecutor in the case against Reiter and Carter, was born in 1909 and educated at Eton and Trinity Hall, Cambridge. Called to the Bar at the Middle Temple in 1932, he had served with distinction (mentioned in despatches) in the Coldstream Guards in the Western Desert, North Africa and Italy during World War II. In 1945, he was one of the British prosecuting counsel at the trial of major War criminals at Nuremberg, returning to London in 1946 to take up a position as Counsel to the Crown at North London Sessions before moving to the Central Criminal Court in 1950.

Griffith-Jones later took on the office of Common Serjeant in 1964, and was Chairman of the Norfolk Quarter Sessions for six years, 1965-71. As well as his legal work, he also served on the Westminster City Council, 1948-54, and was a recreational painter, holding a number of one-man exhibitions in the decade before his death in 1979.

In a career filled with so many achievements, it seems a pity that Mervyn Griffith-Jones is remembered amongst literary historians only as the man who asked in all sincerity of *Lady Chatterley's Lover*: "Is it a book you would even wish your wife or your servant to read?"

The trial concerning *Lady Chatterley's Lover* was the first major test case under the new Obscene Publications Act 1959, and the defendants were found not guilty of obscenity. To some, that seemed poetic justice (but little comfort to Reg Carter or Julius Reiter), since it was Griffith-Jones who had prosecuted the case against Hank Janson – the first of the cycle of cases that had forced the Government to update the outmoded and unsafe Obscene Publications Act.

In 1954, Griffith-Jones opened his case for the prosecution by commenting upon the seven books through the example of *Accused* – perhaps regarding it as the worst "offender" – even before the jury had been offered the chance to read the book.

MR GRIFFITH-JONES: To take *Accused* as an example. That book is the story of a young man who starts off driving a car out on a drunken and rather lecherous evening with some other young men and women. On their way back, he runs over somebody in the road ... indeed, two young girls, if I remember rightly, going at a tremendous speed in the car; they carry on and do not stop; blood, and so on, is found over the bonnet. Then he is on the run and jumps onto a lorry, and goes out into some deserted area of the country ... this takes place in America ... he is dropped off the lorry, he walks a long way and finishes up in a little café kept by a man called Freidman; he is down and out and has no food, so Freidman offers him lodgings and food if he will work for him, Freidman, in the café, and there he settles down to work. The story then revolves around what happens in that café. Freidman is a sadist; he has married a woman, a young girl, who is to all intents and purposes his slave, whom he treats with the utmost brutality. He then treats this young boy with equal brutality and really enslaves him. One has descriptions night by night, as the boy sleeps on the floor outside the bedroom door, of Freidman torturing, in effect, his wife, and one hears her groans of agony coming through the door. Eventually this young man and the wife become attracted by one another; they have sexual intercourse with one another, and they are discovered in the act ... I think upon the second or third occasion of doing it ... on the kitchen floor while Freidman is away; Freidman comes back and they are discovered in the act.

There is then a scene, and Freidman says he will punish them; he puts his naked wife over his knee, and with a knife is going, apparently, to slit her private parts, and threatens to castrate the young man as soon as he has finished. The young man eventually can stand it no longer ... the wonder is that he has stood it as long as that, you may think ... so he seizes a flat-iron, knocks the villain on the head and kills him, puts him down the well. And then the boy and the girl run off. They of course have sexual intercourse at every possible opportunity, until the boy discovers that the woman is older than he thought and becomes less attracted by her; there is a beastly description of a woman's festering foot; eventually she takes an overdose of morphia and dies, the boy goes off and is finally picked up by the police and then beaten-up, and one has a description of the sadistic and ghastly beating-up of the boy imprisoned by the police.

That is the general outline of the book. Now would you look perhaps as an example at page 58. We are in the café and the villain Freidman has gone down to the town to pay his money into the bank; then you see about a third of the way down the page:

I followed him out onto the veranda, watched him come down the steps, cross over to his lorry and climb up into the driving seat. There was maybe an hour to go before closing time. But I turned back into the dining room, closed the door, locked it and switched on the "Closed" sign.

She was waiting for me, her eyes anxious and apprehensive as I closed the door behind me. It was as though she didn't know whether to run to me, or away from me.

I knew we were crazy. But I also knew nothing was going to stop it happening. It was inevitable, something that had to happen, like a car going down hill with no brakes and no means of stopping until it hit bottom. [65]

It appears in a moment, of course, what is inevitable; but if you have read all the book up to now, it is perfectly clear that the only thing that is inevitable is the sexual intercourse that is about to take place:

> I walked over to the kitchen door, closed it deliberately, bolted it firmly. There were shabby, sun-dried and sun-bleached curtains that I drew, covering the glass portion of the door.
> When I turned around, she was staring at me with a kinda wild, desperate look in her eyes. "You can't," she panted. "You mustn't. There's folk coming in all the time."
> I crossed to the only window the kitchen possessed, jerked the curtain across, leaving us in a kinda half-light.
> She shrank away from me, pushed herself back against the table.

And then he goes over and stands by her

> "We can't stop this thing," I said hoarsely. "It's no good trying to fight against it."
> "No," she panted. "You mustn't." There was a thoroughly scared note in her voice.
> It was like it was before, the palms of her hands against my chest but without the strength to push me away. And with the door closed and the sun beating down on the iron roof, that kitchen was boiling us in our own perspiration.

---

[65] This and subsequent quotes by Griffith-Jones are from *Accused*, pp 58-60.

And so on ...

"You mustn't," she whispered. "It's crazy. Anybody can come in."

My shirt was wet, sticking to me like I had been rain drenched. I could feel beads of sweat forming ...

And so on ...

I could feel her skin through her dress, hot and slippery, soft and desirable, the quickening of her breathing increasing the fierce urgency inside me. I did what I'd done before, ran my fingers along her spine, grasped her hair, pulled her lips to mine.

This time she resisted, not too strongly but enough. "Don't be crazy," she breathed. "Anyone can come in."

"I've locked the dining room," I whispered. "Closed down for the night."

I felt the tenseness inside her, the rigidity of shock and fear. "You can't," she whispered. "You can't do that and ..."

I pressed her head towards mine, cut off her words with my mouth. Her rigidity lasted for maybe a couple of seconds, and then she was responding with a savage urgency that was almost frightening, grasping me fiercely, greedily. Her hands were as slippery as mine, and the very fury of her passion was frightening in its intensity, sweeping me along with it.

It was like we were fighting each other. She writhing and biting; me clutching her tightly, our hands seeking and finding each other almost brutally. She panted frantically, "No. You mustn't." But she wouldn't let me go, and the rim of the table was at the backs of her thighs, bracing her, giving her resistance.

There had never been anything like it for me before. I knew that there was no stopping now, that this just had to be.

She panted again: "No. You mustn't." Yet her fingers were in my hair, pulling me towards her, her hands caressing my sweat-soaked shoulders and her lips searching greedily for mine.

Her dress tore. She panted, "No!" Then a few seconds later, "No! It's crazy."

I didn't say anything. I wasn't even thinking. Everything was a hot whirl of emotion, a perspiring whirlpool that grasped me in a delirious embrace, sucking me ever and ever down and down, my senses swimming with ecstasy, as I plunged ever more deeply towards the tranquillity and peace I would find when the urgent, heady whirling ceased.

There are plenty of other passages in that book, and when you have read them you may well think I have selected one that is by no means the worst.

"All authors' words trigger off images in readers' minds," wrote Steve Frances. "The reader usually adds something of his own invention to the author's words. If an author writes 'cold, clear water glistening in the sun,' one reader might think of a fountain, another of a goldfish pond and a third of an Arctic seascape.

"The word 'woman' conjures up visual images in most men's minds, but they are sure to be very different images. An author can write: 'He and she clung to each other,' and in the mind of a reader these words may seem to describe the act of sexual intercourse, although there has not been any such description."

Griffith-Jones's opening statement to the jury included comments on dozens of passages from the Hank Janson books, not all of which he read directly from the texts. For instance:

MR GRIFFITH-JONES: One has descriptions night by night, as the boy sleeps on the floor outside the bedroom door, of Freidman torturing, in effect, his wife, and one hears her groans of agony coming through the door.

The scene appears on page 28 of *Accused*:

I shucked off my jacket, folded it to form a pillow, stretched myself out on the floor, tried to make myself comfortable on the hard boards.

I'd had a long day and I was tired. It wasn't all that difficult for me to sleep. But the thin strip of light gleaming from under their bedroom door disturbed me strangely. I knew I wouldn't go to sleep until it had gone out.

I didn't have to wait long. I heard the faint creak of bed springs and a few seconds later a much heavier creaking as Freidman lifted his bulk onto the bed. Then abruptly, suddenly, the light snapped off,

I was almost asleep when it started.

I lay for a long while wondering what it could be, a kinda low, continual whine.

I sat up, listened. There wasn't any doubt about it then. The noise was coming from their bedroom. I was fully awake now, listening intently.

I'd only heard her speak once, yet I knew instinctively it was her. She was murmuring a kinda low, whining murmur. I guessed they'd be talking about me and wondered what they'd be saying.

Stealthily, silently, I climbed to my feet, crept over to their door. I pressed my ear against the panels, listened intently.

I began to sweat.

I could hear much more distinctly now. She wasn't talking. She was moaning. Giving little moans, punctuated with sharp gasps of pain. And it wasn't what it could have been, a man and his wife roughing each other up a little. She was suffering, really suffering. The moans were breaking through her self-control as she steeled herself against pain.

I stood there in a cold sweat. It was Freidman who was with his wife. What could I do about it? He was a guy twice the size of me, and his wife hadn't yet started screaming for help.

I tiptoed back to my rolled-up jacket, carried it into a corner as far away from the bedroom door as I could get and settled down again.

But I couldn't sleep. The moans went on forever, and I just couldn't sleep while they continued.

"Where are the night by night descriptions of Freidman torturing his wife?" asked Stephen Frances. "There is only the girl giving 'little moans punctuated with sharp gasps of pain,' which prosecutor [Griffith-]Jones misquotes as 'groans of agony'."

Griffith-Jones then read from page 58, referring the "the sexual intercourse that is about to take place," as quoted above.

"If the jury had been listening attentively," said Frances, "it must have noticed that, although there is a description of caressing and kissing in the book, there is no description whatsoever of sexual intercourse."

Again, Griffith-Jones noted another section of *Accused* in which "Freidman puts his naked wife over his knees and with a knife is going, apparently, to slit her private parts, and threatens to castrate the young man as soon as he is finished." ("At what page does this come?" asked the Recorder, eagerly.)

The scene referred to describes what happens when twenty-year-old drifter Harry Farron is discovered with the wife of the much older Alfred Freidman. The two have been love-making on the kitchen floor of a diner (or, rather, it is implied, "She launched herself at me, took me by surprise, gripped me with an incredible strength ... The kitchen was the only place. But this time it was different, without timidity and without restraint. And when it was over it was a gentle parting, reluctant yet peaceful and satisfying." [66]). As they prepare to get dressed, the glass window of the kitchen door is smashed through by her husband.

Freidman.
Freidman!
FREIDMAN
The shattering impact of wood against glass was numbing, paralysing.

I sat up, stared at him wide-eyed, my heart beating madly but my brain numb, dead, refusing to function.

She was sitting beside me, eyes staring, her face white. I could hear her gasping like she was sucking in breath but wasn't exhaling.

Freidman's head and shoulders framed in the smashed window frame looked enormous, his eyes, black and vindictive, smiling with an evil menace. But his voice was quiet, quieter than I'd ever heard it before, almost a purr.

He said softly, "Come over and open this door."

She was trembling, her body trying to obey but fear paralysing her.

"Open this door," he said again, and the note of command in his voice was urgent now, imperative.

---

[66] *Accused*, p 68.

I could feel her body throbbing and vibrating, as her muscles went into action.

"Hurry," he said through his teeth.

She got to her feet, slowly, reluctantly. I wanted to stop her, grasp her by the wrist, prevent her from unlocking the door that was the only barrier between him and us.

But my bones were like jelly, my brain a vacuum, unable to communicate instructions to my body.

In a kinda dream, I saw her crossing to the door, her white haunches quivering, her bare feet treading down the shafts of glass seemingly without feeling, blood spurting, staining the stone floor.

A strangled protest tore free from inside me. I said hoarsely, in a voice that wasn't mine, "No, don't go. Don't let him in."

She was a robot, frightened and numbed, obeying the voice of a man she feared. She turned the key in the lock, and then Freidman was turning the door handle, thrusting the door back with such force it sent her staggering backwards, her shoulders hitting the wall.

There was almost malicious satisfaction in his eyes as be closed the door behind him, turned the key in the lock and put the key in his pocket.

I felt the strength slowly creeping back to my limbs. I crouched, got ready to climb to my feet.

He said, with a dreadful note in his voice, "Just as I thought."

She was staring at him terror-stricken, her hands crossed against her naked breasts.

I was wondering if a flying leap would enable me to reach the kitchen door, so I could bolt through it into the dining room.

161

But he was thinking away ahead of me, his reflexes working rapidly. He circled around me quickly, got between me and the dining room door, bolted it securely.

I didn't climb to my feet. I continued to crouch like I was getting ready to run a race. I was trembling with fear. He walked across to me slowly, his thin lips twisted in a malicious grin of pleasure. "I like you better standing, son," he gritted, and his fingers locked in my hair, dragged me to my feet.

I hadn't any complaints. I deserved it and I got it. His knotted fist uppercutted, scrunched against my jaw, lifted me off my feet, smashed me backwards so my shoulders bit the stone floor and I skidded until my head hit the wall.

In a grey mist of pain I sat up, shook my head. My mouth was full of blood and my head was bleeding. Then, with a coward's relief, I saw that he had left me, had turned his attention to his wife.

"Come here," he said.

She came. Slowly, unwillingly, terror stricken.

But she came!

He locked his fingers in her hair, grinned sadistically. "You decided to play, huh? You betrayed your husband, who's been good to you. Taken on the first little whelp who's come along. And you thought I was stupid, didn't you? Thought I didn't realise what was going on. You're just a no-good bitch, aren't you?"

Her eyes were glazed with terror, her knees trembling, but her hands were passive at her sides.

"You're a no-good bitch," he said.

With her hair coiled around his hand, he kinda strained her on tiptoe while he smacked her face from side to side maybe half-a-dozen times. He wasn't playing. Her lips spurted blood and her eyes became glazed. Yet she made no attempt to avoid the blows, just kinda hung by her hair unprotestingly, arms at her sides.

"You're a no-good bitch," he snarled.

She didn't even whimper, merely half-closed her eyes in pain.

"Say it," he snarled. "You're a no-good bitch. Say it!"

"I'm a no-good bitch," she mumbled through split lips.

"I'm gonna teach you a lesson," he grated. "I'm gonna teach you both a lesson you'll never forget. I'm gonna teach you to be sorry for the day you took your husband for a sucker."

The numbness was leaving my jaw now, replaced by the beginning of pain. The haziness was evaporating too, everything taking on a clear-cut outline.

Freidman hooked a chair over to him with his foot, sat down on it, tugged viciously on her hair to make her kneel at his feet.

"I'm gonna teach you," he snarled. "I'm gonna learn both of you. You're gonna have a lesson you'll never forget. A permanent reminder you won't be able to stop thinking about the next time you start tom-catting."

I wiped the blood away from my mouth, sat up, looked calculatingly at the dining room door. There was just a chance that I could get away if only she would struggle with him, distract his attention.

He repeated slowly, maliciously: "A lesson you'll never forget!" He fumbled in his pocket, produced a jack-knife, flicked it with his thumb so that the short, sharp

163

blade glistened in the sun streaming through the broken window.

I was more scared now. She was a dame as well as his wife, and there wasn't much pain he could inflict on her that she hadn't already received. Even if he did cut off her hair, it would grow again. She was in the kitchen all the time anyway, so she didn't have to worry about her appearance.

But I wasn't his wife. He could get real mean with me, maybe carve me up a little with that knife. The fear was deep down in the pit of my belly, growing stronger and wilder every moment, making me frantic so I was calculating the chances of a headlong dive through that broken window.

He snarled. "Come here, you trollop," and jerked savagely on her hair, toppling her over on top of him so that she sprawled across his knees, face uppermost.

There was wild fear inside me as I stared in amazement, watched his arm clasp across her belly so that she writhed, her head hanging, almost touching the stone floor.

Then he raised the knife, held her in such a way that both she and I understood in the same dreadful moment the horrible, unbelievable intention in his mind.

She screamed, a wild, frantic scream that came from a tormented brain. And the fantastically brutal vengeance he was planning, killed my fear, made me frantic to stop him at all costs.

He saw me coming, was probably expecting me to attack. I was like a crazy thing, while he was quite cool and detached. As my arm crooked around his neck, he smashed his knife hand at me, not the blade but the butt of his hand from which protruded the haft of the knife. It was a huge hand, and he used all his strength. I knew only that the front of my face had been staved in, that I was flying, that my shoulders smashed against hard substance, that I was lying on the floor, arched in pain and the grey mist enveloping me again.

Then through the grey mist I heard her tortured scream, knew that he meant to do this terrible thing, knew that although it was against every instinct of man, he would also do it to me. Cold fear combined with my desperate, outraged horror gave me a strength and a fearlessness that was not a part of me.

The grey haze was edging close around me as I staggered to my feet, lurched unsteadily towards him.

She was screaming, shriek after shriek, terrible tormenting screams that speared down deep into the depths of my soul. I knew I had to stop him, stop this dreadful thing he was doing, stop him somehow, although his strength was ten times that of mine.

The black mist edging in on me flickered, and momentarily I saw a means by which I could prevent this terrible mutilation. I saw the flat-iron she used for tea-cloths, innocent and domestic-looking but a powerful weapon. [67]

Implication and innuendo are open to all sorts of interpretation. What was "the horrible, unbelievable intention" that Farran and Freidman's wife "both understood in the same dreadful moment"? The book certainly does not say.

---

[67] *ibid*, pp 87-91.

Hank Janson, in *Torment For Trixy*, said: "The only thing wrong is the way you folks look at it ... You see rottenness where no rottenness exists."

Mr. Griffith-Jones saw Freidman slitting his wife's private parts, just as he saw Farran and Freidman's wife having "of course, sexual intercourse at every opportunity," following Freidman's accidental death. (In fact, they make love only once more.)

In his comments on *Amok*, Griffith-Jones said: "The hero comes back and finds that the villain has raped the little girl he has picked up by the roadside for about the sixth time." Gerald Howard had to point out that the "little" girl was twenty years of age, that only twenty lines were "suggestive" of rape, and that in the case of the second incident (there were only two), the intimation of rape was based only on the sounds heard by the narrator. Similarly, the shackling of a slave girl in white-hot manacles, as described by Griffith-Jones in his comments on *Auctioned*, is not the scene as it appears in the book.

"If the jury had been allowed to read the books properly, they could have discovered that what prosecutor [Griffith-]Jones said was in the books, was not in the books at all," noted Frances.

CHAPTER TWELVE

THE VERDICT

The case for the defence was simple ... in theory. If one is to judge whether or not a novel is likely to "deprave and corrupt" a reader, one must first establish what is generally acceptable to the public at large, in order to see whether or not that novel oversteps acceptable boundaries. In practice, of course, measuring the morals of a country is not like measuring the temperature, and there are no friendly-faced morals-men and -women to warn us of daily changes in morals across various parts of the country.

To establish a measure of the moral standards acceptable in 1954, the defence, spearheaded by Christmas Humphreys (representing Julius Reiter and Gaywood Press) and Gerald Howard (representing Reg Carter, New Fiction Press and Arc Press), had gathered together a vast library of evidence – a large selection of film stills, bundles of magazines, and fifty or so recently-published books – which, they said, contained scenes very much stronger than anything described by Hank Janson, and which were freely and widely available without raising any complaint.

However, early in the proceedings, the Recorder showed his reluctance to allow any such evidence:

> MR HOWARD: My Lord, I propose to put to this officer [68] a number of newspapers and one illustrated magazine from which, if your Lordship permits it, I would like to read some extracts, in order to ask him whether, to his knowledge, any proceedings have ever been taken in respect of them. That raises the question which your Lordship indicated, as to the admissibility of other matter in the case.

[68] Detective-Sergeant Goodall, the witness.

THE RECORDER: Well, Mr Howard, I should have grave misgivings as to its admissibility, because I cannot see that one publication, whether it may be good, bad or indifferent, can have any influence or have any bearing upon whether some other publication is good, bad or indifferent. But I will not exclude it. I think it is better in a case of this sort that there should be every opportunity given to say what is desired.

MR HOWARD: I am obliged to your Lordship. Your Lordship will recollect that the basis upon which I put it was not that because there may be, to use a more or less neutral phrase, worse publications and, therefore, that involves that these particular publications are not obscene. The basis is this, that if it is right, as in our submission it is right, that the jury, in forming an opinion with regard to these publications, have to have regard to the standard of 1954 and 1953, as the case may be, then any evidence which tends to indicate what that standard is, by way of publications which are read and in respect of which no proceedings are taken, is some evidence tending to show what standard the public is interested in.

THE RECORDER: I do not agree with that either, but I will not exclude anything unless it is outrageously irrelevant.

In his cross-examination of Detective-Sergeant Goodall, Christmas Humphreys also made reference to what was then acceptable in publications:

MR HUMPHREYS: I think you agreed with me before [69], and I am sure you will agree today, that

---

[69] Referring to the proceedings at the Guildhall some weeks earlier, when Reiter and Carter were charged.

the standard of what is legally publishable is constantly changed?

D/S GOODALL: Yes.

MR. HUMPHREYS: You said: "Standards change as time goes on. I know of books that caused public uproar some twenty years ago but that are now sold over the counter."

D/S GOODALL: Yes. The standards have changed.

MR HUMPHREYS: And are changing almost day by day?

D/S GOODALL: Yes.

MR HUMPHREYS: Would you consider that perversion is now openly discussed, and that there are new books on the market which would not be allowed seven or eight years ago?

D/S GOODALL: Yes. But I do not think it would be openly displayed.

MR HUMPHREYS: Would you agree that not only is that standard changing in time but it is also changing in regard to places?

D/S GOODALL: Yes. That does happen.

MR HUMPHREYS: The standards of what is obscene differ from village to village, from town to town and from city to city?

D/S GOODALL: Yes.

MR HUMPHREYS: Could the jury find literature on sale in Leicester Square and Piccadilly Circus which would never be displayed in a provincial town?

D/S GOODALL: Yes.

MR HUMPHREYS: Therefore, a publisher has to consider what standard in relation to what place?

D/S GOODALL: Yes, to a certain extent.

Later in his cross-examination, Humphreys commented on an earlier statement by Goodall that he had "never known any proceedings taken against a book on the grounds of cruelty."

D/S GOODALL: Cruelty alone? I have not known of any myself.

MR HUMPHREYS: Would you agree that the books of such well-known authors as Peter Cheyney, Raymond Chandler and Mickey Spillane are full of brutality from start to finish?

D/S GOODALL: Brutality to a certain extent. Yes.

MR HUMPHREYS: And when plays are made of these books, they follow the pattern of the original story?

D/S GOODALL: Not necessarily.

MR HUMPHREYS: Is it right that there is a film at present called "I, the Jury"?

D/S GOODALL: I have not noticed it.

MR HUMPHREYS: Well, it is up in lights about twenty feet deep in Piccadilly Circus, but you may not have noticed it. And these books of Peter Cheyney, Raymond Chandler and Mickey Spillane are sold in cheap editions?

D/S GOODALL: Yes.

MR HUMPHREYS: In large stores everywhere?

D/S GOODALL: I should think they are, yes.

MR HUMPHREYS: And none has ever been prosecuted?

D/S GOODALL: Not to my knowledge.

Eventually, the jury was sent out, and the Recorder made it abundantly clear that he felt the defence's argument about what was acceptable in publications was irrelevant:

THE RECORDER: I do not think that "standards" have anything to do with it. Sooner or later, I shall be bound to tell the jury so, and Mr Howard and Mr Humphreys can hear what I am saying. I do not think it has anything to do with it at all. The standard of morals may fluctuate from time to time, but it is a pity that it does ... But the law is the same, and it is not much good talking about a case of Higgins, or whatever it was –

MR HOWARD: Hicklin, my Lord.

THE RECORDER: Hicklin – as having been adopted in 1932 and being nineteen years old; it is still law today. It has really nothing to do with standard, but I cannot prevent the defence referring to these matters. I do not think it is relevant. Not a bit.

The bulk of Monday and the following morning was taken up with the reading of extracts from many different books drawn from the list of fifty that the defence had submitted to the court, although their reading was not without interruption from the Recorder, who at one point said: "Well, Mr Humphreys, how many more books have you got to inflict upon the jury?"

* * *

When Mr Humphrey's had completed his closing speech, the Recorder began his summing-up of the case.

> Well, members of the jury, these two men, Reginald Carter and Julius Reiter, and the companies with which they are connected, are charged with publishing obscene libels in seven instances. It is, of course, the duty of the prosecution to satisfy you that these seven books, or some of them, are obscene writings.
>
> So far as any definition of the word "obscene" [is concerned, it] is necessary for you to remember – and I doubt if it is going to help you at all – there is a very simple one in the Oxford Dictionary, which is that it is something "offensive to modesty and decency." In a wider definition in Webster's Dictionary, it says that it is "offensive to chastity or modesty; expressing or presenting to the mind, or view, something that delicacy and decency forbid to be exposed." But the word "obscene" is used in many instances and in a variety of ways. You are not concerned with that. What you are concerned with is whether these books constitute obscene libels. The definitions to which I have referred are supplanted by the legal definition, which has been provided for you by a court of law – eminent judges – which has stood the test of time. It is not a definition which is merely old and has that distinction because it has been used again and again. You have been reminded that it was before the courts in a recorded case as lately as 1932, and apparently used and adopted in a Scottish court even last year. That definition, in the words of Chief Justice Cockburn, was this. I

172

have written it down for you on a half sheet of notepaper so that you may take it with you, as it is quite impossible for you to carry these sentences and this phraseology in your minds. But the definition of an obscene libel is this: "Whether the tendency of it is to deprave and corrupt those whose minds are open to such immoral influence and into whose hands the books may fall."

That is simple enough. Taking the last words first, namely, "into whose hands the books may fall," it has been proved in this case that the books with which you are concerned can fall into the hands of anybody; they can be purchased anywhere by young and old, and indeed it has also been proved that they command enormous sales, no doubt bringing much profit to those who exploit them.

The words which refer to the mentality of persons are these: "the tendency to deprave and corrupt those whose minds are open to such immoral influences" – surely those words must mean mankind in general. Is not the mind of everybody open to the influences of both good and evil?

It was said on behalf of Carter: "How can you corrupt somebody whose mind is already corrupted?" Well, you may think that that is just the sort of mind to which these sort of books might appeal, and that corruption becomes even more corrupt and the individual sinks lower and lower under these baleful influences.

It is said on behalf of these accused that a book is only obscene if it is obscene according to the standards and tests of today. On behalf of Carter, it is put in another way, that the old definition must be applied according to the standards and tests of today, and those were Mr Howard's contentions, the same thing being put in a different way, and it was followed this

173

morning by Mr Humphreys, on behalf of Reiter, who again says the same things in these words, that to interpret the definition – which I have given you and which you shall have – you have got to look at the background of today's publications. I suggest to you that it would be most dangerous to do anything of the kind. No doubt you are quite aware that you are being asked to slide, to let yourselves slide into the degeneracy of modern times, as depicted by these books which have been produced on behalf of the defence. Somebody has been industrious enough to produce and select these books. If they serve any purpose at all, they may indicate to you the sort of abyss into which you are asked to assist by whitewashing these books with which you are concerned and so contributing to the general slide downwards of this type of modern literature to which your attention has been called. I suggest to you it would be a most dangerous standard to adopt; and, indeed, it is not the law, and it is not open to authors, whether in Spain, and publishers to alter the law by writing books of this kind which you have seen this morning.

Fortunately, the law is prescribed for us by better authorities than people who can write descriptions which you have seen. I refrain as far as possible from using language other than that which is strictly judicial, but it is a little difficult. But that is what you are being invited to do, to really disregard the law as it exists today and to substitute another law made for us by these writers and the men who make money publishing this degrading type of literature. One may thank God that it is only a small part of the literature of today, but, as we have heard, of course commands enormous sales. It appeals to the lower instincts and the passions of men, and these men have been making money out of it.

Fashions may alter. Of course they do. The bathing dresses of our grandmother's days are very different from the bathing costumes of today. Reference was made to what is called the bikini bathing costume, which is apparently adopted all over the world. It is different to what it used to be, but unless it is calculated to deprave and corrupt, then there is nothing obscene about it, and nothing perhaps could be suggested as indecent, but we are not concerned with any other word than that which is here in these charges, namely "obscene".

An obscenity is something which tends to deprave and corrupt. It is said here by Mr Humphreys this morning that there is no evidence that anybody has been harmed by these books. That is not necessary. The wording of the definition is something which tends to do it, not necessarily does it at all.

As I have said, standards of morality in particular may change. Alas, they do, very often for the worse, but the law does not; it stands fast. It is a bulwark against the incoming flood of gross immoral writings, if these books produced today are an indication of that flood tide; and no doubt they are. It might well be the privilege of a jury to stand fast against it. When I say the law does not change, it is stating a truism; a happy truth you may think, because how does it help you to hear the people here have not been prosecuted in the case of some of these publications? Does that make any difference to the law? The law of stealing is still the law of stealing, and has been since the days of the great law-giver Moses. It is still stealing, although today you hear about "pilfering" and "scrounging" and the like. That does not alter the fact that stealing is still stealing, and has been for hundreds, if not thousands of years. It is said these people have not been prosecuted. So have a large number of housebreakers not been; but

175

is that any indication that a housebreaker is not a person who breaks the law, if and when he is prosecuted. These arguments are made by those who are instructed by these men to defend them against these charges – eminent counsels such as these men can no doubt afford to employ – and you have listened to ingenious arguments, so ingenious that at times you must have felt as though the old world, the old standards of morals that you have known, was gradually slipping away from you and leaving you and your children a miserable inheritance.

It was at this point that Christmas Humphreys stood up, threw down his papers and angrily strode out of the court with his gown billowing.

Well, fortunately, when we are told that, one is partially re-assured that in the case of *Julia*, the first book with which we were regaled, the first book to which our attention was drawn, a prosecution of the publishers and author of that is now under consideration; and you may feel, perhaps, relieved to know that.

While you have been shown all these books, it is admitted on behalf of these accused men that if they are obscene, these seven books of yours, then it is no defence to say that there are other books which are more obscene. But while that is admitted, and while it is fully admitted that that definition is perfectly good law today, it is said: "Well, it is the background against which you have got to view these new books." I have already dealt with that. If that were so, it is a new standard of law, and it is not the law yet.

It is said you are here as members of the public to decide this case. That is true enough. But you are also here as part of the administration of justice. To administer what? Surely the law, not some fabrication of unknown writers and publishers. Who are they to impose upon us their notions? I think it was said that these are men who formed an opinion that these books are fit for publication, and that it is merely your opinion against theirs. Maybe. But do you think their opinion is in any way warped or biased by the fact that they make money out of it and you do not? That is the difference. And a vital one, you may think.

Then it was argued that cruelty and brutality alone do not tend to deprave and corrupt. Well, if it were necessary to deal with that, you might, perhaps, think that it might well be that they do both. But we are not concerned with books where cruelty alone and brutality alone figure, because here it is a mixture of sex and cruelty and brutality, and possibly sadism all at the same time.

It was said also that there is no suggestion in these seven books with which you are concerned, of perversion or the use of dirty words. Well, it is not a question of what has been left out of these books. You may be very glad that something has been left out. What you have got to consider is what has been put in to them. Almost lastly, it has been argued that the lust and cruelty in these books – which is admitted – has not been made attractive by the writer; that it has not been glamorised, a word which I think was used, and quite a good word to express the argument; and that rape was, made by this particular author in one particular book – I think *Amok* – this man Dexter, you remember – revolting. Well, it is already one of the worst crimes in the calendar, if you want anything more revolting than that. If he does write something which is revolting about rape, and so on and so forth, well then, why write about it at all? Why not choose something that is not revolting? Or does it indicate to you, as I have already said, that it is done because it is one of the things which enables people, readily and easily, as these sales indicate, to trade upon the lower instincts and the baser instincts of mankind in general – men, women and children, old and young? One might perhaps except out of this category of people whose minds are open to such immoral influences, say, possibly, the Convocation of Bishops; I do not know; but that is a very small body of people, and the rest of the world is wide open to these publications. So far as rape is concerned, surely rape must be the very depths of depravity; it is perhaps like tar – you cannot touch it without becoming besmirched. Well, there it is, written and repeated in one of these books, the one I have mentioned.

That, I think, deals with the whole of this case. I have endeavoured to put before you what has been urged on behalf of these accused. It is my duty to remind you of what is said. The whole of the argument seems to me not to be based upon the law as it is but upon a rule which is invented for the benefit of these men, upon an unauthorised alteration of the law. What you have got to see is whether, fairly and squarely, remembering what you have read so carefully and diligently and at length in these seven books, this is matter which tends to deprave and corrupt the minds of persons who are open to evil influences such as I have indicated all men are, into whose hands they are likely to come. That is a point I have already dealt with.

If there is any reasonable doubt with regard to these books that you have seen being obscene, well then, these men and their companies are entitled to have the benefit of your verdict, entitled to be acquitted. But do you think that you are being invited to drag up all your moral anchors in order to enlarge the scope of this type of literature, to open the floodgates and let it submerge – as it might easily do, if this is an indication of what it is – all men, imperilling their happiness and their moral integrity? Because there are influences in life which uplift, and there are others which debase, and in the words of a philosopher and teacher, which may be familiar to many of you, to be carnally minded is death ... death of the mind.

Well, that is the position. As I have said, if there is any reasonable doubt with regard to any of these books, these men are entitled to be acquitted. If, on the other hand, you have no reasonable doubt, it would be your duty to say so. Perhaps you would now consider your verdict, members of the jury. If there is anything which you would want to look at, of course you can; but do not burden yourselves by taking a lot of literature with you to your room; it is all in your minds, and you have seen quite enough. Leave it where it is and you can send for what you want. Take what you want and leave what you do not want, but please yourselves entirely. If you take that definition, Mr Foreman, it will help you to remember it.

* * *

The jury retired at 11.41 am and returned, after lunch, at 2.03 pm.

THE RECORDER: Members of the jury. I understand you are agreed upon one of these counts. I expect that it is the last one, is it not?

FOREMAN: It is count number five. We are agreed on that, my Lord. [70]

THE RECORDER: Is there any point I can help you on with regard to the others?

---

[70] Count five was *Amok*.

FOREMAN: I do not think so, my Lord. We seem to be fully directed as to the questions which are open for answer.

THE RECORDER: Is there any chance of your agreeing about something?

FOREMAN: It seems highly improbable at the moment.

THE RECORDER: All right, Mr Foreman. Of course you realise it is very desirable if you can agree one way or the other, because it involves everybody in a great deal of labour and expense, because it has all got to be tried again, except this one count; somebody has got to go through it all again. I do not know whether it would help you at all, because I do not know how you may be divided, but these words have received the approval of the Court of Criminal Appeal, and it might help if I repeat them to you: "It makes for great public inconvenience and expense if Juries cannot agree owing to the unwillingness of one of their number to listen to the arguments of the rest."

Which is another way of saying that Juries come to an agreement by pooling their ideas, putting their heads together in a process of give and take, mental give and take. I do not know whether that in any way assists you, Mr Foreman, or not. Would you like another five minutes or so to consider what I have said?

FOREMAN: I think so, my Lord. Perhaps if we could retire for a little longer

THE RECORDER: Well, it might be worthwhile. Certainly after that ... well, I will say no more. Just give it another brief review in the light of what I have said. I hope it will help you; I do not know; but obviously I do not want to bring any sort of pressure to bear upon you of any sort or kind.

The jury retired again at 2.10 pm and returned twenty minutes later.

Reg Carter and Julius Reiter were declared guilty on all seven counts.

Before sentence was passed, the Recorder was given one further piece of evidence, learning for the first time from a witness that "the defendants have told me their net salaries were about £2,000 a year." The Recorder seemed to believe that this profit was made solely from the Janson novels, referring to the "thousands of pounds" that the books made.

Evidence was also given about previous convictions (one each for Gaywood and New Fiction Press as detailed in earlier chapters). Dodson also inquired about the number of destruction orders issued against Hank Janson, and discovered it amounted to 1,400 separate orders in respect of fifty-two books since 1950. For the individual titles in respect of which the charges were brought, the figures (with the number of destruction orders issued in London in brackets) were: *Accused* – 24 (2), *Amok* – 8 (1), *Persian Pride* – 12 (4), *Vengeance* – 16 (2), *Auctioned* – 20 (3), *Killer* – 15 (1) and *Pursuit* – 17 (3), all in 1953, bar one order against *Auctioned* in July 1952.

Despite pleas of mitigation from their counsels, the Recorder passed the severest sentence:

THE RECORDER: Reginald Herbert Carter and Julius Reiter, you have had the advantage of being defended by very eminent counsels, and they have been allowed every latitude in the matter of introducing into this trial a quantity of literature to which our attention has been called. This trial is brought, no doubt, at the instance of the Director of Public Prosecutions in an attempt to put down, so far as it is possible for the time being, the publication of this type of literature, which can have only one effect upon those who read it.

These books, irrelevant as I indicated them to be to the issue in this trial, served this purpose; it must have brought vividly to the jury's attention the danger and abuse of filthiness to which the nation is drifting. If it is to be said that an obscene publication is to be judged in the light of modern standards, I profoundly disagree; and, to the credit of the jury, by their verdict they show they entirely disagree also. The jury are to be complimented in making a stand against this tendency, and it must have been some consolation to them for their labours to hear that all these books have been condemned in some fifty-two instances all over the country, and everyone who listened to this case will breathe a little more freely on hearing that. This is literary pollution, and it is high time that it came to an end. The profit of it must be prodigious. This indictment covers a period from March to October, and I am told that in six weeks there is a fresh edition made of a hundred thousand copies. It runs into a very large figure, and if only half the two shillings is profit – or whatever it may be – it runs into many thousands of pounds, and it is monstrous that anybody should be allowed to make money in that way.

Giving this case anxious attention, I have come to the conclusion that it cannot be met by mere payment. Money fines are nothing to people who can make money on this scale, and it is high time publishers realised their responsibilities, as no doubt most of them do. In these cases, we are told you were in doubt, and, notwithstanding the doubt as to the obscenity of these books, you went on with it. One can only hope that this trial will mean a step in the other direction, towards the realm of pure and exhilarating literature and not this kind of debasing stuff, which sooner or later will drag the whole reading public down into a veritable lagoon of depravity. Under those circumstances, the sentence of the court upon each of you is one of six months imprisonment, and a fine of two thousand pounds upon each of these companies.

Carter and Reiter were ushered downstairs from the dock and were locked into different cells. Later, they were handcuffed and led upstairs to the courtyard where, still handcuffed, they were put into a Black Maria and taken to Brixton Prison.

CHAPTER THIRTEEN

THE LAW STANDS FAST

The newspapers for Wednesday 20 January 1954, were full of reports about the case. *The Times, Guardian* and *Daily Telegraph* carried lengthy reports, respectively headlined: "Publishers Sent to Prison. 'Literary Pollution'", "Obscene Books. Two Men Imprisoned: Companies Fined £6,000" and "Publishers of 'Debasing' Book Gaoled".

"It's dangerous to sell these seven books now," reported Frank Smith in the *Daily Herald*. "Until the jury's verdict, they were on sale at many reputable bookstalls, it was stated in court. NAAFI canteens [71] were selling them and had placed repeat orders with the publishers for more." The latter statement – made by Christmas Humphreys during the defence case – was picked up by other newspapers, including the *Daily Mail* ("'Filthy Books'—Publishers Jailed"), and led to a question being raised in the House of Commons by Sir Richard Acland, who asked how many copies of the books "by the so-called Hank Janson" had been distributed by Government representatives to members of the Forces. Nigel Birch, Parliamentary Secretary to the Ministry of Defence, told MPs that only a small number of the books had been purchased, and that all unsold copies had been withdrawn. [72] Elsewhere, the books were selling like hot cakes, according to a *Daily Sketch* reporter ("Jailed Men's Books Still On Sale") who quoted a bookseller in the West End as saying "Since the books were first mentioned in court last week, there has been a rush to buy them. I sold all I had in an hour." [73]

---

[71] The Navy, Army and Air Force Institutes (NAAFI) were set up in the 1920s to run convenience stores and leisure facilities for the Forces at military locations.
[72] *Evening Standard*, 9 February 1954.
[73] *Daily Sketch*, 20 January 1954.

A more worrying connection was drawn by some reports to the case of twenty-four-year-old John Francis Wilkinson who, in August 1953, was charged with the murder of Miriam Susan Gray, aged five.

Charlotte Gray, the child's mother, had only a month earlier married Hermann Schreiber, a chef, and Susan, as she was called by her family, had come to live with them at Boundary Road, Balham, a week later. The house was on three floors, and rooms on the first and second floor were let.

On Friday 14 August, after looking in to see their daughter sleeping soundly on a divan that had been set up in the kitchen, her parents had gone to bed at around 10 o'clock.

Wilkinson had begun drinking after the rest of the household was asleep, taking a bottle of vermouth and a bottle of beer from the cellar and drinking from each alternately until he had reached a state he described as "not drunk and not sober." He had been a persistent drinker since his days in the Army, which he had volunteered to join in 1946 after a troubled childhood. One of twelve children, of which only six had survived infancy, Wilkinson had a long history of nervousness and restlessness and was prone to violent temper tantrums and bed-wetting, which had caused problems when he had been evacuated during the War; after being billeted to a number of different residences, he had been returned home. Leaving school at age fourteen in 1942, Wilkinson had joined the Southern Railway, but had left after two years. From then on, before and after his Army service, he had had many jobs, mostly lasting only a matter of weeks before he became fed-up with them. His Army record had been marred by punishments for being drunk.

In a state of semi-drunkenness, Wilkinson had decided to rob his hosts and armed himself by breaking off the leg of a chair and wrapping it in a piece of flannelette sheet, which he had used for ironing, tied on with two handkerchiefs.

In the kitchen, he had disturbed the girl and struck her repeatedly with the chair leg. He had gathered up food and some valuables into two cases and tried to set fire to the kitchen and bed before leaving. When Hermann Schreiber had awoken at a quarter to six, he had heard someone walk down the stairs and slam the front door, but he had not got up until six-thirty, by which time the house had been filling with smoke. With his wife, he had gone down to the kitchen and, not seeing Sally, gone outside to find her. Called back into the room by his wife, he had seen the girl on the divan where Wilkinson had left her, covered by blankets. After putting out the two small fires, Schreiber had tried phoning the police, only to find that the telephone wire had been cut. The police, however, had been on the scene before 7 o'clock.

Wilkinson had been picked up in the early hours of the Sunday morning by PC David Osbourne, who had been on duty at Hinchley Wood, cycling towards Surbiton, when he had spotted Wilkinson and recognised him as fitting the description of a man wanted for questioning by the CID at Balham. Osbourne had quoted Wilkinson as saying: "I'm glad you picked me up."

Later, at Tooting Station, Wilkinson had made a statement, written down for him by Detective-Inspector Frank Norman, admitting the crime; he had been charged at South-Western Magistrates' Court the same day. As he had given up his job as a furnaceman some time earlier and had no money, he had been granted legal aid.

When the trial had come to court at the Old Bailey, the prosecution had been handled by Christmas Humphreys – who would, soon after, be defending Hank Janson in the same building.

The Janson connection to the case was introduced in a deposition by Detective-Superintendent Charles Morris, who had arrived at the scene of the crime at 9 o'clock and, after examining the ground floor area and garden, had gone up to the first floor and searched Wilkinson's room. "There was a chest of drawers in the room, and in it I found the book entitled *Vengeance* and these two paper magazines." [74]

The Janson novel *Vengeance* had a particularly powerful narrative, returning to a theme that Stephen Frances had explored previously: a wrongly convicted man's vengeance against those who had sent him to prison. In this case the man is former *Chicago Chronicle* reporter Frank Baker, framed for the manslaughter of a woman and imprisoned for five

---

[74] Public Records Office, CRIM 1/2349.

186

years just before he can reveal evidence that he has been gathering for a major story.

Baker has become embittered by his experience to a degree that even Janson finds him impossible to deal with. Given back his old job by *Chronicle* chief Healey, Baker disappears to take out his violent revenge on police officers and others involved in his conviction.

On pages 58 and 59 of the book, and helpfully highlighted by Detective-Superintendent Morris in his deposition, is a description of one of the police officers and the beating he has taken at the hands of an unknown assailant:

> He was lying strangely still. "Listen," he snarled. "I've been lying here in agony for hours trying to figure out who might have done it. I've even figured out some long shots. I passed on my ideas to headquarters, and every suspect they've rounded up so far can give an alibi as sound as a bell."
>
> "Gave you a good going over?"
>
> "D'you think I'm lying on my belly for fun?" he snarled. "Just strip back those blankets and get yourself an eyeful."
>
> "You tell me ..."
>
> "Strip it back," he snarled. "Get yourself an eyeful."
>
> I stripped back the blankets off the wickerwork frame. He was as naked as the day he was born. But there was good reason for it. It looked like the butterfly touch of a feather would cause him to writhe in torment. From neck to knees, his body was swollen up like one gigantic blood blister, the skin ugly with ruptured blood vessels, bruised blue, mauve, violet, and green. It looked like if you pricked him with a pin, he'd explode, spattering the joint with festered fluids.
>
> Hastily I pulled the blanket up over the framework. "Now d'you know what I'm suffering?" he panted.

"What did they do?" I breathed. "How can a guy get that way?"

"Beating," he snarled. "First they slugged me, put me out for a good long while. Then they worked over me slowly, took a long while about it, worked from my neck right the way down."

"How did they do it?" I breathed. "How does a guy get that way?"

"The doctor figures it musta been a heavy stick wrapped in cloth. But what caused the real damage was the steady way it was done. Not savagely or heavily but a calculated, persistent beating that musta gone on for a coupla hours." [75]

Although they were mentioned in court, it was not suggested that the book and two magazines – a photo-magazine called *Showgirls* and a collection of articles, humour and fiction entitled *Bedside Clubman* – caused Wilkinson to commit murder. However, the chair leg wrapped in flannelette and "heavy stick wrapped in cloth" were clearly suggestive to the prosecution.

Wilkinson's statement was accepted as a confession of guilt, and Christmas Humphreys told the jury in court that the facts of the case were not in dispute and that their task was to decide whether or not Wilkinson had been insane within the meaning of English law at the time when he had killed the girl, who had died as a result of shock from having her skull fractured.

The main evidence against Wilkinson was presented by psychiatrist Dr Desmond Curran and the medical officer at Brixton Prison where Wilkinson was held, Dr J C M Matheson.

Curran reported:

I have no doubt that this prisoner should be regarded as the possessor of a psychopathic personality, or what is generally regarded as an

---

[75] *Vengeance*, pp 58-59.

anomaly of character, and I do not believe that he suffers from any mental disease as that statement is generally understood both by medical men and in courts of law ...

He has always been considered the odd man out, has never had any friends, has been solitary, moody and touchy and given, when the opportunity arose, to drinking to excess.

On examination, he was alert and attentive and showed little, if any, evidence of shame. He was not abnormally depressed. He is above average in intelligence, physical examination has been negative and the EEG [76] shows evidence of only very mild abnormality. There is nothing to suggest that he was an epileptic. He did, however, tell me that, in his belief, people avoided him and talked about him and looked at him in a disparaging way. These, however, are not I think true delusional ideas, but rather a paranoid attitude shown by many psychopaths ...

As regards the crime itself, there is I think good reason to suppose that he was under the influence of alcohol when he committed it. It would seem at first sight to be motiveless, but I think this is by no means certain. It must be remembered that he had chucked in his job for no particular reason, as he had often done before, and was near the end of his financial resources. He told me, and I think it is very possibly correct, that he had no idea the little girl was sleeping in the kitchen, and he may for all I know have gone to the kitchen to steal things and to decamp, impulsively killing her and then attempting to have intercourse with her. He denies this and says he never decamped before in this way. He could give no explanation to me about going downstairs with the weapon. There is, however, a past history of arming himself before attempting to break and

---

[76] Electroencephalographic examination, carried out at Maudsley Hospital.

enter, and he may well have had the same idea in his rather fuddled state of mind on this occasion and, as suggested above, killed her impulsively in order to get rid of a potential witness.

He is a man of ungovernable temper, and he said to me once he had started he could not stop, just as you could not stop once you had started running down a steep hill. He emphasised he was not in a state of mind to think whether what he was doing was or was not wrong.

Matheson concurred:

At my interviews with him, I found no evidence of insanity.

He gave an account of the alleged crime which agrees with the statement he made to the police ...

He says that he often got irritable with other people, especially if he were in a crowd, but while under observation here [at Brixton Prison Hospital] he has shown no paranoid trends; that is, he does not appear to think that he is being specially watched here or that he is conspicuous amongst the other inmates of the Hospital.

Mental tests show him to be of average or above average intelligence, and he is not, in my opinion, feeble-minded. While under observation in the Ward, he has been co-operative and well-behaved and at no time shown any evidence of insanity ...

The character defect which I consider is present in this case is due probably to hereditary factors on his mother's side and defective early life and training, due largely to the alcoholic habits of his father.

I am of the opinion that he is:

(1) Sane
(2) Fit to plead to the indictment
(3) Fit to stand his trial.

The suggestion of "hereditary factors" was a reference to Wilkinson's great-aunt and cousin, both of whom had been committed to mental hospitals.

The picture of Wilkinson presented to the court was of a lonely, paranoid man with psychopathic tendencies and a troubled history that dated back long before he would have had an opportunity to be influenced by a Hank Janson novel. At the trial, however, Mr. Justice Hilbery asked whether any action was being taken against the publishers of *Vengeance*, and Reg Carter and Julius Reiter, already under investigation with regard to various Janson titles at the time of the murder, were charged three weeks after Wilkinson was sentenced to death.

* * *

Many juries are under the misapprehension that a case will be reheard by a Court of Appeal if the defence requests it. The Court of Criminal Appeal, however, was set up only as a protection against juries reaching a verdict based on an unfair trial, and a defence can lodge an appeal against a decision only on a point of law or if they believe there has been some misdirection from the court.

The Court of Criminal Appeal had [77] a serious and compromising flaw, in that the three judges who sat to hear an appeal were drawn from a small pool of judges, who consequently would each sit in judgment over each other's cases, leading barristers to dub it a "Court of No-Appeal". "It creates an 'if you don't knock me, I won't knock you' situation," recalled Stephen Frances.

The appeal brought by Reg Carter and Julius Reiter was heard at the Court of Criminal Appeal on Monday 15 March 1954 before the Lord Chief Justice of England Lord Goddard, Mr Justice Slade and Mr Justice Gerrard. Gerald Howard and Christmas Humphreys were again appearing for the defendants and Mr Griffith-Jones for the Crown.

---

[77] The Court of Criminal Appeal was replaced by the Court of Appeal in 1966.

The appeal was brought on six counts, primarily that the Recorder, Gerald Dodson, had misdirected the jury as to what was allowed as evidence and had put his own views to the jury too strongly in his summing-up, in effect ordering the jury to find the books guilty. Dodson had not directed the jury sufficiently to judge each book separately from the others, nor had he differentiated between the seven books accused and the many books the defence had produced in evidence when he had criticised the "incoming flood of gross immoral writing."

Lord Goddard and his fellow judges were not without their own views on the seven Hank Janson books. Goddard, having had the "misfortune" to have read them, said, "I cannot see that any jury could not have come to the same conclusion than that they were grossly and bestially obscene." He later added: "They are filthy, and if they fall into the hands of young adolescents, I do not wonder that there is juvenile crime today."

Mr Howard said that the substance of the appeals was that the Recorder had misdirected the jury as to the way in which the test for obscenity, as laid down in Hicklin's case, should be applied – it was the right test, but the standards of today should be taken into consideration. It was correct that juries should be aware of what was going on around them – for example, in modern films and in other books that were freely available on bookstalls. It was not sufficient for the Recorder simply to read out the test to the jury and to tell them that it was to be applied. They should, said Howard, have been told that it must be applied in accordance with standards which change from day to day and from generation to generation.

Lord Goddard disagreed: "I cannot imagine an age in which these books would not be obscene."

JUSTICE GERRARD: I do not understand the word "standards" of today in relation to this particular case. It seems to me that it is saying the bigger the collection of dirty books you can get together, the better view the jury has of the standards of today. I do not understand that.

MR HUMPHREYS: What I mean is this. My friend has referred to one book, *The Well of Loneliness*, and I can think of another, *Ulysses*, which were banned and years later are openly allowed to be on sale, reprinted again and again and can be bought in London. Therefore, books held to be obscene at English law are now openly on sale. Therefore, today the standard or the test or level of what is indecent or obscene in English law is changing all the time.

LORD CHIEF JUSTICE: I very much doubt that. If a thing is filthy today I do not see why it should not be filthy in five years' time, or, if it was filthy five years ago, why it should not be so today.

Later, Lord Chief Justice Goddard admitted that modern novelists discussed things that would not have been discussed in the days of Queen Victoria, that George Eliot went as far as the tendencies of her time allowed and that Trollope veiled over things that would not have been discussed in his day. But the point, reiterated Goddard, was that it was idle to say that the seven Janson books did not have the tendency described by Chief Justice Cockburn, and that Carter and Reiter had tried to sail as close to the wind as they could and had sailed too far.

During the hearing, the Lord Chief Justice commented on the then recent Scottish appeal case of *Galletly -v- Laird* [78], during which the Lord Justice-General Lord Cooper had said that the character of the offending books or pictures should be ascertained by the only method by which such a fact could be ascertained – by reading the books or looking at the pictures. The book or picture itself provided the best evidence of its own indecency or obscenity or of the absence of such qualities. [79]

Although not quoted by Lord Goddard, the Lord Justice-General had also said that "a glance was sufficient to satisfy

[78] *Galletly* v. *Laird* (1953) S.C. (J.) 16.
[79] *Glasgow Herald*, date unknown, and *The Scotsman*, 27 December 1964.

him that no reasonable magistrate could have formed any other conclusion than that reached by the magistrate," and that, "the mischief lies not so much in the book or picture *per se* as in the use to which it is put, usually deliberately and for gain, by traffickers in pornography who make a business of inspiring and catering for depraved and perverted tastes." The Recorder had certainly been of the same opinion, willing to accept that the jury had read all seven books in under two hours and extending that – but still only to three and three-quarter hours – only at the insistence of the defence. By the Lord Chief Justice's own reckoning, the best evidence available during the trial had not been fully explored.

During the summing-up of the appeal, Lord Goddard said:

> LORD CHIEF JUSTICE: This appeal is brought entirely on the summing-up of the learned Recorder. Let me say at once that the learned Recorder's summing-up was perhaps to a certain extent rather more rhetorical than one could have wished, but he evidently felt strongly, and it is very difficult for a judge to control his feelings when he is dealing with the stuff such as there is in this case. I do not wonder that the learned Recorder spoke strongly.

It is worth quoting here a passage from another appeal heard many years later, this case involving the killing of a police constable:

> The killing of PC Miles had, very understandably, aroused widespread public sympathy for the victim and his family and a strong sense of public outrage at the circumstances of his death. This background made it more, not less, important that the jury should approach the issues in a dispassionate spirit if the defendants were to receive a fair trial, as the trial judge began by reminding them. In our judgment, however, far from encouraging the jury to approach the case in a calm frame of mind, the trial judge's

summing-up, particularly in the passages we have quoted, had exactly the opposite effect. We cannot read these passages as other than a highly rhetorical and strongly-worded denunciation of both defendants and of their defences. The language used was not that of a judge but of an advocate (and it contrasted strongly with the appropriately restrained language of prosecuting counsel). Such a direction by such a judge must in our view have driven the jury to conclude that they had little choice but to convict; at the lowest, it may have done so.

Lord Goddard allowed the highly rhetorical and strongly-worded denouncement of Reg Carter and Julius Reiter to stand in the Hank Janson case because he felt that the Recorder's lack of control over his feelings was justified. The appeal heard in 1998 quoted above strongly condemned the trial judge's – Lord Goddard's – summing-up for precisely that lack of control. Sadly, Derek Bentley, hanged forty-six years earlier, was not around to benefit from the ruling that his conviction was "unsafe".

Goddard's own passion was also evident when he dismissed the appeal to have the defendants' sentences reduced: "It is high time that the publication of this stuff was stopped and stopped in such a way as would indicate that other persons offending in like manner should know the view of the court. We cannot say that the sentence passed by the learned Recorder in any way erred in principle, and therefore the appeals against sentence are also dismissed."

* * *

With the backing of the Publishers' Association, Carter and Reiter requested permission of the Attorney General that their case be taken further to the House of Lords, but they were refused because there was no point of law involved and it was considered to be not in the public interest that such an appeal should be brought.

Instead, Carter and Reiter had to serve their six months' imprisonment.

"After reading the report of the proceedings against Carter and Reiter," recalled Frances, "I was outraged, and all these years later I still believe, perhaps mistakenly, that those who had undertaken to uphold the highest principles of British justice had not only failed to do so, but had actively encompassed its violation.

"What greatly embittered me was the injustice of Dodson. After abusing his power to get a jury to give a decision he wanted, he then proved himself to be, in my opinion, a vile person. In addition to heavy fines and destruction of their business, he then sent Carter and Reiter to jail.

"Everybody knew Reiter as a very happy man, always joking and with a laugh for everyone. He was never gloomy, but always high-spirited and full of fun. He was even happier when he married and had a son. His life had not been easy, but he still had faith in the inherent goodness of mankind. His only slightly worrying problem was the British law about seizing books which were said to be obscene. He could read and speak English, but the subtleties of the language were beyond him. He knew four-letter words shouldn't be seen in print; but what else? He sought guidance from Scotland Yard and lawyers without success. But he had confidence in Carter, who assured him that nothing obscene would be published. He went to court eagerly, because he wished to be vindicated. He was confident that at the Old Bailey, the highest principles of justice were maintained by men dedicated to this sacred trust.

"At the Old Bailey Reiter, heard himself condemned by a high official of British justice as a man monstrously making money by knowingly selling filth. He heard these accusations repeated at the Appeal Court.

"Something was shattered inside Reiter. The happy, high-spirited little man ceased to exist. He was depressed by the distress it had all caused his wife. Not long after he came out of prison, she died of cancer. After he came out of prison, he was completely cowed, and I never saw him smile again."

In an article for the *Sunday Times* in 1964, Godfrey Smith wrote: "Dr Reiter is still bitter about what he considers the injustice of the case, which cost him £20,000." [80]

While Reiter was sent to Wormwood Scrubs, Reginald Carter was sent to an open-camp prison. "I was never able to learn the reason for this," said Frances.

"Carter did not seem bitter when he came out of prison, but he may have felt that he had a grudge against society, and that it should repay him. It was only slowly, over the years, that it became apparent that his experiences were increasingly warping his character and mind.

"When he came out, in my opinion, he had lost all respect for the law and had swung to the other extreme. He saw things in a twisted way. It was clever to be twisted and flaunt the law. I maintained contact with him, unaware that he was so greatly changed, and learned it eventually when it was far too late for me to realise he had broken faith with me. I think it is true to say that after leaving prison, Carter increasingly took advantage of my good faith, until by the time I realised it, he had absorbed everything that should have been mine."

---

[80] *Sunday Times*, 16 February 1964.

CHAPTER FOURTEEN

THE TIDE TURNS

"As far back as I can remember, I have been witnessing injustices," said Stephen Frances. "Poverty too is an injustice. It is not justice that many do not have, while a few have much more than they need. The injustice of poverty caused me to spend my adolescence joining this and that organisation in the vain search for ways to end social inequality.

"If all men cannot enjoy the right to freely express their opinions, I believe that is unjust."

When Frances, back in Spain following his court case in Darwen, heard that Carter and Reiter had been charged over the publication of Hank Janson and were to appear before a jury, he felt he now had a chance to vindicate himself as the author of novels he did not believe to be obscene but which had been judged obscene by the magistrates in Darwen. A summons had already been issued against him but, because he was in Spain, could not be served.

"I wrote to my solicitor that I would come back to stand trial with Carter and Reiter, but that was not possible. Carter and Reiter had already appeared at the Guild Hall and a trial had been fixed for them at the Old Bailey. My solicitor arranged that I should await the outcome of the trial. If it was favourable, the summons would be dropped. If unfavourable, I would return to the UK to stand trial myself."

However, as the Recorder heard the final evidence before passing sentence, he addressed the question of the author to Detective-Sergeant Goodall:

> THE RECORDER: Where is Hank Janson? Do you know?

> D/S GOODALL: He is in Spain, my Lord.

THE RECORDER: He is in Spain? Are there any extradition proceedings which apply?

D/S GOODALL: Not at the moment, my Lord.

RECORDER: He cannot be extradited and brought here?

D/S GOODALL: Not for this offence, my Lord.

MR GRIFFITH-JONES: I thought, in view of your Lordship's question, I might ask if a summons has been actually issued against him?

D/S GOODALL: No, my Lord. I am sorry. I am corrected there.

RECORDER: Has it? Or has it not?

D/S GOODALL: It has been issued. Yes.

Following the failure of the appeal at the Court of Criminal Appeals, on 24 March 1954 a warrant was sworn out for the arrest of Stephen Frances, at the direction of the Director of Public Prosecutions, by an Alderman and Justice of the Peace at the Guildhall Justice Room. "I was a wanted man," recalled Frances. "This was contrary to the agreement made with my solicitor, so I considered that this released me from my undertaking to return at once to London, and instead do so only at my own convenience.

"There was some official concern about the issue of an arrest warrant under unethical circumstances, and when, some time later, I arrived in the UK, my reception was compensatingly civilised."

Flying into Lydd Airport in Kent on Tuesday 14 December 1954, Frances made himself known to a security officer who had been expecting him. A friend, Bob Brackpool, was due to pick him up, and Frances was allowed to drive unescorted to Bishopsgate, where he presented himself to the desk sergeant. From Bishopsgate, he was accompanied by two detectives and his solicitor to Guildhall, where he made a two-minute appearance before a magistrate who immediately bailed him to appear again the following week.

On 22 December he returned to the Guildhall, where he was sent for trial at the Old Bailey on seven charges of publishing obscene books. Frances was released on the payment of two sureties of £500, one paid by a friend of Carter's, Lord Joseph Arthur Smith-Goodwin [81], who ran the Stadium Garage in Pease Pottage, Crawley. It was from Smith-Goodwin that Carter had bought the house – "Restful" – at which Frances stayed during the six weeks he waited to come to trial, and from which Frances had to report to the police daily.

The trial had been intended to begin on 10 January 1955, but was postponed and bail renewed. The trial eventually began on 1 February.

Frances approached the trial with what he believed was a two-pronged defence. First, he would deny writing the books, "which would give the prosecution a headache." He was legally charged with "publishing" the books, which, in legal terminology, also included their preparation as a manuscript rather than simply distributing printed copies. Frances, choosing his words carefully and pedantically, claimed not to have written the books, because it was the "pure" truth – he dictated them. It was a shaky argument at best, but it justified, to Frances at least, a plea of not guilty when he was charged.

The second prong of the defence was that, even if he did write the books, they weren't obscene. When he went to trial, it was in the hope that the jury would have to read all the books all the way through and confound the prosecution by finding them not obscene.

The prosecution case, on the other hand, was to try to prove stylistically that the seven "obscene" Hank Janson novels were the work of the same author who wrote *The Jane With Green Eyes* and *Milady Took The Rap*, which Frances had admitted

---

[81] In this instance Lord was not an honorary title but a Christian name; Lord Smith-Goodwin was known locally as Joe Smith.

to writing in the Darwen case two years earlier. [82] The twelve jurymen (no women) were sent by the Common Serjeant, Sir Anthony Hawke, to their room with orders to read all nine novels – they would have been sent home but, unfortunately, the prosecution had not supplied enough copies of the books.

Except for a break for lunch, the jury were locked in their room from 10.30 am until 4.00 pm each day for a full week, and asked to compare the style of writing and the repetition and use of words and phrases. The prosecution, led by Mr Griffith-Jones and Mr Maxwell Turner, had prepared a comprehensive breakdown of the books, looking for clues, such as the regular use of the word "animal".

The use of the word in *Accused* ...

> It seemed to come out from deep down inside her whistling out over her teeth, a kinda animal noise (p 35)
> ... she was like a young animal, healthy and vigorous (p 45)
> ... she had a way with her, a kinda animal instinct, etc – and lower on page – She was as strong as an animal, etc (p 100)
> ... subjected to her greedy, merciless animal instincts, etc (p 103)

... was contrasted with the use of the word in *The Jane With Green Eyes* (J) and *Milady Took The Rap* (M):

> ... they talked about negroes as though they were talking about animals, etc (J, p 11)
> The grotesque, black figure was still uttering those animal noises, etc (J, p 45)
> She was making ugly animal noises, etc – then lower on page – Virginia gave a low drawn out animal growl – again lower – Virginia started making that horrible animal noise again (J, p 125)

---

[82] The admission ought to have tripped up Frances's case immediately, as he had claimed not to have written any books since Carter took over their publication, but had previously admitted to writing *Milady Took The Rap*, published by Carter under the New Fiction Press imprint.

She gave a gasp of surprise and then
animal-like, began to struggle, etc (M, p 91)
The closer I got the more she reminded me
of an animal, etc (M, p 96)
... snuffling and chewing like an animal.
(M, p 97)
She looked wild, like an animal – and lower
on page – She ate like an animal, etc (M, p
101)
... and yesterday when she'd been wholly
animal (M, p109).

This breakdown was performed for over a dozen words
and phrases: animal, memory, skin, twitching, gouging,
writhing, bodice, lips moist, vibrant, breasts, scent strong in
my nostrils, skin shimmering, biting, scrabbling, sandpaper.

In response, the defence had also prepared their own
breakdown, using forty different crime novels including books
by James Hadley Chase, James M Cain, Mickey Spillane,
Bruno Fischer, Gil Brewer, Darcy Glinto and rival British
Gangster writers like Brad Shannon, Danny Spade, Ben Sarto,
Nat Karta, Hans Lugar, Hans Vogel and Ross Angel.

As it turned out, the hard-working assistants who had
prepared these breakdowns had wasted their time, as indeed
had the jury in reading the books, because when the case
resumed on 11 February, Mr Griffith-Jones announced that
evidence had come to light that appeared to prove Frances's
claim that he was not the author of at least four of the seven
books.

In the earlier Hank Janson trial, the three firms involved,
New Fiction Press, Arc Press and Gaywood Press, had each
been fined £2,000. New Fiction Press had been driven into
insolvency by this. The accounts books of the company were
in the hands of the liquidators and had been examined for
evidence of payments, and this had now revealed two
documents that appeared to be records of payments made to
another author, named Pardoe. The first was for £20 in
respect of a Gangster story, and on it appeared the word
Accused; the second was for £125 for various manuscripts –
Persian Pride, Amok, Desert Fury and *Pursuit*.

Turning to the jury, Sir Anthony Hawke said: "This defendant has sworn that while he wrote a large number of books under the name Hank Janson, he did not write the books which are the subject of this indictment. He has sworn that by the time these books came into existence, he had sold all his rights in the use of the pen name Hank Janson ... and that all these books must have been written by his successor."

Hawke directed the jury to find Frances not guilty on the four counts concerning *Accused*, *Persian Pride*, *Amok* and *Pursuit*, and also suggested that they might take the same course with respect to the other three.

Without retiring, the jury acquitted Frances on the whole indictment, and he was discharged.

* * *

Geoffrey Pardoe had died from peritonitis twenty months earlier at St Thomas's Hospital on 25 May 1953, aged sixty-three. At the time, he had been living in Mordaunt Street, Lambeth. "My father died in considerable poverty," recalls his daughter. "After his death, I collected some items from his room – his typewriter, the complete works of Bernard Shaw and a number of poems he had written." [83]

"He was told that if his leg wasn't amputated he would die. He faced facts, didn't want to limp around, and flatly refused the amputation," recalled Frances.

* * *

The appearance of new evidence was a surprise to all, and, because it caused the prosecution case to collapse, denied Frances the opportunity to tackle the subject that he really wanted to – the alleged obscenity of Hank Janson. It was a turn of events that annoyed and frustrated him to the end of his life, especially in the light of changes in the legal attitude to "obscene" books that began almost immediately after his friends Carter and Reiter had been jailed.

---

[83] Jean Parine, private communication, 19 March 2003.

Much had been happening as a result of that case. During the original trial in January 1954, one of the books introduced by Mr Christmas Humphreys as evidence of changing moral standards had been *Julia* by Margot Bland, which had then recently been the subject of a prosecution in a widely covered case in the Isle of Man.

Douglas had already been the scene of a series of prosecutions in July 1953 (see Chapter Nine), and more activity had followed a month later when Boots Cash Chemists had been charged with supplying two obscene novels through their lending library. The case had begun on 4 August, when Constable Alan Killip had joined the "A" (adult) section of the library and browsed the shelves before selecting two books, *Julia* by Margot Bland and *The Philanderer* by Stanley Kauffmann [84]. He had then gone to the manager of the shop and told him he had reason to believe that the books were obscene and that they would be reported.

When the trial had begun on 3 September, Inspector T A Cringle had sought to persuade the High Bailiff, Mr Howard Lay, that it should be possible for the court to decide the issue on the basis of just two extracts that had been read out. The High Bailiff had disagreed and adjourned the case, saying that he could not decide the issue without first having read the books.

Offering his judgment on 18 September, the High Bailiff had commented that, in his view, the two books were ordinary novels written only to afford the ordinary enjoyment of reading to whoever might peruse them and to provide financial remuneration for their authors. Neither of them, in his opinion, had been published "as being necessary or advantageous to religion or morality, to the administration of justice, the pursuit of science, literature, or art, or other objects of general interest." He had come to the conclusion that both books were obscene within the meaning of the Act [85], but had done so reluctantly, because he was satisfied that

---

[84] The two books had been mentioned in a column by John Gordon in the *Sunday Express* where Gordon wondered why no official action had been taken against such offensive (in his opinion) books.

[85] In relation to the Isle of Man, this was The Obscene Publications and Indecent Advertisements Act 1907.

the defendant company had acted in perfectly good faith throughout, and that the representatives of the defendant company had no improper motive in buying and lending out these books.

The case of obscenity had been proven, but the High Bailiff had imposed a nominal fine of £1 in each case.

Christmas Humphreys had commented on the case during his defence of Hank Janson, saying, of *Julia*, that it had been available in London for at least nine months without being prosecuted and was quite freely available even after the prosecution in Douglas. He had later read extracts from the book. This had (as previously noted) prompted the Recorder to state, in his summing-up: "one is partially re-assured that in the case of *Julia*, the first book with which we were regaled, the first book to which our attention was drawn, a prosecution of the publishers and author of that is now under consideration; and you may feel, perhaps, relieved to know that."

The case to which the Recorder had referred came to court at Clerkenwell on 18 May 1954, and in the face of such criticism from the Recorder of London, it is little wonder that the authoress, Mrs Kathryn Dyson-Taylor, and her publisher, T Werner Laurie, and printer, Northumberland Press, all pleaded guilty. George Greenfield, a former director of T Werner Laurie who had signed the contract for the book, and Alan Caldicott, the managing director of Northumberland Press, both pleaded not guilty to two charges, although Caldicott later changed his plea on one count. [86] All parties were found guilty on all counts except Greenfield, who was found guilty on only one charge and discharged absolutely on the payment of five guineas in costs.

On 26 May, the publishers Martin Secker & Warburg, its director Fredric Warburg and printer Camelot Press were committed for trial at the Old Bailey for publishing Stanley Kauffmann's *The Philanderer* (originally published in America under the title *The Tightrope*).

In June, Hutchinson & Co appeared at Marlborough Street Magistrates Court to answer charges, but the presiding

---

[86] The two charges had been brought because the book had gone to a second edition immediately after the Boots trial.

magistrate refused to deal with the case, because he felt it should be heard before a jury at the Old Bailey. At Clerkenwell, meanwhile, Ralph Stokes, Leonard Slater and Werner Blochert, paperback publishers and printers of *Caressed*, were each given jail sentences, later quashed by the London Sessions Appeals Committee. Stokes had previously worked with Bernard Kaye and had taken over the publishing of Ace Capelli as well as the small offices at 104 Southampton Row that had formerly been home to S D Frances and New Fiction Press.

On 29 June, Secker & Warburg came to trial at the Old Bailey before Mr Justice Staples, who began the hearing by saying that a distinguished publisher like fifty-six-year-old Fredric Warburg should not have to stand in the dock like a common criminal and inviting him to sit with his solicitor. The case, again prosecuted by Mervyn Griffith-Jones, was made remarkable by the judge's summing-up, where he said, in part:

> Members of the jury, as to this there can be no dispute: the verdict that in the course of this afternoon you will give is a matter of the utmost importance. It is a matter of very real importance, in its consequences, to the two companies, the individual, and the individuals who are associated with the two companies charged. It is of importance to authors who, from their minds and imaginations, create imaginary worlds for our edification, amusement, and sometimes, too, for our escape. It is a matter of importance to the community in general, to the adolescent, perhaps, in particular, and ... in addition to that, it is of great importance in relation to the future of the novel, and to future generations who can only derive their knowledge of how persons lived, thought, and acted from the contemporary literature of the particular age in which they are interested. Your verdict will have great bearing on where the line is drawn between liberty and that freedom to read and think as the spirit moves

206

us, on the one hand, and, on the other, a license that is an affront to the society of which each of us is a member.

Members of the jury, in discharging that important duty, I would say two things to you. First of all, that duty rests fairly and squarely on your shoulders. It is not what I think about this book; it is the conclusion that you come to, as representing that diversity of minds and ages composing the reading public of the English-speaking world. You and you alone must decide this case, and if, in the course of this summing-up, I express my opinion about the matter, you are entitled to ignore it.

The next thing I want to say to you is this: during the closing speech of the prosecution, it seemed to me that there was, if I may say so without offence, a certain confusion of thought. It was suggested that you are, by what you decide today, to determine whether books like this will or will not be published in the future. May I venture to say that your task is nothing of the kind. We are not sitting here as judges of taste. We are not here to say whether we like a book of that kind. We are not here to say whether we think it would be a good thing if books like that were never written. You are here trying a criminal charge, and in a criminal court you cannot find a verdict of "guilty" against the accused unless, on the evidence you have heard, you are and each one of you is fully satisfied that the charge against the accused person has been proved ...

Remember the charge is a charge that the tendency of the book is to corrupt and deprave. The charge is not that the book is either to shock or to disgust. That is not a criminal offence. The charge is that the tendency of the book is to corrupt and deprave. Then you say: "Well, corrupt or deprave whom?" To which the answer is: those whose minds are open to such immoral influences and into whose hands a publication of this sort may fall.

Members of the jury, what, exactly, does that mean? Are we to take our literary standards as being the level of something that is suitable for the decently brought up young female aged fourteen? Or do we go even further back than that, and are we to be reduced to the sort of books that one reads as a child in the nursery? The answer to that is: of course not. A mass of literature, great literature, from many angles is wholly unsuitable for reading by the adolescent, but that does not mean that a publisher is guilty of a criminal offence for making those works available to the general public ...

The book does deal, with candour or, if you prefer it, crudity, with the realities of human love and human intercourse. There is no getting away from that, and the Crown say: "Well, that is sheer filth".

Members of the jury, is it? Is the act of sexual passion sheer filth? It may be an error of taste to write about it. It may be a matter in which perhaps old-fashioned people would mourn the reticence that was observed in these matters yesterday. But is it sheer filth? That is a matter, members of the jury, which you have to consider and ultimately to decide ...

I do not suppose there is a decent man or woman in this court who does not wholeheartedly believe that pornography, filthy books, ought to be stamped out and suppressed. They are not literature. They have got no message; they have got no inspiration; they have got no thought. They have got nothing. They are just filth and, of course, that ought to be stamped out. But in our desire for a healthy society, if we drive the criminal law too far, further than it ought to go, is not there a risk that there will be a revolt, a demand for a change in the law, so that the pendulum will swing too far the other way and allow to creep in things that under the law as it exists today we can exclude and keep out? [87]

It took the jury just fifty minutes to decide that *The Philanderer* and its publishers and printers were not guilty.

But before the liberal media could raise a cheer, Hutchinson & Co, publishers, Taylor Garnett Evans & Co, printers, and a director of both companies, Mrs Katherine Webb, were in the dock on 15 September for the publication of *September In Quinze* by Vivian Connell. The case was prosecuted by Mervyn Griffith-Jones and heard by the Recorder, Gerald Dodson. The eleven members of the jury [88] were given copies of the book and told that it was to be "read as a whole" before the case resumed the next day.

In his prosecution, Griffith-Jones said: "There is a great deal that happens in this book besides matters of sex, and it may well be that the book, on the whole, is not a bad book; but gradually, and more and more as one reaches the concluding part of the book, the story is concerned with the sexual intercourse which takes place between the various leading characters in the book."

In his summing-up, Dodson suggested that a book that would not influence the mind of an archbishop might influence the mind of a callow youth or that of a girl just budding into womanhood. Sex was a thing that the jury might think had to be protected and even sanctified, as indeed it was by the marriage service, and not dragged into the mud.

The book was found guilty, and the three defendants fined £500 each. To Mrs Webb, Dodson said that he did not think the case called for a sentence of imprisonment, although the alternative to paying her fine would be six months' incarceration.

Although the courts were now finding themselves at odds with each other – and more guilty verdicts were being overturned on appeal as 1954 progressed – it was the

---

[87] The summing-up by Justice Staples was printed in full in later editions of *The Philanderer* published by Secker & Warburg and Penguin Books.
[88] One jury member was an author and journalist who had previously reviewed the book and was released by Dodson from duty.

destruction order issued against *The Decameron* by Swindon Borough Magistrates in July that galvanised the Government. The book, a 500-year-old classic, had been picked up along with others at a shop owned by Mrs Elsie Foulds, and in defending it, Mr R J Parker had argued that the police would be held up to the ridicule of the whole country if this was considered obscene.

An appeal had been heard on the same day as *September In Quinze* was prosecuted, and Wiltshire Quarter Sessions had overturned the destruction order on the book, but not before a representative of the Director of Public Prosecutions, Mr J T Malony, had made the bizarre claim that the book was obscene because it was in a book shop.

> MR MALONY: I would suggest that this work does, in the setting in which it was found, display an obscene interest in sexual matters, and that some of the stories are obscene in themselves. They were offered for sale in the appellant's shop, where newspapers and periodicals are available for purchase in conjunction with a variety of books the titles of which were certainly calculated to attract those looking for undesirable literature
> ...
> For those who wished to discover what type of material an Italian novelist poured from his pen in the 14th Century, there are places where that can be discovered. But in this place, Commercial Road, Swindon, these books could have been put out only in order to attract people who were looking for obscene literature, and in that setting they were likely to fall into the hands only of those who were so looking.
>
> THE CHAIRMAN (Mr A W Northey): Do you say that a copy of this book in the Swindon Borough Library would be perfectly proper?
>
> MR MALONY: I say it would be, because, although I have failed to discover it, I gather the literary

merits of this book are considerable, and it is perfectly right, I concede at once, that students of Italian social history should have access to it.

The case caused a good deal of amusement in the media and embarrassment at the Home Office, where Sir Frank Newsam complained to the Director of Public Prosecutions (DPP), Sir Theobald Mathew:

> The recent order by the Swindon Magistrates for the destruction of an edition of *The Decameron* has led to some acid comment in the press. According to the *Observer*, the same Bench, on the same occasion, declined to give a destruction order in respect of a number of books with highly suggestive titles, including *Don't Mourn Me, Toots* by the notorious Hank Janson, which has already been condemned elsewhere. I understand that the intention to apply for a destruction order was reported to the Director of Public Prosecutions in accordance with the Prosecution of Offenders Regulations 1946, and that the proceedings were taken with his approval.
>
> The condemnation of *The Decameron* is most unfortunate. It is not merely a world classic, but one which has been widely read for centuries. The ridicule provoked by the incident reacts most unfairly on the Home Office, since the public and press are very ready to assume that the Home Office directs proceedings of this kind. This assumption is completely unjustified – in this particular instance, we had not even heard of the proceedings, let alone directed them, until they were reported in the press – but experience suggests that it is hopeless to try to correct this mistaken impression.

The Home Office seemed to be more worried about being ridiculed than anything else since "the responsibility" was with the DPP, "but the odium tends to be ours."

Sir Frank Newsam's solution was to suggest that works over 100 years old should be disqualified from having destruction orders issued against them. "This will still leave awkward problems with regard to more recent established works of which *Madame Bovary* is an excellent example, but it would be a useful beginning if this rule could be accepted by the Director."

The DPP responded by pointing out the difficulties his own Department was having, since destruction orders were not within his jurisdiction either:

> The sole function of this Department is to inform the police what publications seized under a search warrant (a) have already been the subject of destruction orders, with details; (b) have been before the court and been held not to be obscene; and (c) have not so far been considered by a court.
>
> If asked, we give an opinion as to whether the publications in class (c) are *prima facie* obscene. Generally speaking, Chief Constables act on our advice, but there have been a number of cases in which the Justices themselves, or Clerks of Justices, notwithstanding our advice, have ordered that the material seized should be placed before the court.
>
> Therefore once publications have been seized by the police under a warrant, it is difficult to see how I could justify advising the police to return them, without the leave of the court, particularly those in respect of which destruction orders have already been made.
>
> If Justices cannot be trusted to make sensible decisions the only solution – and I cannot think that it is one that you would favour – would be to instruct the police not to seize certain kinds of publications because, once seized, the matter passes out of their hands and mine and becomes one for the court. [89]

---

[89] Public Records Office HO 302/1 and DPP 6/61.

The solution adopted by Sir Frank Newsam was precisely the one that Sir Theobald Mathew did not think he would favour: he charged Philip Allen at the Home Office with drafting a circular to send around to the police asking them "to be careful of seizing established classics."

On 1 November, Newsam was suggesting to the DPP that even stronger action needed to be taken:

> I think Strutt has mentioned to you the idea which we have in mind of setting up a small working party to look at the law about obscene publications, consisting of representatives of the Home Office, the Scottish Office, the Lord Chancellor's Department and yourself. I hope you will agree that this would be a useful exercise and that you will be willing to help us by joining the working party.

To this, Sir Theobald Mathew replied:

> I shall be glad to join the proposed working party on this troublesome matter, though, whatever the results of our labours, I feel that the HO and this Department will still have to be responsible for carrying this very slippery baby.

This particular "slippery baby" had by then been greased even further with a prosecution, in respect of *The Image And The Search* by Walter Baxter, taken out against Heinemann, whose director, A S Frere, one of the most distinguished figures in London publishing, was on bail for the sum of £100. The trial of the case – prosecuted yet again by Mervyn Griffith-Jones – against this "pornography dressed up as a twelve-and-sixpenny novel" resulted in a hung jury, as did a second held in November and December. The case went back to trial for a third time, but only as a formality, as the prosecution decided to offer no evidence and the jury was instructed to return a verdict of not guilty.

The fifth case against a major publisher – Arthur Barker, in respect of *The Man In Control* by Hugh McGraw – also resulted in an Old Bailey jury reaching a verdict of not guilty.

In June 1954, Graham Greene had written to *The Times* comparing the current wave of prosecutions to the one that had occurred in the late 1920s and early 1930s against *Ulysses*, *The Well Of Loneliness* and drawings by William Blake, which had been seized by police from a London art gallery. "One is tempted to call it all Manichean nonsense," he said. "Is the whole dreary routine to be followed once again – books to be condemned and then resuscitated when a more reasonable official attitude prevails?" [90]

Other "letters to the editor" followed, including one in *The Times* on 27 October under the heading "Censorship by Prosecution," which was signed by Lord Russell of Killowan, Sir Compton Mackenzie, J B Priestley, H E Bates, W Somerset Maugham and Sir Philip Gibbs.

Perhaps Graham Greene's prediction was coming true, as David Maxwell Fyfe was replaced as Home Secretary by Gwilym Lloyd-George in October 1954 and was faced with questions on this subject from all sides – from the House of Commons, publishers, authors and the judiciary. In March 1955, Roy Jenkins MP introduced a new Obscene Publications Bill to the House of Commons as a Private Member's Bill, and a Select Committee was set up to discuss the matter. After much discussion both in Parliament and in the media, a new Obscene Publications Act finally became law in August 1959, and whilst it did not end the arguments over what was considered obscene – as the subsequent cases against *Lady Chatterley's Lover* and *Fanny Hill* proved – it did establish in law that the dominant effect of a book "as a whole" had to be considered in the test of obscenity, and that the artistic merit of a work could be taken into account and expert witnesses be allowed to give their opinion as to the literary, artistic, scientific or other merits of a book.

1954 would go down as one of the most turbulent years in the history of British literature. For Hank Janson, his author, publisher and distributor, it would be remembered as one of the worst of their lives.

---

[90] Graham Greene, letter to *The Times*, 5 June 1954.

PART THREE

WHATEVER HAPPENED TO HANK JANSON?

CHAPTER FIFTEEN

SITUATION – GRAVE!

In late 1954, Reginald Carter began to rebuild his briefly-prosperous publishing empire. New Fiction Press had been put out of business by the fine it received, and Carter shut down the Top Fiction Press imprint that he had set up prior to the Old Bailey hearing in order to keep his businesses running. Under that imprint there had appeared only a handful of Hank Janson novels and a stop-gap anthology, *Deadly Mission*, which had barely made it out of the print works. With the trial having attracted such intensive news coverage, many newsagents were avoiding stocking Janson and similar novels, and publishers soon got the message that Gangster novels were poison in the new climate. Popular writers like Ace Capelli, Duke Linton, "Griff", Brett Vane, Nat Karta, Nick Perrelli – mostly house names used on sex-and-violence novels of dubious quality – were consigned to the obituary desk. When publishers did produce crime thrillers, the covers, language and action were toned down compared with what had gone before. Wives, servants and fourteen-year-old schoolgirls looking for thrills would have to get them elsewhere.

Carter's first task in his efforts to salvage what he could of his businesses was to re-establish his print works. "For a time, Carter dickered with the proprietors of weekly magazines or provincial newspapers, who were attracted by his very competitive quotations," recalled Frances. "But he also warned everybody very loudly that they were dealing with a jailbird, which didn't inspire their confidence. Moreover, he had trade union problems and warned potential clients that he couldn't guarantee uninterrupted production. For a time, he printed a very responsible newspaper, but then had to warn the proprietors to take their printing elsewhere. They did so, just a day before the Printer's Union brought the rotary press to a standstill. When the print shop burned down shortly afterwards, it relieved Carter of a white elephant problem, and his insurance compensated for the material loss.

"'Put it this way,' said Carter. 'Whatever you do, they've got the handcuffs waiting!'

"I thought then that he was joking away his worries. But as the years passed, I realised that the 'handcuffs' had become an increasing obsession."

Alexander Moring Ltd was a defunct publishing company that dated back to the late 19th Century, when it had been known as the De La More Press. Incorporated by Alexander Moring and Walter Skeat in 1903, it had been taken over by Martin Secker and Graeme Hutchinson in 1951 and allied to the Richards Press Ltd, of which Secker and Hutchinson were also directors.

Reginald Carter purchased the company following his release from prison and began plotting a revival of Hank Janson with his author and chief asset, Stephen Frances.

"Carter and I reaffirmed our gentleman's agreement," explained Frances. "We were managing to weather the storm. Everything I'd owned in Britain he'd had to sell or dispose of, even to my endowment policies, which were lapsed, to yield him immediate working cash. I said *adios* to my little boat and to Adrian and Pepita and lived very modestly in Spain on considerably less than a British working man's average wage."

Frances had been working on a novel in the style he preferred: semi-autobiographical. This concerned the fictional exploits of disillusioned Robert Harrison, a twenty-nine-year-old ex-jailbird, conscientious objector and idealist, as he travels through Spain and discovers a new life in a small fishing village. Under the title *Contraband* – it also involved smuggling – this became the first of the new series of Hank Janson novels under the Alexander Moring imprint. It was non-controversial and, unusual for a Janson, not written in the first person.

The cover – depicting a member of the Civil Guard standing

grimly before a mountainous background – was also non-controversial. But Carter and Frances were still nervous: obscene paperbacked novels were still being rounded up and prosecuted. In September 1954, Bernard Kaye (for whom Frances had created the Ace Capelli byline) and his brother Alfred, as directors of Kaye Publications, were sentenced to nine months and six months imprisonment respectively by Gerald Dodson, the Recorder. In October, Leeds Stipendiary Magistrate, Mr R Cleworth, condemned a cartoon magazine, *A Basinful Of Fun*, and ordered 108,000 copies destroyed, saying: "I have never seen in any publication anything so grossly low as two small pictures in this book. It is not a sexual matter, but gross obscenity." One picture was of the winner in the magazine's "Bikini Girl" competition.

Carter conceived an idea to print the books abroad and bring them through HM Customs and Excise for inspection. Customs officials were notoriously tough on obscene material coming into the country, and, the logic went, if they allowed them through, the books were presumably not obscene.

Carter contacted printers L P-F Léonard DANEL, in Loos, France, and a small edition of the new Hank Janson novel was printed and imported in packages with "Hank Janson" very clearly printed on the labels. As Customs officials took no action, a second novel was published, this time featuring the Hank Janson character in an adventure set in Spain. *Untamed* expanded upon a plot that Frances had intended for the "Continental Series" of Janson novels, had they continued from Top Fiction Press in 1953. *Framed*, the second Alexander Moring-published title to feature Janson, was the novel that Frances had completed as a follow-up to *Nyloned Avenger*; it had originally been intended to appear under the title *Woman Trap*. *Escape*, published in 1956, was another expansion of a "Continental Series" story, set in the fictional mid-European country Routania.

Frances gave full vent to his post-trial fury in a number of these new Hank Janson novels. *Menace*, a Janson-less story, dealt with crooked cops, but with more venom than Frances had allowed before; *The Big Lie* featured as one of its characters a bigoted judge named Dobson, whom Janson exposes. A third novel with a Spanish setting appeared, entitled *Deadly Mission.* [91]

Planned as the seventh Special (G) in the original run of Janson titles, *One Against Time* was eventually published in January 1956, and was the third and final science-fiction novel to appear under the Janson byline – a second, entitled *Tomorrow And A Day*, had come out a couple of months earlier, and a reprint of the first, *The Unseen Assassin*, followed a couple of months later. *One Against Time* had the unique heritage of being a second edition, as Frances had sold the novel to a Spanish SF paperback series, Nebulae, where it had first appeared as *La Violención del Tiempo* in 1955.

The new Janson series was off to a flying start, with Frances writing at the top of his form and Carter having no problems importing the books. Alexander Moring Ltd began to expand its line to encompass a wide range of novels: a series of romances by Ursula Bloom; reprints of American hardboiled novels and original thrillers by some of Janson's contemporaries, Michael Barnes and Leslie T Barnard; Westerns; and reprints of British Gangster thrillers from the Comyns list by Mark Shane, Max Clinten and Dave Steel.

In 1955, as protection against any trouble that might face Hank Janson, Frances purchased the rights to the name Darcy Glinto from Harold Kelly. Kelly was the mainstay author for Robin Hood Press, which he ran in conjunction with his brother, Hector, and Ernest Warr, who had been Hector Kelly's assistant in a previous venture, Everybody's Books.

Darcy Glinto had debuted in December 1940 with *Lady, Don't Turn Over*, and a steady stream of new novels – *No Mortgage On A Coffin*, *Road Floozie*, *Snow Vogue* and *"You Took Me – Keep Me"* – had appeared through 1941. In 1942, Harold Kelly had been prosecuted, as had James Hadley Chase, and no more Glinto novels had appeared until the establishment of Robin Hood Press. Hector Kelly, recalling

---

[91] *Deadly Mission* (Alexander Moring, 1955) had no connection with the collection of the same title that appeared from Top Fiction Press in 1953. The Heade cover artwork for the latter was revamped slightly and reused on *Framed*, and the three novelettes from the collection were subsequently reprinted as *Kill This Man* (Alexander Moring, 1958).

his days in publishing, mirrored the disgust felt by Stephen Frances at the persecution of paperback publishers:

> The bulk of the material was published in paperback, but after a year or so, I conceived the idea of binding some of these up for the libraries, and this was quite successful. We carried on this way for some years, until about 1953 when we were summonsed on two occasions for publishing obscene literature, and this so sickened me that I packed up entirely. Apart from which, I had no wish to go to prison, as many quite respectable people did for the same reason. For the life of me, I still can't see how it was even possible to bring a charge against publishers for a lot of the material, let alone obtain a conviction, but it happened. Some of the most well-known of publishers were involved, and convicted, but it was the paperbacks that came in for the stick. As small publishers, they could not afford to go to trial, so that the magistrate's decision was almost inevitably one of guilty, and a prison sentence often followed. It was disgraceful really.
>
> As far as the small publishers were concerned, there is no doubt in my mind that in its application, the law proved to be one thing for the rich and another for the poor. Admittedly there was some crude stuff being published, but it should not have made any difference. But it definitely did and, of course, the cheap paperback style condemned it as well. The law too was so equivocal that you were at the mercy of the magistrate and his point of view, and it appeared to me that just your presence in the dock on that specific charge meant an almost automatic conviction. The law has been changed since then, of course, but it still can't define what is obscene, and no law ever will. [92]

---

[92] Harold Kelly, private communication, 23 September 1983.

Harold Kelly had written a further thirteen Darcy Glinto novels between 1947 and 1953 before Robin Hood Press came to an end. The name was then revived on a series of reprints by Carter and Frances for Alexander Moring Ltd in 1956. At his home, "Restful", Carter had access to a complete set of all the novels that Frances had published, as Frances had arranged with his printers to have a dozen or so copies of each of his titles put into hardback. Thus a number of former Duke Linton and Steve Markham titles were edited and reprinted under the Glinto pen-name.

Carter also reprinted many of Harold Kelly's Westerns under the bylines Clinton Wayne, Lance Carson and Chuck Larsen, and published a previously unissued Glinto novel under the title *She Gave Me Hell*. [93]

The Alexander Moring imprint appeared on the surface to be going well, and Carter began investing heavily in other businesses. "Hank Janson was the mainspring of the business, and it was logical I should be free from all business problems to concentrate on writing," recalled Frances. "Because of this, my only knowledge of how the business was faring had to come from Carter.

"For the next few years I worked hard and lived simply, but was content to do so knowing that economic gains were being ploughed back into the business and establishing it solidly.

"When we started printing in France, the selling price of a Hank Janson was two shillings and sixpence. Since I was delivering a new book every few weeks and receiving only a working man's wage, my investment in the business was considerable.

"I made only brief trips to Britain, and accepted Carter's business reports without question. Nevertheless, I became gradually aware that Carter had some new and odd friends, some of whom he had met in prison, and with whom he seemed to have private arrangements. He now talked incessantly about the 'handcuffs' with a strange relish, almost as though he delighted in flirting with lawlessness. He proposed various and surprising schemes, which I rejected

---

[93] Possibly the novel advertised by Robin Hood Press as *Red Blonde Avenger*, which had never appeared.

because they seemed unsound and probably illegal. Then I learned he was making similar proposals to mutual business acquaintances. Some of them unwisely followed his advice and found themselves on the wrong side of the law, or insolvent.

"During my brief visits, I hadn't been able to extract from Carter more than a bare minimum [of payment]. He hadn't liquid cash, because all the money was locked up in paper and book stocks, he explained. But finally, he had to admit that, contrary to our agreement, he'd invested in other businesses. When these businesses bore fruit, Carter promised, he'd settle up with me. However, from what I could see of it all, he hadn't organised businesses: he'd organised disasters. He'd become deeply involved in a quick-service snack-bar, a small print-shop, rebuilding wrecked cars, a businessman's club, a jeweller's shop, a garage and an exhibition centre. None of these was a paying business, and because Carter had a major say in their management, they were all quite unnecessarily flouting the law.

"I was appalled when he showed me a large warehouse stacked with tons of pulp books he'd bought from Australia and couldn't sell. He'd intended to sell them at a good profit to a large distributor, but the company's buyer had funked out.

"It became obvious that Carter would probably never be able to comply with our gentleman's agreement. Instead of concentrating upon our Hank Janson breadwinner, he'd squandered our gains upon business disasters."

Reg Carter's diverse businesses included New Town Printers (Crawley) Ltd, Sussex Car Breakers Ltd and Stadium Motors (Crawley) Ltd. The latter provides a good illustration of the extent of Carter's business acumen. It was incorporated on 30 January 1957, a mortgage was taken out with G & C Finance Corporation on 11 June, and receivers were called in on 25 September. [94]

In 1956, Carter had incorporated a second publishing company, George Turton (Publishers) Ltd, under which imprint he published a number of children's albums, recycling

---

[94] Public Records Office, BT 31/40036/577788.

old comic strips and stories bought up cheaply from companies now out of the waning comic publishing industry.

Frances, in Spain and unaware to what degree his finances were in peril, was still writing excellent Hank Janson novels. Titles like *Situation – Grave!* and *Sugar and Vice* showed him to be still on top form. And Frances was not afraid to experiment with giving his readers something different every now and then. *Revolt* was a Janson-less story of an Army private named Tom Hugget, who rebels against harsh treatment by refusing to accept orders and eventually escapes the guard house to go on the run from the Army and police. *Invasion* took a step back in Hank Janson's history and involved him in the D-Day landings of 1945. *The Amorous Captive* was a rambling three-volume historical series set in the times of Queen Elizabeth I, focusing on the exploits of a simple peasant girl sent to the Old City of London, where she is robbed, both of her virtue and of her money. Later she falls in with thieves, and later still she becomes involved in the war with the Spanish Armada.

Most bizarre of all was the idea of Hank Janson writing the biography of real-life British crime boss Jack Comer, better known to the public as Jack Spot. Comer was an East End Jew who had fought Moseley's blackshirts in the 1930s, been discharged from the Army as mentally unfit and, after a period as a strong-arm man in Leeds, returned to London after the War to open a gambling club before expanding his interests in the control of the betting at Ascot racecourse. Comer, physically large and expensively dressed, had married a young Irish model and announced his retirement as the "King of the Underworld". One of his lieutenants, Billy Hill, had been waiting in the wings to take over. In the early 1950s, Hill had enjoyed a close relationship with crusading crime reporter Duncan Webb, who had ghosted his memoirs under the title *Boss of Britain's Underworld*. Spot had felt was a calculated insult. He had beaten up Webb and soon found himself in court; the fine had been only £50, but the incident had not improved his image with other underworld figures, who had already been questioning his leadership. In 1956, he had been viciously attacked by razor wielding thugs (amongst them, an up-and-coming "Mad" Frankie Fraser).

In 1957, he had been declared bankrupt. Refused entry to Canada, Spot had opened up a club in Lancaster Gate, only to have it burn down a few months later.

The Hank Janson biography *Jack Spot, The Man Of A Thousand Cuts* is one of the oddest biographies ever published. Frances wrote the book like a novel. In it, Hank Janson claims that he contacted Spot, and that: "in accordance with a pre-arranged plan, Jack Spot and I made our way by devious routes to a secret *rendezvous* somewhere in Europe." Living in a discreet commercial hotel, Janson says, he "mercilessly probed" Spot about his life for day after day, until "I had absorbed so much of Jack Spot I could almost think in the way Jack Spot himself thought."

> The Jack Spot Story is worth telling. But Jack Spot hasn't the know-how to write a book. I've merely stepped into his shoes, dressed myself in his personality and experiences and placed my writing ability at Spot's disposal.
>
> But I'm not forgetting that an author's *first* responsibility is to give pleasure to the reader. It's a curious fact that true stories, written as true stories, never possess the tension and excitement that straight fiction provides.
>
> But why shouldn't I write the true story of Jack Spot as though it was fiction? [95]

As an example, here is Janson's version of events when Jack Spot was attacked in 1956:

> On 3 May 1956, me and Rita were enjoying a temporary lull in the pursuit by reporters. We'd been out walking together, and were then returning to our flat in Hyde Park Mansions, which we would soon have to vacate. We were not more than fifty yards from the steps leading up to our flat.

---

[95] *Jack Spot* (London, Alexander Moring, 1958), p 8.

I saw the cars from the corner of my eye, and wouldn't even have looked towards them except that the doors were opened simultaneously and loudly. There came a swift and ominous rush of feet.

I stared unbelievingly as they rushed towards me, ten or twenty of them with handkerchiefs tied loosely around their faces.

There was no time to defend myself. No time to do anything!

I went down beneath the weight of them, the sharp pain ripping and tearing at me. An iron bar opened up my skull, keen steel sliced evenly through flesh, and their weight was bearing down on me, crushing me, forcing the air from my lungs so that I was suffocating.

The weight was enormous and inescapable. They hacked, and I was choking and unable to breathe. All at once, I was back there in that cul-de-sac all those years ago, feeling yet again the panic and fear of death. I was gibbering, and the panic was trying to rear up inside me, held down only by the tremendous weight that was choking me and the red haze that enveloped me as again my skull was split.

They intended to kill me!

This wasn't a run-of-the-mill cutting job. They intended to kill me. The razors could only slash me to ribbons. But the chopper, the iron bar and the coshes were intended to finish me.

It was Rita who saved me yet again.

Any other woman would have run fear-stricken from the murder that was taking place.

But not my Rita!

Already she'd proved again and again her loyalty to her husband, no matter how worthless he might be.

Now she proved it once more.

Without a thought for her own safety, she flung herself on my attackers and at the same time

226

screamed like a train whistle. She herself was injured, but she fought on desperately, pulling them away from me and screaming all the time.

It was the screaming that helped most. There's nothing like the awful, frantic screams of a woman to draw attention. People came running, others dialled 999, faces appeared at windows, and my attackers hastily scrambled back to their cars and drove off. [96]

Frances – as his alter ego Hank Janson in the shoes of Jack Spot, and with one eye over his shoulder to avoid litigation for libel – had penned a strangely fascinating, if flawed, book, which did little for Jack Spot's reputation. Billy Hill had had his memoirs ghosted by well-respected crime-busting journalist Duncan Webb and serialised in the *People* before reaching hard covers. Spot's biography, on the other hand, didn't even dare call itself a biography, and Hank Janson, for all his thirteen million sales, was still remembered as a writer of "dirty books".

Janson was, however, still perfect material for Daniel Farson, who was running a series of half-hour television shows entitled *Success Story*. In December 1958, Frances was interviewed in a Soho strip club, sat at the bar with scantily clad girls in the background. As he was, in reality, slightly built and looked nothing like the beefy tough guy Janson was portrayed as, Frances wrapped himself up in two thick overcoats for this appearance; and to cap off his act as the broad-shouldered and heavily built Janson, he wore a fedora hat and insisted on his features being covered by a mask.

Carter, on the other hand, had no need for this Elephant Man-style disguise: he was nattily dressed and showed Farson around a large warehouse, pointing out piles of Hank Janson books, parcelled and ready to ship out, reciting sales totals for each title, although by then they were far below their heyday of selling 4,000 copies a day.

* * *

---

[96] *Jack Spot*, pp 165-66.

One reason for the falling sales was undoubtedly the loss of Hank Janson's main cover artist.

Reginald "Heade" Webb had been responsible for Janson covers since 1948, producing artwork for all but a handful of the titles in the five original series. For years he had lived and worked at Queen's Mansions in Brook Green, a suburb in the Hammersmith area of West London. His studio was on the top floor of the imposing Victorian mansion, up a long flight of stairs. In his wire-framed spectacles and the white coat he wore while he worked, he looked like a teacher at school. His wife, known to all as Paddy and still only in her thirties, had died suddenly from cancer in 1951, and he had found it impossible to raise a young daughter alone; he had decided to send her to foster parents, and afterwards had become a virtual recluse. Financially stretched by medical and schooling bills, suffering from grief and worsening health, he had continued to carry out commissions with incredible resolve and no visible reduction of quality.

Following the Old Bailey trial in 1954, Webb had found work at the Amalgamated Press, providing covers for *Thriller Comics* and the *Sexton Blake Library*, and from early 1956 had begun producing two covers a month for Panther Books, signing them "Cy Webb". He had also painted covers for Pan Books. When Reg Carter had relaunched the Janson series in 1955 and tried to re-establish the winning team of Janson and Heade, Webb had agreed, but only on condition that he was paid double what he had previously received for a painting.

The covers that Webb produced for the Alexander Moring Hank Janson titles were unsigned and obviously rushed, lacking the depth and detail that had given the earlier Heade covers such an erotic charge. Now that charge was seen only occasionally, for instance in the covers for *Escape* and *Cactus*.

Overwork and constant smoking steadily creased Webb's features and destroyed what was left of his health until his heart gave way. He died on 14 October 1957 at the age of 56. At the time of his death, he was working on a head and shoulders portrait for a Pan cover. His body was discovered by the daily help who cleaned his studios. A neighbour had the sad task of searching through stacks of magazines looking for a will; mostly she found only birthday cards, Christmas cards and letters, still in their envelopes because Webb could not be bothered to open them.

* * *

By the time the *Success Story* television programme aired in December 1958, Stephen Frances was having serious doubts about his continuing relationship with Reg Carter. In the spring of 1959, he convinced himself that, finally, they could no longer continue to work together. In the early months of that year, Alexander Moring had published the second volume of *Amorous Captive* and the War-set novel *Invasion*, followed by the release of two reprints [87] It is possible that the split between Frances and Carter prompted Carter to switch the publication of Hank Janson at this point to his other publishing company, George Turton Ltd. The third and final volume of *Amorous Captive* was published by Turton in August. It was the last original Frances-written Janson that Carter would publish – he continued briefly with two more original Hank Janson novels, *Wild Girl* and *Torrid Temptress*, both written by another author attempting to ape Frances's style. Then *Bad Girl*, a retitled reprint of *Frails Can Be So Tough*, ended the brief Turton imprint and, in October 1959, Carter sold the Hank Janson byline.

Recalling one of his conversations, Stephen Frances quoted Carter as saying: "Put it this way, whatever you do, they've got the handcuffs waiting. You might as well be hung for a sheep as a lamb. Scotland Yard was on the phone this morning. They want to see me this afternoon, and they've warned me to bring my solicitor."

"He didn't seem disturbed. On the contrary, he seemed to be looking forward to the visit and skating on thin ice.

"I had been foolish to trust Carter, but I couldn't condemn him. He'd been influenced by his experiences, and his thinking had become warped. He wouldn't do anything straightforward if there was a twisted way to do it. All his

---

[97] By coincidence, these were the same final two fifth series Janson novels published by Top Fiction Press, *Silken Snare* (aka *Silken Menace*) and *Sultry Avenger* (aka *Nyloned Avenger*).

other business ventures were failing amidst similar undertones of illegality."

Reg Carter had seen the writing on the wall. The Lend-Lease agreement between Britain and America, which had been so important to Britain's efforts during World War II, had been a millstone around the country's economy ever since. Rules set in place to restrict the amount of material imported into the UK were not relaxed until 1959; but after that point, it again became economically viable to import books and magazines from the United States.

America had also had a paperback boom since the War. This had been led by Fawcett Publications, whose Gold Medal books had sold by the hundreds of thousands during the 1950s. Many publishers had switched from producing pulp magazines to the new, thriving paperback market, and, as the decade came to a close, the market was overburdened with hundreds of new titles being released every month.

One such publisher was Monarch Books, set up in 1958 by Allan Adams, Fred Fell and John Santangelo of Capital Distribution Co, with author and editor Charles N Hecklemann, then Vice President and Editor in Chief of Popular Library. Hecklemann became Monarch's President and Editor, and later recalled:

> We started out slowly at Monarch, issuing just a few titles every month to get our feet wet. The competition was heavy – Pocket Books, Bantam, New American Library, Dell, Avon, Pinnacle, Fawcett, [and] Popular Library among others – and Capital had to make a mighty effort to break into the distribution pipeline to newsstands, chain stores and bookstores. And we had to fight for rack space at a time when many publishers were issuing eight to ten titles a month – admittedly more than the market could assimilate.
>
> Though Monarch did publish both reprints and originals, the tremendous demand for softcover titles soon compelled us to resort to taking on many originals in all areas – straight fiction, Westerns, detective stories, science-fiction and a

wide range of non-fiction. Many of the Monarch novels carried strong adult themes and dealt with social and behavioural problems such as juvenile delinquency, drugs, political corruption, unusual phobias and sex. That was the norm for the time.

The Monarch Human Behavior Series covered many and varied aspects of the human situation in a group of carefully crafted non-fiction volumes such as *Medical Problems of Women* by Martin James MD, *Girls and Gangs* by Don James, *The Sexual Revolution* by Benjamin Morse MD, *Sex and Hypnosis* by L T Woodward MD, and *It's Cheaper to Die* by William Michelfelder. [98]

The average print run of a Monarch title was 100,000 copies – "Economically, it wasn't feasible to print less than that number," noted Hecklemann – but there were distribution problems:

> Monarch had a smaller distributor and it took more effort, more checking of the marketplace, to get good exposure for our titles, particularly since by the time Monarch came along, all the paperback companies had grown bigger and were publishing more titles. Every company was trying to crowd competitors out of the field. It was a rat race. There was – and always will be – the problem of returns. It is a situation endemic to the paperback book business. Wholesalers get flooded with titles month after month after month and – except for certain well-advertised bestsellers, which find five or six exposure slots in the racks and for a good period of time – many paperbacks are lucky if they get a month or two of exposure before the newsstand operators bundle them up or tear off the covers and return them for credit. And one of the continuing problems publishers face is what are called "premature returns". Often

---

[98] Gary Lovesi, "An Interview With Charles N Hecklemann", *Paperback Parade 35*, August 1993, p 16.

when newsstand operators are overloaded with titles and have big bills owed to wholesalers, they will ship back to the wholesaler cartons of new books that they *did not even open*, in order to get credit for them and lower their monthly bill.

The lifting of import restrictions in the UK opened the floodgates for American paperbacks to pour in.

Soon after selling the Janson byline, Reg Carter travelled across to the United States and netted a deal with Capital Publishing Inc to buy remaindered Monarch titles and import them cheaply into the UK. He approached Godfrey Gold, who had taken over the lease on Carter's former Borough High Street offices, and secured a distribution deal that would eventually lead to many problems, some of which were directly and indirectly to influence the future course of the Hank Janson series.

CHAPTER SIXTEEN

A RISKY BUSINESS

Jim Roberts was a chef. A master chef, in fact, who had served on the Queen Mary during World War II, and later worked in the same capacity for British Railways. By the mid-1950s he had become disillusioned with work and, with his wife, had set up a wholesale business, A & P Roberts. The business was on a small scale to start with, Jim Roberts himself driving around in an old Ford A, buying and selling books. But by 1959, paperbacks were booming. Penguin, perhaps the most famous name in British paperback publishing, had made huge advances during the War. This was largely thanks to their Services Editions, which had guaranteed them additional paper beyond that available to any of the newcomers. After 1950, Pan Books, Corgi Books and, later still, Ace Books and Panther Books, had begun to grow and prove that Penguin were not the only game in town. By the late 1950s, Panther had begun to aggressively chase potential best-sellers, paying £5,000 for the rights to *The Bramble Bush* by Charles Mergendahl. This payment was later dwarfed by Corgi, when they paid £15,000 for *Lolita* by Vladimir Nabokov.

It was boom time for the wholesalers, and about to become more so with the arrival of cheap American paperbacks.

Jim Roberts's business, known as "the newsagent's friend", was growing rapidly; and as his customer base grew, so did his workload. Roberts hired a friend, Derek Vinter, to manage the business for him. Vinter, whose parents lived next door to Roberts, was an engineer, but grasped the opportunity to change his life. "I was told by somebody 'You get one chance in life, and if you don't take it, don't grumble'," he later recalled. [99]

---

[99] Derek Vinter, interview, 4 December 1998.

One of Jim Roberts's suppliers was Reg Carter, whose Alexander Moring company had just hit the rocks and whose chief asset, Stephen Frances, no longer wanted to deal with him. Carter planned to sell up. Roberts and his manager set up a publishing business, Roberts & Vinter Ltd, and bought the rights to Hank Janson for £15,000. "If my memory's right," says Vinter, "Steve Frances was out in Spain, and [Carter] sold the copyright to get money out to him. Jim Roberts realised there was potential in Hank Janson and decided to buy the copyright and start a publishing firm."

"From the proceeds of that sale," recalled Frances, "I was able to extract some cash from Carter to live on while I was finding some other way to make an income.

"I had been very lucky and had escaped from the treadmill with the help of Harry Whitby. But Carter's failure to honour our agreement put me right back on it again. I had no possessions in Britain, all my good business contacts had been severed or soured by Carter, and I had only enough cash to keep me alive. Certainly not enough capital to print a book, even if I'd had one ready for publication. Ironically I'd made my home in a country where there was no chance of practising my profession. I could make myself verbally understood in Spanish, but writing grammatically correct Spanish for Spanish readers was quite impossible.

"The new owners of Hank Janson were willing to discuss carrying on with my authorship, but they wished to change the image of Hank Janson. They also insisted on buying the copyright outright for anything I wrote for them. We never reached agreement.

"I either had to return to London and find a job, or write something and find a publisher for it before my money ran out. I chose the more risky alternative, because I liked Spain and I liked writing."

* * *

Frances had been living in Spain for most of the decade, and much had changed over that period in the fast-moving world of paperback publishing. There was still a market for original paperback novels, but nothing like the early days of Hank

Janson. The "Gangster thriller" was no more. Even Ben Sarto, who had been a constant rival to Hank since they had both launched in 1946, had come to an end in 1958.

One of the steadiest markets for crime thrillers in the UK was the *Sexton Blake Library*, which had been publishing novel-length adventures of the "schoolboy's Sherlock Holmes" since 1915. The series had struggled through two wars, but by the early 1950s had been on its last legs, not least because schoolboys had found a far more exciting literature to read in Gangster novels. Hank Janson had been hot property, currency in any playground, even if you had to tear the covers off; being caught in possession of a Janson novel had been instantly punishable in most schools.

The readership for Blake was growing older. Even during the War, the word had gone around to the regular authors to consider that they were writing for adults; and, in 1955, former Panther Books editor William Howard Baker had joined the Amalgamated Press to revamp the character even further. Out had gone the old-fashioned Baker Street office, with its comfortable armchairs resting close to the fireside and its motherly housekeeper; in had come spacious new offices in Berkeley Square. The youthful Tinker of old had become a young man with a full name, Edward Carter – although Blake still called him by his old nick-name – and the previously all-male crime-fighting team had been supplemented by female secretaries and assistants.

The "new order" instigated by Baker had also introduced a new team of writers to the Blake saga, some (George Mann, Jack Trevor Story) from Baker's days at Panther, others newly blooded to detective thrillers. Into this circle came Stephen Frances. The bulk of his Blake stories appeared under the house name Richard Williams, the titles – *Vendetta!*, *Torment Was A Redhead*, *Somebody Wants Me Dead!*, *The Slaying of Julian Summers* – belying the light touch he brought to the saga. His first story was told, first person, by Marion Lang, Blake's secretary, the second by Tinker; one – *High Summer Homicide* – allowed Frances to slip back into the familiar role of newspaper reporter, as Arthur "Splash" Kirby of the *Daily Post*.

The switching of narrators allowed for some stories that were out of the ordinary. In *Torment Was A Redhead*, Tinker is conned into believing he has colluded in the robbery of a consignment of diamonds; in *Somebody Wants Me Dead!*, a successful boy's story writer by the name of Harry Snogg witnesses a bank robbery but finds it hard to separate his own reactions from the actions of his fictional creation, detective Ryley Steele; *The Slaying Of Julian Summers*, on the other hand, was a more formal "whodunit", based around the publication of a fictional novel entitled *The Headless Corpse*.

In contrast to the light-hearted Blake novels, Frances also began writing tough thrillers for Consul Books, the paperback imprint of World Distributors Ltd of Manchester. These allowed him to play to the strengths he had learned from years of writing Janson: chiefly the depiction of how people act and react when they are pushed to their emotional limits. In *Day Of Terror*, Doris Leston has her world invaded when she is trapped in her home by a wanted murderer. In *Bad Boy*, Charlie Cooper is a seventeen-year-old probationer in the custody of Sam Chasters, a strict disciplinarian who treats his ward as a slave; Charlie's affair with Chasters's wife, and the terror he is put through when he is caught, are, however, only a pale reflection of the events of the Hank Janson novel *Accused*. The *Pattern Of Life* of John Denham is one of rapid destruction, as the wheels of Authority grind slowly onwards towards his hanging after he has been falsely accused of rape.

For Consul's editor, John Watson, Frances also wrote three tie-ins to the television series *Naked City*. "Because I lived in Spain," recalled Frances, "I had never seen *Naked City*, so while in London I spent some hours in a small, private cinema where the episodes were projected for me. I was also given the scripts to work from. There was a snag. The scripts of these television episodes never had enough meat in them to provide a full-length book, so I had to pad and pad and pad. I complicated the plots, wove incidents and dialogue into the story that had never been featured in the original episodes to provide the book-length required."

As Danny Stephens, Frances wrote two novellas dealing with little-known aspects of the War. These appeared together under the title *The Whore Of Dalsburg*. The title story was about a small French village liberated from occupation only to be retaken, and about the retribution carried out by both French and Germans against those seen as collaborators. The second story, *They Did Not Pass*, told of a Chicago newspaperman who escapes from the Spanish Civil War and finds himself in a French concentration camp at St Jean.

A number of Frances's early non-Janson novels were reprinted by Consul under new titles and bylines, and *Not Everybody Died* was intended as the first of a new series of stories set in Prohibition-era America as recorded by Chicago newspaperman Danny Stephens. As it turned out, this attempt to revive the Hank Janson style fell flat and lasted only the one novel.

With the demise of the *Sexton Blake Library* in the summer of 1963, Bill Baker brokered a deal between the owners, Fleetway Publications, and Mayflower Books to continue the series in paperback, with Baker as editor. At the same time, Baker launched Press Editorial Syndicate to provide original paperback novels from his stable of writers. As well as writing three more Sexton Blake novels, Frances also wrote two Westerns and a story called *The Disorientated Man*. The latter novel was conceived by Howard Baker and published under his pen-name Peter Saxon, Baker having heavily edited Frances's manuscript for it. It was a bizarre and melodramatic mixture of science-fiction and horror, with a plot that jumped between the British police search for a blood-drinking monster, a mysterious East European agent called Konratz, and the slow dismemberment, one limb and then one sense at a time, of a young man called Ken. The book was found by American producer Milton Subotsky, who snapped up the film rights and co-produced the movie – as *Scream and Scream Again* – with his partner Max J Rosenberg through their British-based horror film company Amicus, although the majority of the budget was put up by American International Pictures, who hired director Gordon Hessler. Hessler's script followed the book's fractured storyline, and he cast three heavyweights of horror movies, Vincent Price, Peter Cushing and Christopher Lee, although none had an especially meaty role. The evocative title and star cast helped make it one of Amicus's biggest successes.

Frances had by this time also, briefly, hopped back onto the Hank Janson treadmill.

* * *

Jim Roberts was of the entrepreneurial disposition. "He was a character," recalls Derek Vinter. "He had a finger in this, a finger in that, and if ever there was a man who could turn nothing into something, he could do it. I remember there was a firm that was printing a magazine called *Pep*, which was a rival in those days to *Spick* and *Span* [semi-pornographic magazines of 'saucy' artwork, stories and photographs (nude and semi-nude)] and the firm went up the spout; they'd produced twelve numbers, and I believe Jim paid something like one tenth of a penny per copy. There were thousands of them. He brought them back, and we didn't know what we were going to do with them. We packed them up, and he went out to [distributors] Gordon & Gotch, and when he came back, he'd doubled his money in one visit, selling them 500 of each number to be sent to Canada. That was the sort of man he was. He would see a line, know where to place it or what to do with it, and that was the way he carried on."

But the business became too diverse and too big. "That's why he shed it and came out of publishing." One pie in which Roberts had a finger was livestock. "His wife was an ex-RSPCA inspector. They went over to Ireland because she wanted a horse, and they came back with, I believe, twenty-seven donkeys. They lived at Godalming in Surrey at the time, and these donkeys were going to be delivered to the railway station. He paid someone to let them loose down the high street so that he got some publicity." Publishing was set aside as Roberts helped bring donkey derbies to holiday camps.

As a part of the shedding of Roberts's interests, Hank Janson was sold again, to Godfrey Gold and David Warburton.

Godfrey Gold had been associated with Hank Janson for many years as a wholesaler, dealing with Julius Reiter and Reg Carter. When Carter had given up the lease on 139

Borough High Street following the demise of Alexander Moring and George Turton, it had been taken up by Gold and used as a storage warehouse for his stocks of pin-up magazines.

Gold, like Jim Roberts, had a finger in many pies. Born in Mile End in East London in 1916, he had spent his early years as a market trader, operating without a hawker's license – a risky proposition, as he never had the money to pay fines and would have to put up the rent book on his home as collateral until the debt was cleared. During the War, he set up a small workshop in Leytonstone, manufacturing "Golden Brand" starch substitute. This was sold on the black market, and made Gold and his partner enough money to open a small factory. Towards the end of the War, he was arrested for receiving stolen goods and served a four-year sentence at Dartmoor.

Following his release, Gold ran a confectionary business, while also wheeling and dealing in any commodity that came his way. Buttons, books and comics proved to do a steady trade, sold from a stall outside the front of Gold's house in Upton Park by his wife and two young sons, David and Ralph. In 1950, Gold and his brother Gerald bought up a transport company that was about to go into receivership, although the partnership split within a few years. In July 1954, Gold was again sentenced to four years imprisonment, this time for his part in the robbery of 100 tons of copper ingots from a barge on the Thames.

Released in 1958, Gold used £200 capital to buy a second-hand van, from which he began distributing comics. By the following year, Godfrey and his son David had bought a "hole in the wall" science-fiction bookshop in John Adam Street in London's West End with the help of Godfrey's brother, also called David, who was likewise in the book distribution business.

Building up their business on paperbacks and pin-up magazines, the Gold family – Ralph having joined the firm following his National Service in the Army Pay Corps – set up Books Immediate at 4 East India Dock Road, Limehouse, which they used as a warehouse for their stock and as a store front.

The Golds, as Goldpoint Ltd, then began publishing their own pin-up magazines, with titles like *Petite* and *Sleek*, in runs of 3,000-4,000. By the end of 1959, they were printing 60,000 copies of a range of "art" books every month. Sales were low, although the company still made a reasonable profit. The huge overstocks of pin-up magazines that found their way to Borough High Street were disposed of only after David Gold realised that he could ship them out as new titles for the price of printing a new cover. Thus old issues of *Sensations* became new issues of *Jade*, with an even higher price (3/6) that attracted more readers on the principle that the higher the price, the stronger the material.

Godfrey Gold was found guilty and fined £50 for publishing an obscene magazine in 1960, after a copy of *New Look* was seized from a shop in Southwark. A new company, Ralph Gold Booksellers Ltd, was set up to avoid problems should there be any further charges.

It was at about this time that Reg Carter and Godfrey Gold struck a cash-up-front deal to import copies of American paperbacks – 500 copies each of a dozen titles. Within two days of the books' arrival at Borough High Street, they had sold out, and customers were begging for more.

Two weeks later, a second shipment of Monarch Books arrived at Tilbury Docks, only to be seized by Customs officials and destroyed. The Golds arranged another shipment, this time to come in through Southampton, which it duly did without any problems. Godfrey Gold then flew to America to set up an exclusive deal with Capital, the American distributors. The immediate success of these American titles had meanwhile prompted Ben Holloway, a rival bookseller and publisher of pin-up magazines, to sign a deal with Midwood to begin importing their sexually stronger novels.

The Customs action against American paperbacks was as heavy as, in earlier years, the police action had been against British Gangster novels. In 1961, Customs officials seized 677,000 copies of 721 different titles. By May 1962, they had added a further 234,000 copies of 201 titles. To try to circumvent these problems, Holloway began printing his books in England, but the police were just as voracious as

Customs, seizing 171,723 copies of 1,026 different titles in 1961.

Only half the shipments were getting through, and the price of the books jumped to 5/- to compensate for the number of copies being seized.

But the difficulty for both the police and Customs was also one of numbers – over a million books seized in the space of seventeen months. Before Customs officials could bring legal action in relation to a seizure, they had to read each new title; and the importers were exercising their rights under the Customs Consolidation Act to have their cases heard before a jury. The judge and jury would then also have to read every single title – and in one High Court action, the case involved 350,000 copies of sixty-nine different titles.

With only a limited number of officers available to read the books, Customs, with the approval of the Director of Public Prosecutions, devised a scheme whereby they would seize consignments from particular publishers in America to particular importers in the UK (the grounds for which being that these particular transactions in the past had been found to consist of upwards of 90% of obscene works) and inform the importers that the books were being held until such time as they could be examined. "They will then be placed in a warehouse *sine die*" [100] – which meant indefinitely postponing any need to make a decision.

It was against this background of stock seizures that Godfrey Gold and David Warburton purchased Roberts & Vinter Ltd and the rights to Hank Janson from Jim Roberts. Janson was relaunched in a "New '64 Series" under the imprint Compact Books, and two new Janson novels continued to appear every month.

Godfrey Gold also had interests in a bingo hall and in manufacturing a cosmetic called Fame Perfume, which took up much of his time. Most of the publishing and distribution business was therefore handled by his sons David and Ralph Gold; and, from the start, David Warburton, a wholesaler from Oxford, was left in charge of the Compact line, along with Derek Vinter, who remained with the Roberts & Vinter

---

[100] Home Office, internal memo, 19 June 1962.

imprint as manager until he eventually left to return to the engineering industry.

Chief amongst the authors of the Hank Janson novels at the time was Harry Hobson, nick-named "Hank" at the offices of Robert & Vinter. Keith Roberts, who worked at the company as an editor, recalled: "[Hobson] took all of the Chicago newspapers, I think at his own expense; we had a great stack of them in the office. He was a tremendous expert on the city, although he never visited it; he seemed to know everything about it, even to the names of the officials in the police and fire departments." [101]

Hobson, born in Sheffield in 1908, had been a professional musician, travelling twice around the world and appearing on both radio and television. He had started writing in the mid-1950s and established himself with *The Gallant Affair*, published by Cassell & Co in 1957. He turned to writing full-time in 1958 and wrote a further four thrillers for Cassell, one of which was made "Thriller of the Month" by the London *Evening Standard*.

His association with Janson began in 1961, when, he said, "I had this cock-eyed notion that it would be more beneficial to eschew prestige and become Number One with a small company and grow up with it." [102]

Other writers who worked directly for Jim Roberts, and later for Dave Warburton, on Hank Janson novels included Harold Kelly – the former Darcy Glinto – and, from 1964, a prolific Canadian called Jim Moffatt, who had been an editor and writer in New York before relocating to the UK. But many of the Janson novels of this era were sourced indirectly through the literary agency of Charles Jackson, a teacher, author and part-time agent who had been writing for the then dwindling American pulp market. "Hank Janson came along because I was writing 'thick-ear' stuff for the American market; mainly Westerns but also some thriller stuff. Steve Frances used to write in an American idiom, and I thought, 'Well, I could write this.' I met up with Jim Roberts, but he sold his business to Godfrey Gold, and Dave Warburton

---

[101] Keith Roberts, private communication, n.d. [c.1985].
[102] Harry Hobson, private communication, 26 April 1985.

stepped in." [103] Jackson had become a literary agent by default. Interested in crafts and hobbies and spurred on by a desire not to see children wasting their time watching television inactively, he had tried writing some scripts for a BBC hobbies programme. "Back came the script with a note saying they only considered submissions sent in by literary agents. So I said, 'Bugger that,' and formed a literary agency myself. It was quite easy to do – think of a name and pay a solicitor to do it, and there you were with your own limited company. My wife and I became shareholders, naturally, and the next thing I sent into the BBC, they were interested in."

Jackson attracted a number of young writers to his agency, as well as some established authors. The latter included Victor Norwood, who had written Gangster thrillers for Reg Carter's Comyns Publications in the early 1950s. Norwood was as colourful a character as one could hope for – and if reality was not colourful enough, he was happy to tell as many tall tales as he could get away with. At various times, he claimed to be a boxing, wrestling and judo champion, and an expert swimmer, archer and shooter who had spent a year singing baritone in operas around the world.

Born in 1920, Norwood served with the British Merchant Marines during the War as an anti-aircraft gunner in the Atlantic and Malta convoys. He began writing after being invalided, and his first novel appeared a few years after he was discharged from service, whilst he was working at a local steel works. Norwood used the income from his Westerns and Gangster novels to finance a trip to Guiana to search for diamonds – an exploit that later became the basis for his book *Man Alone!*. A prolific and fluent author, Norwood began writing Hank Jansons after Charles Jackson became involved in their supply in 1962. He continued writing, mostly Westerns, for the British market until the late 1960s, when he began producing a steady stream of pornography for Greenleaf Classics in America.

"Norwood's writing was all right, but he needed a bit of editing," recalls Charles Jackson. "But once [his books] were edited, they were acceptable."

---

[103] Charles Jackson, interview, November 1999.

Soon after he began supplying Warburton with Hank Janson manuscripts written by Norwood and others, Jackson suggested to him that there was a large, previously untapped market for the novels. "By the time I got involved, they had about fifty or sixty titles, so I said, 'Have you ever tried selling foreign rights?' They hadn't even thought of it, so I asked if I could try, and they said, 'Yeah, all right. What will you want for your share?' I said the usual commission, 15% for literary sales.

"So I sent some Hank Jansons to a pal of mine, a literary agent in Copenhagen, and asked if they were any good, and he told me that he could sell all Scandinavian rights in all four languages: Finnish, Norwegian, Swedish and Danish.

"After that, every time Roberts & Vinter published a [Hank Janson] book, they would send me six [copies] of [it], and I used to send one for each country to be translated."

Translations of Hank Janson began to appear in Scandinavia in 1963, in book form in Sweden and Denmark and in the magazine *Magasinet For Alle* in Norway. Dutch and German translations followed soon after. Some titles were continually reprinted in these countries until as late as 1988. Gold Star Books also produced a series of American editions, with additional sex scenes especially written in, although this lasted for only seventeen titles (1963-1965). [104]

In September 1963, the directors of Nova Publications, who published *New Worlds* and *Science Fantasy*, agreed that the two titles would have to cease. *New Worlds*, which had begun life with Steve Frances's Pendulum Publications in 1946, had been relaunched by Nova, a company set up by a group of determined fans of science-fiction, in 1949. By 1963, the two magazines (*Science Fantasy* had been launched as a companion title in 1950) were struggling, and Nova

---

[104] One Hank Janson novel, *Lady Mind That Corpse*, had been reprinted in America in 1949 when Frances struck a deal with New York-based Checkerbooks Inc. Unfortunately, Checkerbooks almost immediately collapsed before Frances was paid. A second title sold to Checkerbooks, *Honey, Take My Gun*, later appeared from Pony Books in Canada under the title *Orchids To You*, again with no payment for the author. *Smart Girls Don't Talk* was published in America by Flamingo Publications, New York, as the first issue of 'Hank Janson Detective Magazine' in 1951, but no further issues appeared.

was forced to announce their imminent demise to their printers.

Amongst the printers' clients who were told that the presses would soon have some additional capacity was David Warburton, who promptly bought both titles. John Carnell, editor since *New Worlds* had first appeared, turned down an offer from Roberts & Vinter to continue his editorship but suggested a possible replacement, Michael Moorcock.

Moorcock was then only twenty-four but already had many years of editorial experience, having edited *Tarzan Adventures* for two years from the age of sixteen before spending another two years on the *Sexton Blake Library* under William Howard Baker. A prolific writer for both *Science Fantasy* and *New Worlds*, Moorcock joined Roberts & Vinter in February 1964 with an aim to make science-fiction a credible and popular part of the literary mainstream, eschewing old ideas – or radically reworking them – and encouraging experiment to revitalise what he saw as a stagnant genre.

Science Fantasy, meanwhile, was to be edited by Kyril Bonfiglioli, an Oxford-based art-dealer and antiques shop owner, who also wanted to produce a magazine of literary quality. This matched the ideas of David Warburton, who, according to Moorcock, was looking to "upmarket" Roberts & Vinter:

"They thought that *New Worlds* would be an inroad into Smiths, which had refused to take any of their books. We were to be the respectable front which would help them get the likes of Hank Janson and their magazines into Smiths.

"David Warburton, as much as anyone did, ran the Janson series, though [it was] also run at odd times by others such as myself." [105]

The Compact Books line had, by then, expanded beyond Hank Janson alone, and the instigator of this had been none other than Stephen Frances.

Frances was still struggling. The money he had retrieved from Reg Carter from the sale of Hank Janson went only so far, and finding markets for his work was not easy from his base in Spain. Short stories sold to the *Evening Standard*,

---

[105] Michael Moorcock, private communication, 1 August 1998.

Today, *Argosy*, the *Evening News* and *Reveille* supplemented the writing of Sexton Blake yarns, but his hope was still to establish a new character that he could take to the heights that Hank Janson had previously enjoyed.

Although still unhappy that Roberts & Vinter required their authors to sell them all rights in their novels for a flat fee of around £150 per title, Francis needed to make a living. By now, he also had a family to support – he had married a Spanish girl, Teresa Barbara Prenafeta, and had two sons, David and Stephen. And his familiarity with Hank Janson at least guaranteed a sale. Writing *Nymph In The Night*, his first novel with the Janson character for over three years, must have felt like slipping into a pair of comfortable old slippers.

In the aptly titled *Second String*, Frances introduced a rival to Hank in the shape of Hilary Brand. Although she first appears only two chapters from the end of the book, Hilary – a reporter on a local paper, the *New Lidton Courier*, "young, boldly and proudly beautiful and so full of vitality that it seemed to brim out of her green eyes" – quickly manages to scoop Hank on a story. She sticks to Hank in *Brand Image* as he travels through Missouri on a working holiday, at the end of which he persuades the Chief of the *Chicago Chronicle* to hire her at local rates as he heads down to Texas on an assignment, chronicled in *Hilary's Terms*. When Hilary scores another scoop, there is nothing the Chief can do except hire her.

As did Roberts & Vinter. For a further four novels, Frances became Hilary Brand, switching his narrative voice from that of grizzled veteran Hank to that of young, auburn-haired Hilary.

During this brief run, Frances persuaded Warburton to experiment again with the Janson Special, and produced *Daughter Of Shame*, a historical set in Elizabethan England. This was intended to be the first of a trilogy (like the earlier *Amorous Captive*), following the adventures of comely Mary True after her parents have been burned for witchcraft, but no further volumes appeared.

After producing nine novels for Roberts & Vinter, Frances left Hank Janson – and Hilary Brand – for good in 1965.

The Brand novels were handed over to James Moffatt, who had also branched out from writing Hank Janson and was penning a series of detective tales under his own name featuring a character called Johnny Canuck. The Compact Books line was further diversified by Moorcock, who had been handed a novel that he felt so poor that it needed to be re-written from the ground up. *The LSD Dossier* appeared under the byline Roger Harris and introduced a new character, secret agent Nick Allard, whose adventures Moorcock then continued to write under the pen-name Bill Barclay.

Compact also published a diverse line of science-fiction novels, ranging from reprints of titles by L Sprague De Camp and Charles L Harness to originals by John Brunner, Thomas M Disch, Judith Merrill and the ever-prolific Moorcock.

The quality of the Hank Janson books of this era was decidedly patchy. Norwood had departed in 1964, and Harold Kelly had followed shortly afterwards. Moffatt, whose Janson novels often needed an overhaul, was more comfortable when allowed to create his own character. Harry Hobson was consistently the best writer on the series at this time, and tried not to let the formula of Hank being a Chicago newspaperman limit his plots. One notable tale, *Lake Loot*, concerning treasures looted by the Nazis during the War, even attracted some unwelcome official attention.

Hobson himself, however, was less than happy with some aspects of the Janson production line. "Publishing-wise it was a very sloppy operation; there was no direction, no advertising, very few suggestions, and I soon found no-one bothered to read the bloody books, so that misprints and page transpositions went unheeded, [at least] until Parks Press of Manchester took over [the typesetting and printing] after Richmond Press (deservedly) went skint. Then the distributors, Thorpe & Porter of Leicester, went skint too."

Thorpe & Porter's 1966 bankruptcy brought the Compact Books line to a skidding halt. The company was in debt to the various Gold-run businesses (Roberts & Vinter, Dagg Books and others) to the tune of £260,000. The Golds decided to rethink their publishing policy and abandon their "posh" front in favour of a return to the soft pornography market. A relatively "respectable" men's magazine entitled *Golden Nugget*, one of the first in Britain when it was launched in March 1966 and intended by its publishers to be a British

Playboy, disappeared. Its contents had by this point been thoroughly subverted by its contributors to include articles on William Burroughs and J G Ballard and a series of Janson short stories, mostly written by Jim Moffatt, as padding between the naked ladies. The science-fiction novels also disappeared. Hilary Brand and Johnny Canuck were put out to pasture, and Compact returned to being the sole province of Hank Janson.

The Janson novels of this latter era were written by only two authors, Harry Hobson and Colin Simpson.

Born in 1914, the son of a bank director, and educated at Harrow, Simpson had formerly been an actor [106]. In 1962, as Colin Fraser, he had co-written (with Philip Ridgeway) the movie *The Switch*, featuring Anthony Steel as Customs officer Bill Craddock. Later, he had adapted the script as a novel for Compact, where he worked as a layout designer and copywriter.

Hobson had, for the most part, maintained the Janson character as he had inherited it, but changes accelerated following the departure of David Warburton in 1967. Warburton, having made a brave attempt to keep *New Worlds* afloat with Mike Moorcock, had finally thrown in the towel and departed for Scotland, where he set up book wholesalers Clan Books.

The covers of the Janson novels immediately switched from artwork to photos. Then, in 1968, Hobson gave the saga its most radical change since 1950, as Janson quit the *Chicago Chronicle* to move to London and take over "Special Assignments Limited". Hobson had directed Janson through a number of stories that tried to capitalise on the popularity of spy fiction in general and the James Bond movies in particular. He had involved Janson with US and UK intelligence services, and had initiated a series of eight novels that detailed the activities of WASP, the "World Association for Scientific Progress", a secret organisation of top scientists whose wish was to disrupt governments and stop war. Another, more sinister outfit created by Hobson was The Organisation, although this featured only briefly in the Janson saga.

---

[106] His only known film role was in *Pink String and Sealing Wax* (1945).

The new, London-based series, launched in *Sprung!*, was intended to update Janson; Special Assignments Ltd (SAL) was a press agency, with a large, smoothly-running office in Holborn, who would take on assignments for any newspaper or seek out hard-hitting stories themselves. Hobson treated it more like a private investigation service that Janson made available to anyone. Simpson, on the other hand, seemed to prefer Janson simply as a reporter.

A change of a different kind came in 1970: Janson switched imprints from Roberts & Vinter to Gold & Warburton, and a few months later, with *The Big Round Bed*, eschewed all innuendo regarding sex in favour of a more frank approach. The final eight Janson novels, published in 1970 and 1971, left nothing to the imagination.

Caribbean Caper was to be Janson's final adventure, and Hobson, between the sex scenes, still managed to give Hank some dignity. He even slipped in a few references that long-time fans would appreciate, having a character commenting on the books that Janson wrote and noting that he was not American ("I never took papers out"). Two further titles advertised as "in preparation" failed to appear.

CHAPTER SEVENTEEN

"IT TAKES TIME TO BUILD THE MILLENNIUM"

"Picture yourself with an enormous sum of money that you can spend like water. What would you do with it? Would you buy a large and luxurious house and stock it with the most beautiful girls you can obtain ...? But don't confine your financial excesses to sexual indulgence. Think about everything you could do with the imaginary inexhaustible fortune you possess. How many private swimming pools will you build for yourself? How many luxurious private aeroplanes will you own? How many chairs do you need to sit in, how many beds to lie in and how many houses to shelter you from the elements?" [107]

Think about that scenario and you may respond, as John Gail does in *This Woman Is Death* – not the first Hank Janson novel, published in 1948, but a new Stephen Francis novel of the same title, published in 1965 – that: "A man's only got one ass to sit upon. Every additional chair is superfluous. A man needs only one bed to sleep in and just one roof to shelter him. Even for a gourmet, the number of exotic dishes he can relish is limited by the size of his stomach." [108]

Take fifty-eight of the world's most wealthy men, who have reached the same conclusion. They have all the money they could want, and have sampled every experience. After the excesses comes boredom, and then the desire to do *something*. "Does it seem *impossible* to you that these men, bored and unemployed, knowing the enormous extent of their power and influence, should have combined secretly to use their wealth to make our world a better place to live in?" asks Gail's mysterious questioner, George.

---

[107] Stephen Frances, *This Woman Is Death*, p 40.
[108] *ibid*, p 41.

"If such an organisation existed," notes Gail, "with so much power and influence, there'd be no problems; no racial hatred, no economic problems, no misers and no wars." Such an organisation, Gail concludes, is possible – but unlikely.

"It takes time to build a millennium, John," says George. "We've only been working for five years, and the human race is terribly cussed." [109]

* * *

"I could no longer use the character Hank Janson nor write anything that might seem to be plagiarism [of that character]," said Stephen Frances. "I gave a great deal of thought to inventing a new character, named him John Gail, and constructed him bit by bit, making him a person with good points and human failings. He was anti-war and like me in other ways. If I'd met him in the street, I would have known him."

When readers first meet Gail, he is a door-to-door salesman, trying to sell the twelve volume *Children's Pictorial Encyclopedia* to a housewife with a young boy. An expert at hard-sell salesmanship using a combination of flattery and encouragement, he attacks the woman's conscience at its most vulnerable point, through her son. That leaves him in something of a moral dilemma: he knows she cannot really afford the fifty guineas for the book, but his own financial situation makes the sale important. He makes the sale, but returns later, more to assuage his own guilt than to help the woman. His subsequent visits are mistaken by the woman's irate husband as evidence of an affair, which loses Gail his job.

Gail's home life is also in flux: for two years he has lived with his ex-lover Laura, who is now planning to marry, which means that the comfortable flat they still share is in peril. These circumstances coincide with Gail finding an advert in the newspaper:

---

[109] *ibid*, pp 42-43.

> Excellent financial rewards await young man,
> physically fit, reasonably intelligent, naturally
> non-conformist and totally devoid of any undue
> respect for the law. Write to Box 503.

Gail replies to the advert on a postcard with two words: "What else?"

The secretive "Advertiser" reveals himself only after Gail has filled in a questionnaire and submitted himself to a full physical examination. Gail meets George, a small grey man with a round, pink face and gentle, blue eyes, at Westminster Bridge. George wears a hard-brimmed bowler hat and an old mackintosh that needs replacing. He speaks softly, probing Gail for his thoughts and views, and asks him to imagine a situation in which he has so much money that he could change the course of world events. Gail's reaction is one of disbelief that an organisation that links together men with such power could exist, and George tells him: "The strength of our organisation is its improbability."

The organisation in question is called PLEADON and is financed by fifty-seven multi-millionaires (one of the original fifty-eight having died recently as the debut story opens [110]). PLEADON has a world-wide network of agents, men and women dedicated to the betterment of humanity, culled from all levels of society. Unlike most spy networks created in fiction, this is a group whose work is not government-sponsored and goes far beyond political and territorial boundaries.

Gail is very much an everyman character, who has struggled through life without causing deliberate harm to anyone; a connoisseur of fine things, but only when he can afford it. George sums him up as: "Talented, but only mildly. You like drawing, music interests you and you have a slight flair for literature. But intuitively, you know you're merely mediocre. You have charms and you're physically fit; you're intelligent and you're idealistic; and as long as you have money, you won't find life too bad ... But what will you do without money, John?"

---

[110] Later books open with an explanatory paragraph, which gives the figure as 54.

252

As an anti-authoritarian with a sense of duty only to the world, Gail is in a moral dilemma when faced with the reality of PLEADON. George admits that one day Gail may be asked to kill, and pacifist Gail is unsure if he can condone an organisation that freely admits to operating that far outside the law. Its targets are, however, death-merchants of the worst kind – not necessarily working for governments, but usually individuals who can sway the balance of power and will do so for personal profit.

Gail's first "assignment" is to remove from circulation an arms dealer who is supplying weapons to a revolutionary cause. This is done with the aid of the age-old spy gadget, the drugged cigarette, but leads to the accidental death of an innocent motor cyclist when the arms dealer smokes the cigarette while driving and falls unconscious at the wheel.

Brought face to face with the outcome of his actions, Gail falls apart; and the plan to douse the sleeping arms dealer with whisky and have him jailed for drunk driving also collapses. It is left to Gail's "wife" for this assignment, the seemingly professional Vanda, to hold both Gail and the situation together.

The anti-heroics were not intended by Frances to be humorous, but to be a character flaw with which Gail had to cope. Not that the John Gail novels were without their humour. Following his first assignment, Gail decides to become a writer of articles, but, as rejection follows rejection, his theories about editors grow from individual stupidity to a full-blown conspiracy; in *Cry For My Lovely*, an electronic surveillance device causes Gail's house-cleaner to ask nervously if she can plug in the vacuum cleaner without fear of electrocution; and the opening of *Hate Is For The Hunted* sees the inactive and very bored Gail indulging in a spree of senseless spending – on everything from a camel to 125 fathoms of galvanised chain, guaranteed rustless – and having it all delivered to the luxury suite of his London hotel. The comedy element was often slight, as it had been in Frances's Hank Janson novels, but necessary to balance the otherwise emotionally heavy storylines and Gail's doubts about the morality of what he is doing.

Although published in the era of super spies, Gail's adventures were as far away from those of James Bond as Fleming's creation was from Chandler's Philip Marlowe, although inevitably comparisons were made: "Agent 007 Had Better Watch His Step" was the headline to one interview published shortly before the first novel was released in 1965. Unlike Bond, Gail is not particularly a patriot of his country and is active in the nuclear disarmament campaign. His love affairs are rarely successful, and working with or meeting women often leads to tragedy and more moral guilt, as with the deaths of Diana in *To Love And Yet To Die*, a nun (who is mistaken for Gail's accomplice and operated on by a drunken surgeon) in *The Sad And Tender Flesh*, and Kate (who is kept heavily doped and her needle wounds rubbed in dirt to cause infection and death) in *The Caress Of Conquest*. The trappings of success are often held by those who least deserve them: the Hampstead art-crowd in *The Sweet Shame Of Fury* pander to each other's quirks endlessly and emptily, and Gail's own desire for economic freedom and materialism leads only to bored frustration when it is achieved.

"In my books, I have usually tried to present some aspect of morality – a grain-sized pill with a thick sugar coating," said Stephen Frances. "Unlike Mike Hammer and similar tough heroes, Hank Janson did not run around shooting and killing frequently and casually. A killing is a very serious matter, and Hank Janson treated it as a very serious action. This attitude reflects my own convictions."

The seven books that made up the John Gail adventures were, at times, heavy going; at other times they exploded into action that could be extremely violent and sadistic. The plots ranged far and wide, from political blackmail to the infiltration of a private sect whose members are involved in ritual flogging and human-hunting, and from the destruction of a narcotics gang to the search for a serum to cure cholera.

"My hope was that John Gail would become as popular as Hank Janson," said Frances, "and that I would once again be happily dictating yarns that would revive my finances." By the time he completed the first novel in the series, money was again tight: Frances had an interest in a nightclub, but his writings for the past year had netted him very little, with no royalties, and he had a seven-year-old son at school in England and a seven-month-old baby to feed.

"If Carter had kept faith with me, I could have printed the book myself, made an agreement with a distributor and seen the book on bookstalls within a few weeks. I could have used my publishing experience to give the book a good start, and, with luck, it could have caught on like Hank Janson. In anticipation of this, I'd given the first John Gail book the same title as I'd given the first long Hank Janson book – *This Woman Is Death*.

"The book was written, but I had to wait while the manuscript was kicked around between editors and readers. Eventually I was told it would be accepted, subject to certain alterations. I made the alterations and received an advance royalty payment, which, by then, I badly needed."

The publisher was Mayflower Books, now under the editorial direction of John Watson, Frances's former editor at Consul Books. "Having to find a publisher brought home to me forcibly the enormous difference between being on the treadmill and being your own boss. I had no say in the publishing, I was merely a wage-earner, producing work for which I was paid and thereafter having no control over the handling of it. I couldn't compose the cover drawings, decide how often the Gail books would be published or intervene in trade publicity and distribution."

This Woman Is Death appeared in May 1965 with a cover that can be most politely described as uninspiring. Later Gail novels had better covers, but the momentum and impetus of a best-selling first outing were lost.

"There were half-a-dozen or so paperback publishers in Britain, issuing about a hundred new titles every month," reflected Frances, "but few booksellers and newsagents can display a hundred new titles, and their display space is even more restricted if they also handle newspapers, magazines and bound books. So it's a matter of luck which new books are displayed and can catch the readers' eyes. Those that don't get displayed, don't get sold. The problem becomes even more acute after a month, when another hundred new titles come onto the market. The booksellers return the 'unsolds' and display as many of the new titles as they can.

"It is important to an author that his book sells well, but not necessarily so to publishers, who produce books like sausages. They print a total of books every month which is estimated to yield an average profit. This satisfies the accountants, who don't care which author gets the best bookstall display. The exception to this is, of course, the best-sellers. The publisher prints large editions of these, knowing they will be widely displayed, some booksellers building pyramids of them in the shop window.

"I couldn't visit distributors and offer incentives for them to display and stimulate sales of John Gail. Like all wage earners, I had to accept my wage and leave the rest to the boss, and John Gail enjoyed the average sale of an average sausage.

"This was not what I'd hoped for, but it enabled me to carry on living my simple way of life in Spain."

* * *

"I was so accustomed to writing the Hank Janson books and enjoying large sales that it was a big disappointment that John Gail was just an average seller," Frances later wrote. "I'd put a lot of planning into Gail, and was convinced I could have made him into a reasonably good-selling character if I could have published him myself. The saddest aspect of it all was that I'd lost my big chance to get off the treadmill. Now I was back to the plodding labour of working for others."

In between writing the John Gail books, Frances found work elsewhere, including writing scripts for children's comics and what he euphemistically called "specialised material" for United States publishers – in other words, pornography for the American paperback market.

With the lost opportunity for John Gail to become another Hank Janson, Frances was determined to gain some control over the publishing and printing of a new series in the hope of re-establishing himself as a one-man band. In July 1966, he reaffirmed a deal with Harold Kelly to take over the popular Darcy Glinto byline and titles, and was able to gather together a set of the books with the help of a friend, Janson collector Derek Thomson. Thomson sent copies of the books to Charles

Jackson, who was acting for Frances through his Bookland Company Ltd literary agency. "I remember going with Steve to see this bloke with a large web-offset printing machine who used to print the early Hank Janson books," recalls Jackson. "By then, things were getting a bit dicey for Steve, and he was trying to get this printer to accept a deal, [under which] Steve would write characters under another name, but I think he turned it down. The web-offset machine was run into the ground."

Frances had convinced himself that the popularity of *The Untouchables* on television [111] and *Bonnie and Clyde* at the cinema indicated an impending revival of interest in Gangster fiction, but the Darcy Glinto scheme came to nothing, and eventually Frances had to admit: "The paperback trade at the moment is in a terrible state, with millions of 'unsolds' and new books being disposed of at less than cost. There simply isn't room on the bookstalls for anything like the number of titles still being printed every month. A little man with Gangster stories couldn't get his nose in. He'd be ruined at once if he tried." But he would keep trying, and it would be until 1970 that he would eventually concede defeat: "Darcy Glinto seems to be a dead duck. Nobody's interested in reviving him."

By late 1967, only three John Gail novels had appeared over some eighteen months. Frances had already delivered the fourth, *Hate Is For The Hunted*, and had two more written, but was faced with the reality that "books of mine due to be published might not appear for perhaps two years."

* * *

"The Spanish Saga" was the label Frances gave to a novel that he had longed to write for years: a novel that he thought might take him off the treadmill, make his name a bestseller in hard covers and relaunch his career as a writer. With Mayflower Books and John Gail, he might at least achieve royalties rather than the flat fee offered by Compact for the Hank Janson or Hilary Brand novels – but only if the books

---

[111] Originally broadcast in America from 1959 to 1963, the series did not reach British television until 1966.

he was writing were published, and not a single one of them had appeared between November 1966 and July 1968.

He felt confident that he could write the book and bring something to it from his unique position: "I had lived for many years in Spain, had travelled it widely and had talked with scores of Spaniards who had lived through the Spanish Civil War. I'd soaked up facts and emotions like a sponge, and now had them all locked up inside me. Not many foreigners, dependent upon newspaper reports, have gained an accurate picture of that war. Even the Spaniards knew only what had happened in their own limited circle. I knew that Britain's left-wingers' political opinions about the war were quite mistaken.

"I set out to write a big novel – big because it would show what happened to half-a-dozen families of different social standing, from just before the outbreak of war until some years after the Second World War ended.

"It was an enormous amount of material to handle. With Hank Janson and John Gail, I could carry all the characters, action and incidents in my mind while I was writing the book. But this was quite impossible for what I mentally labelled 'The Spanish Saga'. A complicating feature was that I had to write to earn a living. I couldn't devote myself to a book that would take many months to complete. I had to write it piecemeal in between comic scripts, short stories and other, paperback books."

The Spanish Saga was to embrace the period 1934 to 1964, during which time the half-dozen fictional families about which Frances was writing went to war, married, had children and behaved in many extraordinary ways, through which Frances hoped to build up an accurate and true picture of Spain's civil war. "It was a writing venture quite different from anything else I had tackled. I imagine that an architect who is accustomed to designing bungalows would face similar construction problems if asked to design a hospital with dozens of entrances and passages and wards, all integrated within a ten-storey building.

"One of the attractions for me about Spain was the universal contempt for the clock. Nobody was willing to be ordered around and dominated by Time. We ate at night when

258

we were hungry, usually around ten or eleven. Then we sat out in shirt-sleeves in the warm night air, talking, telling of experiences or telling jokes. We went to bed when we were tired, not when the clock said it was bed-time.

"When I first moved to Spain, sometimes I set my alarm-clock and sipped tea while waiting for the sun to rise. As dawn broke, Adrian brought the boat over from its moorings and I went down to join him. We steered a course from Rosas lighthouse to Escala for about three miles out into the bay, throttled down and put out lines for mackerel. We always caught a few, and if we hit a school we caught a great many. On occasions, we hauled in two or three hundred within an hour or so.

"When the fish stopped biting, we turned around and headed for Al Madrava, a beautiful bay with a wide, white-sand beach. It was accessible only by boat or by a footpath, and we usually had it to ourselves. We could imagine we were on a deserted, tropical island. We put down lobster pots, swam or lazed in the shade, and when we were hungry, we built a fire, cooked fish and drank wine.

"I never ceased to feel lucky that I could enjoy all this natural beauty while I worked, instead of labouring under electric light in a grimy factory.

"There were usually two stages to my book-writing. The first stage was mainly mental. The second was the physical registering of what was in my mind on to dictated records.

"The mental stage I could carry on with almost anywhere: holding a fishing line, swimming, walking, listening to music or steering a boat.

"To stimulate my mental plotting, I would think of an unusual situation. What would be unusual and startling? Well, let's suppose that Hank Janson is walking along the road when a girl runs out from a building and rips off her clothes in broad daylight. It would be a good start to a book and demand the reader's attention. But there has to be a sensible reason to justify the girl's behaviour. Why should she tear off her clothes? Are they wet? Is she hot and sweating? But why doesn't she go to her room and strip off? I'd concentrate on this situation until the action took shape and could be summed up as a scene. The girl goes to the hotel reception desk and a small parcel and a message are given to her at the same time as her room key. The message is about an urgent phone call she must make. She phones from a call-box in the hotel lobby. While on the phone, she rests the package on the writing ledge and opens it one-handed. It contains a cardboard box, and when she removes the lid, a spring-gadget sprays her with acid. She drops the phone, rushes out into the street seeking help and, because her acid-soaked clothing is burning her, she rips it off [112].

"Such a book opening must trigger off plot development. Why was the girl sent an acid-spraying package? Inventing a logical reason for it introduces characters and sub-plots. And all of this I could do while breathing through a snorkel tube and watching fish flee from my pursuit.

"But I was not only seeing fish. I could also see the girl walking over to the receptionist. I see her receive the key and the package. I see her mentally, as though watching a film, and if something's not right, I rewind the film and run it through again and keep running the film, rewinding and correcting until I can run the scene right through without a fault.

"When I'm in the middle of a book, fragments of film frequently intrude into my thoughts. I have no control over them. A scene will edge into my mind while I'm talking, or interrupt a chess move I'm about to make, or cause me to drop whatever I'm doing and rush away to make a note. This means that effectively I'm working sixteen hours a day. The only rest I might get is in between books.

"Very often, I deliberately complicate an already complicated plot so that I myself am mystified by what the outcome will be. On occasions, I've come close to the end of a book with the action so complicated that I'm unable to unravel it logically. Then I have to spend days trudging the deserted beach while my mind works overtime thinking up changes that will give the story a sensible finish."

The Spanish Saga was the most complex book Frances had ever attempted. It was nothing like running a Hank

---

[112] This is the opening scene to *Scarred Faces*, Janson's second outing in 1946.

Janson movie mentally through his mind. It was more like a festival of David Lean movies shown back to back.

"Simply working out the chronological order in which all my characters would do their thing made me acutely aware of the complexity of plotting a big book. I spent a solid month composing a chart, which showed me at a glance where my characters were, in what year and what they were doing at that time. This chart helped me enormously to maintain the correct relationships between my characters, and to avoid confusing my readers.

"Although this book was fiction, I wanted it to be historically correct. The story is told through its major characters, but whatever they experience has happened at some time, somewhere in Spain. For example:

"One day, when I was visiting a friend, he invited me to go shooting. He owned several large vineyards, and we trudged across them under a blinding sun, hopeful for a glimpse of a partridge or a rabbit. We came upon the ruins of a stone-built house, and beside it was a well that still seemed usable. I was thirsty. 'Is it dried up?' I asked.

"'No. I don't think so.' My friend picked up a stone, dropped it, and it 'plonked' into water.

"'It's drinkable?'

"'Probably, by now. But during the war, the Committee brought a priest out here, shot him and dropped him down the well. We prefer not to use it.'"

"In the novel, a man is killed and dropped down a well. It really happened.

"When the book was published, a critic jeeringly commented that its Gangster-story-writing author was still writing Gangster stories and had even called one of his characters 'Scarface'. Well, my Spanish 'Scarface' was a real person who, after Franco won the war, made so many daring guerrilla raids across the border from France that his name became a household word. He was eventually trapped and killed by the Civil Guard. I personally know the officer who was in charge of that operation. Through the press and radio, that guerrilla was known as 'Cara Quemada' (burned-face) because of the ugly scar upon his cheek caused by a severe burn. Cara Quemada doesn't translate well into the English language. So I gave this real person the name Scarface, and gave a critic a peg to hang a Gangster-writing comparison upon.

"The Spanish people suffered a violent upheaval during their civil war, tragedy assailed many, and disruption, death and hunger became a way of life. The civil war impressed its impact upon all Spaniards, and by encouraging them to talk, and sometimes confide in me, I obtained an authentic background for my book.

"I wanted the book to be accurate and objective. I had no intention of white-washing the Left and blackening the Right, and because of this, there was an element of risk. The Franco Government would relish the crimes of the Left being set down in print, but it wouldn't be happy about the atrocities of the Right being published. Hemingway's novel about Spain and the film [adaptation] *For Whom The Bell Tolls* were banned. Not even an English language edition of the book was allowed to enter the country.

"Franco's censorship was very strict. It was of two types; political and religious. Kisses and embraces were cut from films, and quite often their plot was unintelligible because a girlfriend was portrayed as a sister to avoid a relationship unacceptable to the censor.

"Exasperated publishers, who waited months for censors to decide the fate of the books they submitted, learned by trial and error which censors concentrated upon religious themes and which ones were concerned with politics. The trick was to submit a political book to a religious censor and vice versa. But even this ruse didn't get the better of the Franco regime. A publisher managed to steer a book that was slightly critical of the Franco regime through a censor noted for his piety and disinterest in politics. He anticipated a brisk sale and printed a large edition, only to have the entire edition seized and destroyed. The publisher was heavily fined, his defence – that the book was passed by a censor – waved aside, because although the book may have been approved, the publisher should have known it wasn't fit for publication.

"Franco's Spain was extremely sensitive to criticism. Even a book published in English that was critical of the Franco regime might have consequences. I didn't expect to be shot or imprisoned, but I might be expelled from Spain, which by now was my home. But it was a risk I decided to take."

Completed in 1967, the first part of The Spanish Saga was published by Mayflower Books in July 1968 under the title *Criminals Of Want*, described as the first of four "separate but interlinked novels." Three more volumes – *Until The Grapes Bleed*, *Where The Sun Dies* and *The Bitter Seeds Of Hate* – duly followed, the last of them in December 1968.

Frances expected little of the British paperback editions – Mayflower was in the process of being absorbed by Panther Books, and The Spanish Saga was "lost in the maw" – but had high hopes of an American edition in hard covers. During 1969 he prepared an American edition, edited for length and some language, and spoke hopefully of it: "The publishers are very enthusiastic about it and are making it their lead book."

When it finally appeared in August 1970, under the title *La Guerra*, it had all the appearances of an epic: the Delacorte Press in New York released it in a finely-bound edition with spot illustrations by Paul Bacon; the 629-page volume was priced $7.95, and both publisher and author eagerly awaited the reviews.

Very few appeared.

On the same day that *La Guerra* came out, Albert Speer's *Inside The Third Reich* was also published, and received almost the entire attention of the national press's book critics, to the exclusion of all else.

Where *La Guerra* was reviewed, the critical response was extremely complimentary:

> Not since *For Whom The Bell Tolls* have we been privileged to share in the experience of the Spanish people, and incidentally to learn what the struggle was about. Mr Frances, an Englishman twenty years resident in Spain, describes the total picture better than Hemingway ever did, without sacrificing one iota of a story-telling ability that matches the Master's. (M A R, *Iowa Gazette*)

In what must be the most penetrating look at the horror and futility of war since *Dr Zhivago*, author Stephen Frances describes actions of both Loyalists and Rebels ... It is a powerful book, one which will leave a strong impression on the reader. Even 630 pages is too short. (R L Tracey, *Sacramento Bee*)

This is a massive but compellingly readable novel ... War emerges stark and terrifying from these pages. Writing of it with tight control, Mr Frances achieves heights of incredible power." (*Book Views*)

The consensus of comparison was to Hemingway, although the *Miami Herald* chose to compare Frances's "literary skill and vivid characterizations" to those of Ernie Pyle. More than one reviewer found parallels with Margaret Mitchell's classic *Gone With The Wind* and remarked that the book would make an epic movie.

"I should be so lucky!" said Frances dolefully.

CHAPTER EIGHTEEN

GHOSTS

One day, Frances was asked to call upon a Spanish official at his office. The official gestured towards the chair on the opposite side of the desk, and Frances sat down. The official then read slowly through a letter on the blotting pad before him, looked up and asked: "Can you tell me anything about a British car with the registration number ...?" He read the number from the letter.

Frances, who couldn't even remember the registration number of his own car, said, "Sorry, I can't help."

The official stood up and excused himself, deliberately walking to the door and closing it behind him. The letter was left on the blotting pad.

"I could read it upside down," recalled Frances. "It stated that the Metropolitan Police had reported to Interpol that Mr X, a clever confidence trickster, was probably in Spain. He was driving a Ford car and would probably contact an accomplice, Stephen Frances. I had met Mr X – he was a friend of Reg Carter."

The official returned, rattling the door-handle. "Sorry to have kept you waiting," he said, and the two shook hands before Frances left.

"I wrote to the Commissioner of Police in London. I stated that it had come to my attention that libellous charges had been made against me that could seriously affect my social standing in the community. I demanded that these charges should be withdrawn; or else I would come to London to meet any criminal charges he wished to make."

The letter was ignored. So were letters to the Metropolitan Police and Scotland Yard.

Reg Carter had been busy since his publishing company George Turton Ltd had gone into receivership in 1960. The importing of books from the USA had helped revive his fortunes, and in 1962, he had bought shares in South Shields Greyhound Stadium Ltd, enough to give him a prominent place on the board of directors. He had brought with him his usual drive and foresight, not to mention a considerable amount of his own money, and the boardroom had reacted approvingly to this wind of change. "That was the birth of the sports stadium, costing £383,000, an elaborate futuristic social asset which from tomorrow will be part and parcel of the South Shields scene," recorded the *South Shields Journal*. [113]

Carter was convinced that the new sport of ten-pin bowling was going to sweep the nation, and the South Shields stadium was to be a massive complex incorporating a twenty-four-hour garage (Stadium Garage) which opened in 1962, a greyhound racing track, a casino, the Scottie Room (a pub), the Congress Room (a functions hall), and, central to the complex, the Dog's Bowl, a twenty-lane ten-pin bowling alley, which Carter leased to Ten Pin Bowls (Durham) Ltd (director: R H Carter). Carter even had a flat built above the stadium for himself.

South Shields Sports Stadium Ltd, as it became known in 1963, owned the freehold on the property, subject to a £201,000 mortgage taken out with Epic Southern Properties Ltd. The latter company began legal proceedings against the stadium in July 1964. [114] A compromise deal was reached that would involve Avenue Road Securities, a subsidiary of Epic, taking over the freehold but allowing South Shields Sports Stadium to rent back the sports centre dependent on a valuation of the worth of the property; by agreement, if the valuation was low, it would be treated as £250,000. The valuation fell short, but Carter felt that even a quarter of a million pounds was still unjustifiably low and refused to implement the terms of the compromise.

One reason why Carter felt that the valuation was low was that an independent valuation had placed the figure at nearly £650,000. This was based on a plan presented by one Mr F R Cradock, who had shown an interest in buying the stadium "lock, stock and barrel" and then leasing it out to a

---

[113] *South Shields Journal*, 27 September 1963.
[114] 1964 S. No. 2215.

subsidiary company: the purchaser would be Star Explorations Ltd, a wholly-owned subsidiary of Town Centre Properties Ltd, who would then sell the property to the latter company and take out a twenty-one-year lease to rent it back, splitting the various functions of the stadium between four companies, each a subsidiary of Star.

Reg Carter put this offer to the stadium's creditors in January 1965, and a deal was struck between South Shields and Star later that month and completed in February.

In April 1965, Brunswick Corporation (UK) Ltd commenced legal proceedings against South Shields for debts incurred over the credit-sale of bowling equipment. The Stock Exchange quotation for the company was temporarily suspended. In May, the Stock Exchange also suspended dealings in Town Centre shares, and the Board of Trade announced in October that it was to investigate both Star Explorations and Town Centre Properties. [115]

Carter's company, Ten Pin Bowls, was also in negotiations in 1964 with West Hartlepool Greyhound Racing Company Ltd to purchase the West Hartlepool greyhound track and a rugby field, which had the potential for developing into another sports centre; negotiations had reached the stage of a formal contract before they were suddenly broken off in May 1965 when Ten Pin Bowls stated that they were unable to raise the necessary finance.

On 15 February 1966, the last game of ten-pin was played at the Dog's Bowl, and the South Shields Stadium was officially closed the next day. Ten Pin Bowls was wound up by court order that year.

The Board of Trade enquiry report issued on 1 February 1968. In March, the South Shields Finance Committee approached the Board of Trade for an opinion as to whether or not there should be an investigation into other companies involved in the Stadium. The Town Clerk, Mr R S Young, reported that, after consulting the Borough Treasurer, "it was considered desirable that there should be an inquiry into the activities of the various companies with which Mr Carter was associated." [116] The investigation was not pursued.

---

[115] HM Stationary Office. (S.O.Code No 51-420)
[116] *Shields Gazette*, 30 March 1968.

"During this period," recalled Frances, "Carter was being visited at frequent intervals by Scotland Yard's dicks, and revelled in it. Getting the better of the law, he seemed to think. But he had all the trouble and risks for nothing, because as far as I can make out, his companions in crime faded out leaving him to hold the bag, and, I believe, took the swag with them."

Soon after, Carter suffered a stroke, which half-paralysed him. A second stroke some six or seven years later caused his death, after rendering him unconscious for several days, at the age of 55.

"It's sad to think of such a lively bloke dying so young. And, of course, while he lived, I always had the hope that I'd be able to get back at least a small part of the money that should have come to me and that I did not get, the lack of which has kept me hack-writing to pay the rent.

"I wonder if Dodson would have been pleased with his product."

* * *

On 29 May 1970, Frances returned to London to headlines. "Hank hits town" announced the *Daily Mirror*. Next to the headline, a photograph showed fifty-three-year-old Frances, jacket open, tie unkempt, smiling as he made a shooting gesture at the photographer with his fingers.

The Spanish telephone system had improved enormously over the years. "A messenger came to the café where I was playing chess. There'd been a telephone call from London, and the caller would ring again in half an hour. I went home to take the call, and I was asked if I would go to London to write a film script.

"To those with little experience of writing film scripts, such a question might conjure up images of a luxury air-flight to Hollywood, meetings with stars, hordes of luscious starlets besieging my hotel suite, and receiving my Oscar and a trunkful of hundred-dollar bills under the spotlight of world publicity.

"But I've had experience!"

Getting to the point straight away, Frances asked the important question: "Will you pay my fare?" Of course. "Return fare?" Naturally. "And my accommodation and living expenses?" They'll be taken care of.

Frances agreed, and a few days later, a return flight ticket was waiting for him at Barcelona Airport. "The ticket was waiting for me in Barcelona, and Barry, the producer, and Sir Somebody and other interested characters were waiting to greet me when I reached Heathrow Airport. After drinks in the bar, a Rolls Royce drove me to the Cumberland Hotel at Marble Arch, where I was booked in. 'The Company pays,' said Barry. 'Order anything you want and have it put on the bill.'

"There was a cocktail reception in the hotel's conference room, attended by totally disinterested reporters who propped up the bar, pretty girls and handsome boys who gushed on about their acting, Sir This and Lady That and a surprising number of guests who didn't know why they'd been invited or what it was all about.

"Barry introduced me to a handsome young man. 'This is the King of Russian Georgia,' he said.

"'His Majesty the King of Georgia,' corrected one of the King's aides. The King offered me a disdainful hand. I shook it vigorously. 'Wotcher, cock!' I greeted him heartily, in my best working-class accent. Without looking, I could sense Barry curling up agonisingly.

"The King snatched his hand away and gave me a frosty look. 'Is that a common British greeting?' he asked stiffly.

"'It couldn't be more common,' I assured him. Immediately Barry was at my side.

"'Don't muck it up,' he pleaded. 'Don't rock the boat.'"

The movie was to be shot in Mauritius, a tropical island east of Madagascar in the Indian Ocean, and the President of the country was said to be very enthusiastic about the project. Every facility for the filming would be provided. A handsome Mauritius actor distributed pictures of the President shaking hands with him. Nobody at the party seemed very interested.

"A reporter did tear himself away from the bar long enough to come over to me. 'Is it true you're Hank Janson?'

"'Well, I used to be.'

"'You pornographic old sod!' he said chummily, and went back to the bar."

Not a word about the reception was ever printed.

"An attractive young woman with a Rolls Royce was placed at my disposal to chauffeur me wherever I wished to travel," recalled Frances, "and another young lady was provided to take my dictation of a synopsis of the film script." The film's title/was originally announced as *Pamplemousses*. Frances wrestled with the outline in his room at the Cumberland and eventually emerged with a story that he called *The Avenging Sun* before returning to Spain.

He flew back to London in July, on another return ticket, to get involved with the production, meeting directors, actors, technicians ...

"There wasn't a hotel or restaurant in Park Lane where we didn't lunch or dine with somebody.

"I became aware of an atmosphere of magical suspense; as though everybody was acutely conscious that we were all part of a precious, yet delicately brittle project that we must handle with the utmost tenderness lest its fragile substance be shattered. Everybody except me rigorously avoided mentioning money, as though it was the most likely subject to destroy the magic."

"What about a few quid for odd expenses?" asked Frances.

"Handing out cash isn't the way we do things," was Barry's response.

"I couldn't get even one solitary pound note from him," recalled Frances.

July turned into August.

A director was flown in from New York, and Frances heard that half a million dollars was being sent over from the United States in a fortnight's time. The producers flew in some Mauritius businessmen, who dined at the Grosvenor Hotel while they discussed finance. Frances met a second director. A third director was on his yacht in the Mediterranean and could be contacted only by radio.

"This was too much," recalled Frances. "Three film directors had been given to understand that they were going to direct the film, although out of reverence for the 'precious project' nothing so crude as cash and contracts had been mentioned."

Frances was to accompany Barry on a visit to James Mason, who was to star in the film. The trip was called off and arrangements made to visit Herbert Lom instead. That visit didn't materialise either. Barry, meanwhile, was casting other roles, although the rough draft of the script hadn't yet outlined any of the characters.

It was now mid-August.

At lunch in a modest Chelsea restaurant one day, the head waiter came over to Frances's table and announced that a car from the BBC had arrived. "I've fixed for you to have an interview," said Barry. "Useful publicity. Sorry I forgot to tell you."

Frances was whisked off to the BBC studios at Wood Lane to appear on *Face To Face*, a popular interview programme fronted at this time by presenter Tony Bilbow.

"In the interviewing room, I was received by a pleasant, lively young man who was quite put out when I asked him his name. He was Tony Bilbow, who was mollified when I told him that, living in Spain, I never saw British television.

"We sat in chairs facing each other, spotlights were switched on and Tony asked questions. A camera circled around us while we talked. I was almost tongue-tied with stage fright, acutely conscious that millions of eyes would be watching us. But Tony gently coaxed me along until I'd settled down and started recording.

"Afterwards, I saw a quick run-through of the recording. Tony and the rest of his staff thought it had gone off well, and I was relieved because I couldn't see that I'd committed any atrocious acts.

"When the interview was televised a few days later, I discovered what I hadn't known at the time. The interview preceded a group discussion about pornography. One of the group was C H Rolph, whose articles in the *New Statesman* I've always enjoyed reading. But he disappointed me. He sympathised with me that I was indignant because what was considered pornography in Hank Janson's day, was not so today. He had missed the point. I didn't think that Hank Janson was obscene, neither then nor now. My complaint is that the trial was unjust."

Frances suddenly realised that he was due to be paid for his appearance. "I telephoned the BBC, believing myself now to be within reach of fish-and-chip money."

Yes, agreed the BBC. He was entitled to a fee. It had been paid to the film company, and they had sent somebody around to collect the cheque.

"The company arranged the interview," explained Barry. "It's all part of the picture deal."

A film distributor impressed Frances: "He seemed to have dedicated himself to shattering 'precious projects' with hard, economic facts. He was very good at it. But Barry confidently parried his ruthless financial analysis with talk of the dollars that would arrive from the States very soon. The conversation then turned to the 'End' money. The distributor asked my opinion about the 'End' money. 'I don't care a damn about the End money,' I told him. 'What I'm after is some Beginning money.'"

The next day, a cheque for £250 was reluctantly handed over. "The cheque didn't bounce, and that restored my faith. I became enthusiastic and joined in the happy planning of our filming trip in a tropical paradise. We visualised long weeks of shooting; sea and sand, waving palm trees, dusky beauties and luscious tropical fruits. We rounded up everybody who would be on the first flight to Mauritius and went to Harley Street in a body to have our anti-tropical fever shots. I even became a little worried when a beautiful Mauritius actress warned me that at that time of the year the tropical heat might be too much for those not accustomed to it."

The date arrived for the money to be transferred from America. The money did not arrive. The directors of the project also failed to arrive at their office that day. On the third day, the office was packed with creditors.

"I went back to my hotel, packed my case and set off for the airport, congratulating myself that I'd had the foresight to insisting on a return ticket." Unfortunately, the bill for his final stay at the White House hotel wasn't paid, and Frances was stuck with a demand for £150 he could ill-afford.

The Avenging Sun had one last sting to its tale: "I was sorry for all the disappointed creditors, with the exception of the Harley Street doctor who gave us our jabs. My arm was infected and painfully swollen for more than a month."

* * *

In 1969, Frances began a collaboration with Joseph Bernard Hutton that was to last seven years, although his name was never mentioned in any of Hutton's books, outside a brief acknowledgment to "S Frances" in one.

Hutton was born in 1911, in a small town some forty miles from Prague, Czechoslovakia. His family moved in 1920 to Berlin, where Hutton was educated at grammar school before graduating to Berlin University and going on to work as a reporter for several Berlin newspapers. He was an active member of the Communist Party of Germany, and this led, in 1933, to his fleeing from the Nazis back to Czechoslovakia, where he worked as the foreign news editor on *Halo Noviny*, a Czech Communist evening paper.

He was elected Deputy Member of the Central Committee of the Czech Communist Party in 1934 and sent to Moscow to the Comintern and for "schooling". He worked for a time for the Moscow evening newspaper *Vecherniaya Moskva*, before returning to Czechoslovakia in 1938.

Hutton arrived in England, via Poland, in June 1939 as a refugee, and worked under Jan Masaryk in the Department of Information of the Czechoslovak Ministry of Foreign Affairs in London. He also began writing for various British and foreign newspapers and made freelance contributions to the BBC. After the War, he became an attaché at the Czechoslovak Embassy in London before turning freelance in 1948. In 1957, he became the Diplomatic and Special Correspondent for Kemsley Newspapers. Later, he fulfilled the same role for Thomson Newspapers.

"As a young man," said Frances, "Hutton moved freely among the influential Communists closest to Stalin, among them Lenin's wife, Stalin's third wife and numerous of the original Bolsheviks such as Radek and Kalinin.

"When Stalin launched his infamous purges directed against his old comrades, it left him virtually the only survivor and therefore the unchallenged leader of the country. Hutton became increasing dismayed as, one by one, his friends, the old Bolsheviks, vanished, were executed as traitors after being condemned on trumped-up charges, or died suddenly of mysterious illnesses. Hutton was wounded while reporting upon the Red Army in action and, after hospitalisation, returned to Prague. He became an official of President Jan Masaryk's Government, and when it took refuge in London after Germany invaded Czechoslovakia, he went with it.

"Throughout the following years, Hutton became increasingly convinced that Stalinism was a world menace. He remained in Britain after the War, but Jan Masaryk returned to Prague and later committed suicide. Hutton was convinced Masaryk had been murdered by Russian agents, and without him the Czech Government was completely Russian dominated.

"Hutton became a naturalised Briton, and drawing upon his intimate knowledge of the Soviet Union, and information from underground contacts, he set about writing a series of books that exposed the truth about Stalin and the Soviet Union. He wrote a biography of Stalin, an account of the Moscow trials, and books about the activities of the KGB. When [the actor] Buster Crabbe mysteriously disappeared after last being seen wearing a frogman suit close by a Russian warship anchored in a British port, Hutton published a startling book entitled *Frogman Spy*. [117] Through his underground contacts, Hutton had learned that Buster Crabbe had been detected by the Russians, seized and whisked away to Russia.

"Although he spoke English fluently, Hutton could not write good English prose. Only very talented people can write well in a language that is not their mother tongue. Also, his presentation of information was often dull and unexciting. When I met Hutton, it was for the purpose of collaboration. I was to correct his manuscript and make them more presentable for readers.

"For some years, Hutton had been attacking Russia and the KGB in print, and as a result he lived warily. He knew he was watched, cars followed him, at times his home was entered and documents stolen. He could never feel safe.

---

[117] Published in Britain as *Frogman Extraordinary*.

"Like Hutton, I had long since concluded that Stalinism was corrupting Communism. But I wasn't so indignant about it that I was willing to place my head upon the political block for the KGB to swipe at. I was more than willing that all the credit for our collaboration should be attributed solely to Hutton."

Frances had been introduced to Hutton by John Watson, Frances's former editor at both Consul Books and Mayflower Books, who, following the takeover of Mayflower by Panther Books, had launched his own company, David Bruce & Watson. Hutton had approached Watson with the idea of writing a biography of Rudolph Hess, the Deputy Führer of the Third Reich who had mysteriously landed in Scotland in May 1941 and become a prisoner of war until he was returned to Germany for the trials at Nuremberg. Hutton, who spoke fluent German and was still in touch with many who had gone underground during the regime of Hitler, spent much time and a good deal of money making phone calls to Germany, and had long conversations with Hess's wife and son.

The book was to be entitled *Hess: The Man And His Mission*; and, finally, the manuscript arrived in Spain for Frances to correct.

"I grappled with this for days," recalled Frances. "All the sentences were expressed the wrong way round, were excessively long and rambling, and involved two or three different ideas. To create sense out of confusion, I found myself re-writing every sentence. But even then, the result was still bad. The facts weren't being presented readably. I couldn't make the manuscript satisfactory.

"I told Hutton, 'There's only one way I can work with you. The basic facts are the guts of a book. But those facts can only be presented in a racy, readable style if I chuck away your manuscript and re-write everything.'"

Hutton agreed, and Frances found the task of writing the book, rather than trying to re-write it, far more enjoyable.

Other books followed: *The Subverters Of Liberty* was a study of Communist infiltration into Western society and institutions; *Women Spies* examined the techniques used by female spies who had been trained at secret establishments inside the USSR.

"It wasn't easy working with Hutton. Sometimes he was strangely elusive, vanishing for a week or two. I suspected he was dodging his creditors, but his explanation was that he had been preparing a special underground report for the CIA. I have no respect whatsoever for the CIA, but I do know it squanders a great deal of money. As a poor, hungry author, I'm always eager to get my hands on a few bob. So I suggested to Hutton that he should propose to the CIA that I provided regular reports about the Spanish political scene. Hutton didn't seem enthusiastic, and nothing resulted. I wasn't greatly distressed. The way Hutton remained only two jumps ahead of his creditors strengthened my impression that he earned very little from the CIA, if anything.

"There was another side to Hutton that strongly contrasted with his anti-Communist political activity. In 1964, he was virtually blind. He'd received every possible medical assistance and had been tactfully advised to resign himself to the inevitable. As a last, desperate resort, Hutton visited a Spiritualist healer. Subsequently he wrote: 'A miracle occurred!' He was able to see again. He wrote *Healing Hands*, a book about this remarkable cure, which had a very wide sale.

"All this happened before I met Hutton, but he was still a strong believer in Spiritualism and wanted to write another book about it.

"When I was in my teens and searching for answers about how we should live in society, I had probed into Spiritualism, as I had into many other 'isms. I have never witnessed events that could be described as supernatural. But on occasions, I have heard mediums make accurate statements about past and future events of which I am quite sure they could not have had knowledge. My conclusions are that amazing coincidences occurred and correct facts were stumbled upon accidentally; or else there is more to Spiritualism than anybody seems to be able to find out about it. So I was quite happy to collaborate with Hutton [writing] about Spiritualism."

The book, *The Healing Power*, was a study of Mrs Leah Doctors, a Brighton-based spiritual healer who claimed to channel the healing powers of a spirit guide called Dr Chang.

It was followed by a second book, *Step Into The Unknown*, on the study of parapsychology.

"Almost all the collaboration between Hutton and me was conducted through the mail. We met only when I visited London. He was very hazy about business matters, seemed quite unable to keep proper accounts, could never tell me what payments had been made for foreign rights, nor how much of my share was owing to me. Getting accounts from Hutton was difficult. Getting money due to me was much more difficult. Always, it seemed, he was on the verge of bankruptcy, and paying me would wipe him out. So we always reached a compromise that was unsatisfactory to me.

"We'd worked out a collaboration method. Hutton sent me factual matter. I studied it, and then wrote a first rough draft of the book on tapes. I sent the tapes to Hutton, who had them typed up and sent me back the typed sheets. I altered, corrected and prepared this manuscript for the final typing and sent it back to Hutton. Hutton then had the final typing made and visited publishers with the finished manuscript. He should have sent me carbon copies of the final, finished manuscript, but often forgot to do so.

"The last time I saw Hutton, he was very frail, but undeterred. He had cancer, he told me. But he also had his Spiritualist faith. He intended to ignore his illness until it went away. He died six months later. He dropped down while crossing the road, and those who went to his aid found that he was dead."

CHAPTER NINETEEN

CLOSE TO THE BREADLINE

In 1970, Frances had irons in many fires. He had written a spy thriller, *Red Star Over London* (as by David Roland), which was due to be published in hard cover by the company set up by former *Sexton Blake Library* editor Howard Baker; he was planning a sequel to *La Guerra* in anticipation of it hitting the best-seller charts; and he had mapped out a series of horror novels designed to follow up the success of *The Disorientated Man*, which had been released to British cinemas as *Scream And Scream Again* in December 1969.

As the year progressed, Frances was also working on *The Obscenity Of Hank Janson*, an exposé of the unjust Janson trial, but he had few hopes for it, admitting to a friend: "I don't expect this book to make more than enough to pay for typing and expenses – if it finds a publisher at all. I am working on it only when I can spare time to do something fruitless."

At that time, writing *anything* was proving pretty fruitless for Frances. The seventh John Gail novel, *Cry For My Lovely*, originally scheduled for release in July 1970, finally slunk into the shops in 1971, and an eighth, due to come out in December 1970, never appeared at all. Howard Baker went bust with *Red Star Over London* held up by the printers, who had not been paid. The book was eventually published in November 1971, after the company was taken over by Hutchinson, by which time Frances had long since completed a second novel under his David Roland pen-name. This was another of his works that never appeared.

Apart from his collaborations with J Bernard Hutton, Frances seemed unable to get a book into print. "One of my problems," he noted, "is that I'm so far away from everything here, and half the time I don't know what's going on. There's a book I've ghost-written based on a television play. I finished it six months ago, but I don't know what's happening to it and am waiting for news."

By late 1971, Frances was even talking of possibly writing for the by-now-pornographic Hank Janson line. "Things are very bad financially. So bad that I may even investigate writing for Gold & Warburton. The trouble is that publishing has felt recession before any [other industry]. Despite magnificent reviews, *La Guerra* has only sold enough copies to pay the advance royalty that I long ago spent. Although British publishers like it, it's too big and expensive for them to publish. Foreign countries can't afford the translation costs on top of the printing costs. All paperback [publishers], Mayflower, New English Library, etc, are severely reducing their print titles. In short, I'm finding it hard to find markets. For six months, I've been waiting for a publisher to give me the go-ahead with sci-fi books, children's books and a political book, but they're planning and stepping very cautiously.

"At the moment, my one outlet is in the US, where I'm about to send a couple of books. But they do not commission them, so we'll see what happens. In other words, boy, I'm very close to the breadline, and will be on it if something good doesn't happen soon. This *Subverters* book, for example. If the *Daily Mail* serialises it, I shan't do badly. But if they don't, and if the book sells averagely, I will barely get enough out of it to pay my writing hours at the rate of a semi-skilled labourer. That's the way writing is today!"

Frances made similar pleas over the next few years: "I'm going all out on badly paid stuff that I can get cash for quickly, because I'm in trouble with my bank overdraft and in danger that they'll stop all my cheques until it's settled. Since my agents have to pay all cash to my bank by an arrangement, this move would castrate me!"

* * *

Frances had been writing pornography "to earn quick money to pay the rent." Not the kind of short stories he had previously sold to *Exclusive* and other British glamour magazines, but "really hard porn, not to let the kids handle."

In some cases he was able to indulge in his interest in history: *In The Hands Of The Inquisition*, published by Charles Skilton's Canova Press, was the story of Maria Deluz, a twenty-one-year-old Spanish girl, sold into the service of a goldsmith, who on a trip to Lisbon falls foul of the Inquisition in 1502. Aimed at the bondage/flagellation market, and priced accordingly at 15/-, the book was relatively tame erotica, as one might expect from British "smut". A similar charge could be aimed at *A Study Of An Arab Nymphomaniac*, written by Frances under the pen-name Ullrega de la Garbia. This was the story of Anna, a young, seemingly frigid wife suffering from loss of memory. Anna is referred to D de la Garbia, a radical Spanish psychiatrist, who, through a series of consultations, discovers her to be repressing memories of her (very active) sexual past. Although the publisher's imprint was given in this book as "Pamar Enterprises Inc" of New York, the publisher was actually Godfrey Gold, to whom Frances at around the same time sold a number of novels in a similar vein, three of which seem never to have been published – the pornography market perhaps suffering the same problems of cutting back as the mainstream paperback market.

Frances found a steadier market in the USA with Bee-Line Books, founded by David Zentner in 1965 and one of the most prolific of America's paperback pornography lines. Unlike the paperbacks that had first appeared in the early 1960s, which had sex scenes written into a more-or-less (depending on the author) reasonably coherent novel, the Bee-Line titles of the early 1970s had eschewed any semblance of plot and were little more than chapter after chapter of relentless coupling. Frances was fairly adept at turning out what the publisher was after, but took no pride in it. The books were dressed up differently, but the action was interchangeable: "Tasty piece! Meet Rita, the horny red-head! She does everything you've always wanted to do – but were afraid to admit" (*Oral Antics!*) ... "They were switch hitters! These are the chicks who dig both men and women and who communicate without ever saying a word. When they meet someone they want to bed, they just rub up against the person until they drive them into a frenzy of passion!"

(*Double Header!*) … "A lusty lesbian teaches a hired stud that five orgasms a day keeps the doctor away" (*Wet & Ready!*).

Frances could not take writing these books seriously, and the boredom shows in his lack of invention in any of the scenes, and occasional disregard for the serious business of intercourse ("Elaine believes live male sperm supplies vital vitamins. She likes a regular ration, to keep physically fit." "Taken *internally?*" "How else?").

Humour was definitely the intention in his two novels starring Hugh Pecker. Frances had met a director of Lancer Books during one of his increasingly irregular visits to London. The two had spent an evening chatting, and Frances had been asked to write a light-hearted, sexy series for the American market. The result was Hugh Pecker, a social scientist, the chief executive advisor to a major American university, whose specialised subject is sex. As a sexologist, he is totally dedicated to assisting his female students to achieve the highest qualifications in this branch of the social sciences, working long hours and always willing to give a backward student his personal tuition. Pecker is also the founding president of the Whango Athletic League (motto: "Keep Healthy, Keep Happy, Keep Whanging"). Pecker has also been coerced into heading a little known branch of the CIA known as the "Peckerton unit" thanks to the accumulation of some 723 years' worth of imprisonment he might face if his enthusiastic research into sex should ever come to court.

In Pecker's debut title, *Oh! Hugh Pecker*, the Chinese have initiated a secret training school where girls of all nationalities are taught modern methods of espionage and lovemaking techniques that no normal man can resist. These ultra-seductive Mata Haris are then sent out to tempt high-ranking officers of the American fleet. Pecker's assignment is to find the school and destroy it.

The second book, *Come Again, Pecker*, involved subverters who are undermining Britain by encouraging strike action, causing unemployment and provoking working-class discontent. By infiltrating the Lilywhite Purity League, these subverters are using it as a vehicle to make Britain joyless: "Comrades. Every book that is burned, every film that is banned and every strip-teaser deprived of an audience, brings Britain closer to revolution. We must foment unhappiness, misery and discontent. We must plunge Britain into narrow-minded Victorian despair and deprive the working man of his lust for living." Thanks to the Whango Athletic League and its parallel organisation for women, the Pussy Health and Culture Club, Pecker is able to destroy the reputations and influence of the subverters.

The third book, *Pecker's Arabian Nights*, would have seen Hugh penetrating the Arab kingdom to investigate espionage in the oil industry and discover the secret of the harem. (The secret being that the reason harems are locked and bolted is not to keep out men but to stop sex-hungry hordes of frustrated wives from getting out.)

Of the three, this third title was Frances's favourite – but, as with so many of his books written during this period, it never saw the light of day. Lancer Books went into liquidation.

* * *

In February 1974, Frances was visiting England when he was rushed into hospital in the middle of the night suffering from pneumonia. After returning to Spain to recuperate, he was again hospitalised for the removal of a kidney stone. This left him so weak that during his recovery he fell and broke two ribs, and shortly afterwards contracted pneumonia again. By September, he claimed to be "in action again" but "waging a constant fight against the weakening side-effects of being pumped full of drugs so many times."

His latest novel, an Elizabethan historical called *Avenging Daughter* (actually a heavily revised version of his earlier Hank Janson novel *Daughter Of Shame*), was sold to New English Library, who also accepted a proposal for a series of books set in the violent and erotically abandoned world of Ancient Rome. "I took care to ensure that the background was historically correct, and I worked real people into the story alongside my fictional characters," recalled Frances. "One shelf of my bookcase is devoted entirely to well-thumbed reference books about life as it was lived in Ancient Rome."

The series – *Barba The Slaver*; *Haesel, The Slave*; *Brotan The Breeder*; *Gracus The Centurion*; and *Corissa The Vestal Virgin*, all published as by Dael Forest – sold only modestly when it appeared in 1975-1976; but a reissue in America in 1978, noted Frances, "helped to keep the wolf from my door." A sixth novel, *Alicia The Concubine*, failed to appear.

Avenging Daughter was eventually published in 1977 under the title *The Witch Mark* by S F Roland.

"I must start chasing up publishers," said Frances in early 1975. "I have out what I think are four good books, but none of them seem to be moving. The US seems even more depressing than the UK." Even the US market for pornographic books had received its biggest blow in years. William Hamling, Earl Kemp and others had been found guilty, in December 1971, of violating Federal obscenity laws about sending obscene material (in this case, a flyer advertising *The Illustrated Presidential Report Of The Commission On Obscenity And Pornography*) through the post. Hamling had taken the case to the Supreme Court in April 1974, where the decision had gone against him on a 5-4 vote and both he and Kemp had been jailed. "Recent US judgements have now prevented more of these types of US publications," recorded Frances despondently.

As always, Frances had a catalogue of projects on the go: *The Voyage Of The Explorer* was a science-fiction novel (he had recently sold a short story to *Science Fiction Monthly*, which promptly folded); *Success In A Can* was his first attempt at writing a humorous novel, which he had hopes of turning into a television series; *A Butterfly In Pamplona* was another large novel set in Spain.

On the non-fiction front, he was ghosting for Hutton a book about a man who claimed he could levitate, but Hutton was by this time already suffering from the cancer that would eventually kill him, and very ill. "When he died," lamented Frances, "Hutton had received from me three manuscripts which he'd presumably had typed and submitted to publishers, so somewhere there are another three books floating around which I have written but for which I have not been paid."

Another non-fiction project not related to Hutton was a book, entitled *Take Your Pickism*, "about Pacifism, Mormonism, Anarchism and a great many other 'isms."

Sex came to Frances's rescue again. In Britain, the Longford Report had opened a few eyes to sexual matters, and the daily dose of "Page 3" newspaper nudity in the early 1970s, welcomed by many and tolerated by most others as a bit of fun, had helped make sex more accessible.

The British sex comedy, exemplified by Brian Rix's underwear and Sid James's throaty approval of comely actresses, was widely appealing, not only for its saucy antics but also for its pricking of the hypocrisy of authority. In 1971, Christopher Wood, a former accounts executive with a couple of novels already to his name, launched the "Confessions" series of books with *Confessions Of A Window Cleaner*. This series, through the exploits of lead character Timothy Lea in various occupations, brought sex to the man in the street. The staple in theatrical farce of catching ministers of religion and bank managers with their trousers down gave way to the antics of window cleaners, taxi drivers and driving instructors. Timmy Lea was the common man with a working class attitude to booze and birds, and Wood set the tone for every "Confessions"-style series that would follow: quick-fire, colourful gags every few lines, rough-and-tumble sex every chapter, and a different job every book.

Bawdy rather than sexually explicit, the books were a huge success – garnering three million sales in three years – and the film rights to the series was snapped up by Columbia Pictures, who turned *Confessions Of A Window Cleaner* into a major theatrical hit and cheeky lead actor Robin Askwith into a star.

Former photographer Stanley Long had been in the film industry for many years, originally shooting 8mm girlie films before spending £8,000 in 1961 to produce a feature entitled *Nudes Of The World*, capitalising on the then current craze for nudist films. As a cinematographer, Long was best known for his work on *The Sorcerers*, a 1967 horror film starring Boris Karloff, but it was with sex films that he made his biggest impact on British cinema.

Long decided to capitalise on the success of *Confessions Of A Window Cleaner* with his own series of films, and released *Adventures Of A Taxi Driver* in 1975. The film, starring Barry Evans as a randy London cab driver, was a hit, and Long almost doubled its budget to produce *Adventures Of A Private Eye*, filling the screen with well known stars, led by Jon Pertwee as a flamboyant detective forced to leave his assistant in charge of the business while he is on a case in Beirut. The assistant was played by Christopher Neal, a Dublin-born but Manchester-bred songwriter who had penned two top-10 singles and an album for Paul Nicholas.

Although less successful than *Adventures Of A Taxi Driver*, *Adventures Of A Private Eye* still netted Long considerable profits, and a third film was planned. This was originally intended to be called *Adventures Of A Roving Reporter*, but in the event became *Adventures Of A Plumber's Mate*, written by Stephen Frances and rewritten by Aubrey Cash.

Released in June 1978, *Adventures Of A Plumber's Mate* starred Christopher Neal as Sid South, assistant to B A Crapper (played by *On The Buses* star Stephen Lewis, complete with the moustache and hangdog expression the actor became famous for as "Blakey" in that series). Sid is deeply in debt and being threatened with eviction from his flat and with violence by his bookie's hired thugs. His problems escalate when he is sent to replace a toilet seat for bored, bondage-loving Janice (Prudence Drage); Sid is almost caught "on the job" by Janice's violent husband, recently released from prison for his part in a gold bullion robbery. Sid narrowly escapes, not realising that the toilet seat he has removed and sold cheaply to a junk shop is made from the melted-down gold.

The toilet humour continues through a series of groan-inducing puns and occasional nudity, at its best when Sid is caught in a shower room by four young tennis players and endures the attentions of a topless masseuse, at its worst when attempting to move the largely incoherent plot forward. Most critics felt that humour associated with hard-nosed, violent criminals was pushing the formula into uncomfortable areas. Frances, uninvolved with the production beyond writing the script, was unhappy: "I'm annoyed with the film director for the balls-up he made of the film. I haven't seen it myself, only the shots, jumbled up and without sound, but it's enough to get me protesting."

The movie, however, proved to be the most profitable of the three in the series, largely thanks to a tiny role played by Elaine Paige as barmaid Susie, who lends Sid a sympathetic ear and becomes his girlfriend by the film's end. Just as *Adventures Of A Plumber's Mate* was released, Paige hit the big time as Evita in the Andrew Lloyd Webber musical of the same name, and attempted to get the movie pulled from distribution. This just made it an even bigger hit.

Frances – writing as Sid South – novelised the movie for Mayflower Books. It proved to be his swan-song as a novelist.

* * *

Easter Saturday 28 March 1964 saw the debut of Radio Caroline, a pop music broadcaster operating from a ship, the *M V Caroline*, moored off the coast near Harwich, outside the then three-mile limit of British territorial waters. The first record played, following an introduction by DJ Chris Moore, was the Beatles' 'Can't Buy Me Love'. Caroline was Britain's first commercial radio station, but had been set up against the recommendations of a 1962 Government White Paper, which had rejected the idea of a "sustained" and "broadly-based" trial to test the potential popularity of local radio stations. Until then, the BBC's monopoly on radio broadcasting had been challenged only by Radio Luxembourg, which broadcast from mid-Europe but primarily in English and relied on many British advertisers for its success.

During its first few weeks of broadcasting, Radio Caroline attracted seven million listeners over the age of seventeen. Within weeks, a rival station – Radio Atlanta – had started up from a ship, the *M V Mi Amigo*, anchored fourteen miles away.

Officialdom took a dim view of what it termed "pirate radio stations," claiming the vessels were a hazard to maritime shipping and interfered with a Belgian station used for broadcasting to ships at sea. It seemed however that the only possible legal obstacle to their operation was that listeners might be contravening the Wireless Telegraphy Act 1949; and this would be all but impossible to enforce, since the Post Office could not take action against people who accidentally tuned in. Still, the Post Office cut off Radio Caroline's ship-to-shore radio and refused to lay in a telephone line, making supply ships the only means of communication between the on-board crew and the shore.

In July 1964, Radio Caroline and Radio Atlanta reached an agreement to merge, and the *Caroline* sailed to spread the music of Radio Caroline to a new anchorage off the Isle of Man, while the *Mi Amigo* remained to broadcast from its original location.

The Government's response was to try to starve the two ships out and make it an offence to supply food, fuel or advertising. A request that the Manx Government take the same approach in respect of Radio Caroline North, operating from the *Caroline*, was turned down, but the law was passed in the UK as the Marine &c Broadcasting (Offences) Act 1967. As the law came into force on 14 August 1967, many smaller stations that had sprung up in the wake of Radio Caroline bid their listeners a tearful farewell. Radio Caroline itself, however, decided to tough it out and move its base to Holland.

Other problems had faced the *Mi Amigo*, anchored nine miles offshore – or not, as its operators discovered in 1966, when the ship drifted towards the coast and grounded itself fifty yards off Frinton beach. Radio Caroline had survived this crisis, but could not survive mounting debts incurred through supplies now needing to take a longer and more difficult journey. On 3 March 1968, both Radio Caroline ships had their anchors cut and were towed to a port in Holland and impounded.

In 1972, the *Mi Amigo* was sold for a knock-down £2,400 at auction. The authorities having been informed that it was to become a museum, it left port in Holland, only to anchor in the North Sea and, eventually, begin broadcasting again. It was a stick-and-string operation – problems with the radio mast and generator meant that it was off the air more often than it was on – and its distance from England dictated that it should become a Dutch service.

The Dutch authorities, which had tolerated the long-running Radio Veronica, found themselves with three new broadcast services: the rival Radio North Sea, forced away from England because its signals were being jammed in 1970, and now both Radio Mi Amigo – a Dutch-language broadcast operation run by a man named Sylvain Tack – and Radio Caroline, broadcasting in English. Against public protest, they drafted new anti-pirate laws, which came into effect in August 1974. The *Mi Amigo* was towed away from the Dutch coast to anchor in the Thames Estuary. After briefly adopting a base in Belgium, Syvain Tack decided to move his operation to a villa in Playa de Aro in Spain.

Concentrating on playing album music rather than singles, Radio Caroline was financed through donations and a touring Caroline Road Show. The Radio Caroline of old was unrecognisable in this new operation – the early DJs of the 1960s like Johnny Walker, Robbie Dale, Simon Dee, Tony Blackburn, Gerry King, Dave Lee Travis and Tommy Vance were long gone. In their place were Tom Anderson, Mile Hagler, Tony Allan – and Loving Awareness, an ideal established by Ronan O'Rahilly that promoted love, peace and happiness..

Steve Frances became involved with Radio Caroline after seeing Dutch DJs recording programmes for Radio Mi Amigo in a shop window in full view of the public in Playa de Aro, forty kilometres from Rosas. "I was passing, visited them casually and was given a warm welcome. They were quite willing to explain their set-up and show me what they were doing. They enjoyed the interest they aroused. They received hundreds of listeners' letters every day, and they encouraged me to read some of them.

"I was astonished by the emotional response Radio Caroline aroused within its listeners. They were entranced by its music, and by a kind of social philosophy named 'Loving Awareness'. It seemed to me that here was a nucleus of young idealists who desperately yearned to express themselves but lacked the means to do so.

"I had never heard Radio Caroline, but nevertheless I toyed with the idea of publishing a magazine for its readers. The Dutch disc jockeys were helpful and gave me a mailing list from which I could circularise the launching of *Caroline Newsletter*."

The first issue was published in 1977, the 32-pages a mixture of articles from DJs, reviews, poems, comments and letters from Radio Caroline listeners. Frances knew that this venture was never going to be financially rewarding, "perhaps even costly." The compensation was: "The nostalgic smell of printers ink and the whirr of a Heidelberg printing machine. I set the typescript and prepared the layout myself in a small print shop in Figueras." The editorial address was TBP, Apartado 321, Rosas [118] – which Radio Caroline began to use as a contact address. News of the newsletter was broadcast, and Frances began to receive subscriptions.

"Almost at once, the Post Office informed me it was illegal for postal orders to be sent out of Britain. I didn't want potential readers to have their subscriptions confiscated in the post, so I changed my plans. The second and subsequent issues of the *Newsletter* were printed and published in Britain.

"There was a secondary reason why I was publishing *Newsletter*. From the letters I'd been given to read, I'd learned that the Home Office was conducting a reign of terror against young people. School-kids who enjoyed listening to Radio Caroline enthusiastically wrote slogans praising the station, or drew pictures of *Mi Amigo* on the envelopes of letters they sent their pals. These letters were being intercepted in the post and eleven and twelve-year-olds were receiving official letters on Home Office notepaper, threatening them with prosecution. It may even have had a traumatic effect upon some; others were extremely indignant and wrote their protests to Playa de Aro. These letters I had read.

"These Home Office threats seemed preposterous until I looked up the law. Special legislation had been introduced in 1967 to prevent Radio Caroline operating. If disc jockeys and others flouted the law and operated Radio Caroline, they could not complain if they were punished. On one occasion when the disc jockeys were forced to abandon ship, they were arrested and handcuffed as soon as they put foot ashore. But they were prepared to face the consequences. What law had the school-kids broken?

"I looked it up. Marine Broadcasting (Offences) Act. Section 5(3)(f) declares as an offence:

---

[118] TBP were the initials of Frances's wife.

"Publishing the times or other details of any broadcasts which are to be made or (otherwise than by publishing such details) publishing an advertisement of matter calculated to promote, directly or indirectly, the interests of a business whose activities consist in or include the operation of a station from which broadcasts are, or are to be, made.

"It will be obvious to everybody that this clause was intended to prevent Radio Caroline buying newspaper space, or television time, to advertise its programmes.

"However, some demonically-minded Home Office official had realised that the intention of this clause could be perverted so that school-kids who enjoyed listening to Radio Caroline were transformed into criminals. It had become a crime for school-kids to scrawl comments about Radio Caroline on the backs of envelopes.

"I believed that *Caroline Newsletter* would perform a public service if it drew attention to this dangerously anti-social interpretation of the law. June Sutton, a close friend, offered to help me print and distribute in Britain, and obtained a [Post Office] box number in Crawley. She received correspondence and subscription at this address, and I edited from Rosas."

The *Newsletter* published three issues in 1977, with little to distinguish it from most fan magazines. However, the fourth issue became critical of the Home Office and its kid-scaring letters, which had now been reinforced by legal action against the users of stickers and badges that promoted Radio Caroline.

"A young man, John E Jackson-Hunter, was prosecuted and convicted for displaying a sticker in his car," recalled Frances. "The sticker measured one inch by one-and-a-half inches. He was sentenced to three months suspended imprisonment and ordered to pay court costs. Hunter was outraged by what he regarded as social injustice and refused to pay the costs. Just before he entered prison to spend Christmas in a cold, bleak cell, he issued the following statement, which *Newsletter* published:

DECLARATION OF INTENT

I, John Edward Jackson-Hunter, after spending eight days in courts at a cost to the taxpayer of £10,000 for the offence of displaying one Radio Caroline car sticker on one vehicle, have decided not to accept my punishment of three months imprisonment suspended for two years, plus a £500 contribution to the court costs.

I refuse to pay this money as this would be defeatism and a scar on the Face of Freedom.

After writing to numerous MPs in vain, the only course open to me is to go to prison for sixty days.

Whilst in prison I most definitely intend to go on hunger strike in protest of the way I have been badgered by the Home Office.

Nothing in this declaration must be interpreted as bearing any malice or hatred towards the courts, judges, stipendiary magistrates, magistrates, prosecutors, police or any officials of the Home Office or Post Office.

I go through this course of action to make the Home Office think twice about prosecuting anyone else.

J. E. Jackson-Hunter.
WALTON GAOL
Liverpool. 24 November 1977. [119]

"*Caroline Newsletter* had urged all readers to write to their MPs complaining about the lunatic extremes to which the British law had been brought, and, as requested, readers sent photocopies of all their correspondence with the Home Office and their MPs to *Newsletter*. This correspondence indicated that MPs were concerned about the matter. One MP wrote that he had consulted legal experts who had told him it was quite impossible for anybody to be sent to prison for displaying a sticker. He said he was investigating the

---

[119] *Caroline Newsletter 4*, 1977-78.

matter. But he never wrote again, and never replied to subsequent letters.

"Since *Newsletter* was being sent photocopies of all the correspondence, it had a panoramic view of what was happening. Upon receiving their constituents' complaints, MPs wrote to the Home Office requesting confirmation of the facts. MPs were informed that Jackson-Hunter was not sent to prison for displaying a sticker, but for some other reason. Therefore, *Newsletter* began a campaign to have a Government Committee appointed to enquire into Civil Servants' behaviour. MPs were told that no credence should be given to *Newsletter*, because it wished to further the interests of Radio Caroline, with which it was associated.

"Quite independently, a number of young people formed a group with the name 'The Caroline Movement,' which also had the intention of supporting this campaign."

Caroline Newsletter became increasingly critical of the Home Office. Then, June Sutton was informed that her box number was being withdrawn. The fifth issue of *Newsletter* quoted a Post Office spokesperson as stating: "It was brought to our attention that this box number was being used in connection with a magazine about Radio Caroline." Who brought it to the attention of the Post Office?, asked the *Newsletter*.

"After a protest, it was suggested that the box number would be restored if June signed a statement that *Newsletter* was not connected with Radio Caroline. June said she would sign, on condition that every other box renter was also required to sign. The box number was not restored, but June persisted with using it. The letters that arrived were not put in the box but instead were delivered to June's home. Her cheques for box rental were returned, not accepted.

"Two detectives swooped down upon June, talking about prosecution and advising her to consult a solicitor. They left her, she reported, 'Shaking like a jelly.'

"Two detectives descended upon the printer of *Caroline Newsletter*. He at once stopped printing *Newsletter* and said he would never do so again, even if Scotland Yard gave him permission. He was in fear of being prosecuted, he stated.

292

"Two detectives called upon the chairman of the Caroline Movement and left him with the impression that he was in imminent danger of being prosecuted."

These attentions of officialdom had the desired effect, and issue seven of the *Caroline Newsletter* failed to appear when it was due in 1978. "It's been suppressed by Scotland Yard,' the printer informed me. The members of the Caroline Movement were also uneasy, and ceased pressing for an enquiry into the behaviour of Civil Servants.

"This Scotland Yard intervention was clearly improper and, following the correct procedure, *Newsletter* presented a Schedule of Complaint against a police officer. He had already been transferred to some other section. Two detectives swooped down upon June and induced her to sign a statement. When they, left she telephoned me, so distressed that she didn't even know what she'd signed. I obtained a copy of the statement from Scotland Yard. June had withdrawn all complaints."

A "Special Edition" of the *Caroline Newsletter* appeared, dated Winter 1979/80, the cover prominently displaying its contents:

> This is a summary, prepared for the Home Secretary, Mr William Whitelaw, of the incidents, events and facts relating to Scotland Yard's suppression of issue number seven of *Caroline Newsletter* and of other improper actions taken by Government officials to prevent Members of Parliament enquiring into the consequences of Government officials' enforcement of the Marine Etc. Broadcasting (Offences) Act.

"Again *Newsletter* presented its Schedule of Complaints," reported Frances, "and added a new complaint, that June had been harassed into withdrawing her first complaint.

"Scotland Yard has never investigated this complaint, and does not answer letters referring to it. However, a pleasant man telephoned me from Scotland Yard, giving me his name, rank and telephone extension. He wanted to chat. 'What have you got against us?' he asked.

"'You know as well as I do,' I said. 'Somebody in the Home Office spoke to somebody in the Director of [Public] Prosecution's office. He spoke to somebody at Scotland Yard, and then somebody ordered: "Get out there and scare the shit out of those people." They did a good job on June and the printer.'

"He chuckled. 'You know we wouldn't do anything like that!' he reproached."

Meanwhile, the *Mi Amigo* was in a bad way. In 1976, bad weather had breached the ship, and the captain had abandoned ship aboard the supply tender, leaving only three DJs and an engineer. Over the next few years, the ship broke anchor and grounded a number of times. On 19 March 1980, *Mi Amigo* broke anchor one final time, and its almost-wrecked hull was pounded on the seabed in shallow waters. Tom Anderson continued broadcasting throughout, until he was taken aboard a lifeboat just before the sea engulfed the ship.

Frances's contact at Scotland Yard phoned: "What do you think now about *Mi Amigo*? She sank yesterday. We've wound up our investigations. We're not going to prosecute anybody."

"It would have been fun if you had. What leg would you have stood upon?" asked Frances.

"We would have found one," replied the man from Scotland Yard. "We always can."

CHAPTER TWENTY

"ASK ALL THE QUESTIONS YOU WANT"

Fifty years after the Old Bailey trial, the early Hank Janson novels have become collectors items. The phrase "Heade cover" is guaranteed to start a bidding war on the online auction house eBay. Stephen Frances would have been 86 if he were still alive today – not an especially great age. In Rosas, finding an active 86-year-old is not uncommon. The *tremontana* climate, never damp and often very dry, has given the inhabitants the reputation of being very healthy and long-lived. One proud boast of the villagers is that Rosas is so healthy that in order to start a cemetery, a volunteer had to be put to death.

Frances liked his cigarettes. When in England, he swapped a *porrón* of wine for a glass of whisky, which he took "unspoiled". No-one can guess what legacy the deprivations of his early years left to his health.

"Change is inevitable. Nothing stays the same. It gets better or gets worse. That's life," wrote Frances, looking out over the bay at Rosas, the population swollen to 200,000 in the summer tourist season. "Put it this way. Any time anybody has anything worth having, all the other rotten sods are fighting each other, or conspiring to take it from him, or destroy it. That's what life is all about!" he said, quoting Reg Carter.

"I can still sip my breakfast tea while looking out of my window at the sea – but I look out now on a New York skyline of ten-storey hotels," said Frances.

"The roads are jam-packed with cars that overflow onto almost all the pavements. Walking anywhere is hazardous, because of the cars treading on your heels. If traffic lights hadn't been introduced, it would be almost impossible to cross the main street, which is as busy as Oxford Street!

"The mountainous coast overlooking Rosas has also been invaded by builders, who have almost obscured it with all types of residential constructions that cling to the steep slopes with the aid of retaining walls and concrete piles.

"Eighty extra municipal police are drafted in during the summer to cope with an average of twenty robberies every day, as many traffic accidents and countless drunks and parking offences. A two-storey State-built post office with a staff of twelve handles millions of postcards and letters.

"Al Madrava and Canyelles Petites are so overbuilt and overpopulated that they seethe with life like a broken-open anthill, and all the little bays and coves that were once so naturally beautiful swarm with bathers searching for space to sun themselves. The sea is torn up by surfers, skiers and speedboats that put in peril all swimmers who venture into deeper water. Speakers howl advertisements, and the air reeks of scented sun-tan oils. The once-transparent sea is murky and seeded with indestructible plastic bags that daily increase in number.

"Rosas has changed. Almost everything that made it attractive has been destroyed. It is overbuilt, over-populated and over-commercialised.

"If I were to enter Rosas today for the first time, I would instantly turn around and speed away.

"Some friends from London dropped in on their way south to Almeria, and during the conversation one said, "On television a few weeks ago, somebody asked 'Whatever happened to Hank Janson?' Why don't you write your autobiography?"

Frances laughed at the idea: "Why should anybody want to read about me?"

"Nobody is likely to be interested in me," he later wrote. "But from time to time, I found myself rethinking the suggestion. Some things that have happened to me could be of interest to others. People might like to know how a slum-kid could have reached the threshold of wealth and might have become a rich man if he had concentrated more upon making money and less upon friendship."

Hank Janson had been branded a prolific writer of filthy books, and Frances had spent the next thirty-five years trying to make the point that the books were not obscene. "Obscenity is still a matter of opinion, not a matter of law," he told a reporter in 1968 [120]. "My stuff was done by innuendo. One minute a man and a woman were sitting side by side. You'd read a whole page and get the impression of physical contact, but you couldn't pin it down." "The Innocence of Hank Janson" was one headline to a *Guardian* interview in 1970 [121]; "The Truth About Hank Janson" the title of another interview in 1971. [122] By then, Frances had already mapped out a book to be called *The Obscenity Of Hank Janson.*

Frances had often considered the idea of reviving Hank Janson, but was faced with the problem of obtaining the rights to the name: as early as 1970, he had commented to a friend: "I have made tentative attempts to get control of Hank Janson again myself. I had a moneybags who had some capital he was willing to invest, with me doing an overhaul of Hank Janson. But the present owners asked ten thousand quid for the rights in the title, which was ten times what we were willing to pay, and they wouldn't consider discussing a lower figure."

In 1975, he noted: "Again I'm in financial straits, and again because somebody hasn't paid me a substantial amount that is owing. So I can't think now of perhaps doing something about Hank Janson. But if there is a chance, I'd like to get hold of the title again through other people with whom I can co-operate."

Janson was never far from his mind, even if he could write "Janson" stories only obliquely: "I'd appreciate your opinion about Roman slaver books," he asked a friend. "Do you think they might catch on like Hank Janson? It has the same ingredients. It's a little, carefully constructed, but quite fictional world in which sex and strong emotions are blended with a great deal of action. I feel it would appeal to Hank Janson readers, but I'd like to know your opinion."

The Obscenity Of Hank Janson was proving elusive to someone who was capable of writing a novel in a few weeks. Ten years after starting the book, Frances wrote to a young

---

[120] *Sunday Times*, 25 February 1968.
[121] *Guardian*, 4 July 1970.
[122] *Parade*, 3 July 1971.

fan: "I never think about the past, factual checking of my memories would be exasperatingly tedious, and what I would be paid wouldn't justify it."

There was also a moral dilemma in writing the book. Should he, or should he not, discuss writing the seven novels the court had deemed to be obscene? He had, after all, denied writing them in court, and the sudden and surprising discovery of payments made to Geoffrey Pardoe for a number of novels had brought the prosecution case tumbling down. "Anyone who tells a lie on oath is guilty of the serious charge of perjury," he told his young fan as he described the case against him. "So, although the grossly unjust procedure at the Old Bailey might make a defendant feel justified in committing perjury, Frances had no intention of doing so himself. Frances, quite correctly because it was the 'pure' truth, denied that he wrote the books."

But at other times he confessed: "How many [novels by Pardoe] Reg Carter published under different names I don't know. I am quite sure that, if alive, Pardoe would deny he wrote the six Hank Jansons you refer to, and I would think your best plan is to do what so many people have done [and] assume that I am the author. I won't mind."

The "six Hank Jansons" – actually five – were those titles for which Pardoe appeared to be paid: *Accused*, *Persian Pride*, *Amok*, *Desert Fury* and *Pursuit*. None of them, it should be noted, featured Hank Janson as lead character, and Pardoe's payments (£20-£25) were well below the going rate for Gangster novels, which should have earned their author twice that amount.

Frances's hedging disguised his collaboration with Pardoe, which he admitted when discussing the novels he wrote as Duke Linton: Pardoe almost certainly provided an extensive outline for each book. Indeed, the outline format can still be seen in *Pursuit*, which takes a couple of very obvious digressions from the main narrative to fill in the background detail about some of the characters: "Gil Taylor. Thirty years of age, slim, good-looking, dark and handsome, with black eyes that could be as soft as a woman's or as hard as diamonds." [123]

---

[123] *Pursuit*, p.26.

Working from an outline was not unique to Frances, even in the days of Duke Linton. One of his prolific contemporaries at Scion was John Russell Fearn, who had begun writing Westerns for the firm before switching to science-fiction; in order to keep both lines going, Fearn had invited Matthew Japp, a friend from the local writer's circle, to supply him with outlines for Westerns in return for 25% of the money he received for the finished books.

Could Frances therefore claim that the 'pure' truth was that he did not write *all seven* of the Hank Janson novels accused of obscenity? The characters and situations were outlined for him by Pardoe – sometimes (whether Frances knew it or not) heavily influenced by other novels: *High Sierra* by W R Burnett, for example, was the basis for one of the Duke Linton novels; and *Accused* by Hank Janson owed more than a tip of the hat to James M Cain's *The Postman Always Rings Twice*. From these outlines, Frances dictated his novel, editing the manuscript once it was typed up by his secretary to make it ready for the printers.

Frances chose to say he did not "write" them. But he wanted to defend them, and chose to return to England knowing that there was a warrant out for his arrest.

In 1984, at a time when "my life is dominated by resistance to starvation," Frances was still determined to prove somehow that his Hank Janson books were not the filth they had been portrayed as, and conceived a more audacious plan than simply pointing it out in a book.

"Seven Hank Janson titles have been declared as obscene," he wrote to Janson fan Steve Holland. "Obviously, they mustn't be published. But if I was to come through the UK Customs and draw an officer's attention to seven obscene books, together with proof they had been declared obscene, he would be duty-bound to confiscate them. I would challenge the confiscation on the grounds that the books were not obscene, and the Hank Janson trial would be heard all over again. Like you, I am convinced the books were not obscene in 1954, and I am sure it can be proved in 1984."

Frances was sixty-seven-years-old at the time, and not in the best of health. "I am not eager to go through Customs with the books, although I will do so if it's considered more effective. I would think a solicitor would be the best person to do this.

"D'you feel like getting some newspaper editor to take up this idea?" Frances asked Holland.

And I said, "Yes."

* * *

Since this is the story of Hank Janson rather than the biography of Stephen Frances – although the lives of the two, character and author, are inexorably entwined – I do not regard this personal intrusion on my part as breaking any convention of biographical writing. I have a small, and as it turned out rather insignificant, part to play in this narrative, and it is best told without trying to confine myself to being a character in someone else's story.

I had developed an interest in Hank Janson following a school assignment, part of an English Literature class, for which I had chosen to write an essay on the development of British SF magazines. Stephen Frances was, of course, involved, both as publisher of *New Worlds* in 1946-47 and as the creator of the pen-name Astron Del Martia in 1949. Following my first letters to Frances, I thought I would try out a Hank Janson or two to see what they were all about; and I very quickly became a fan.

"Ask all the questions you want," replied Frances to my letter. I asked many. In 1984, I had a draft of an article that I thought might be worth submitting to a collecting magazine. I showed it proudly to Frances, who commented: "I do congratulate you on having done such a thorough job of investigation, but even so, there are factors which you can't possibly know about, and which can never be clarified. Although Carter and I had a very close relationship, after I went to live in Spain, his activities quite escaped me."

"Publishing is so bad that I can no longer make a living by it," Frances bluntly stated in a later letter. Occasionally I would receive a message asking if I could track down copies of a book and send it off to a publisher for reprinting. "I'll make sure you get paid." I never was, but Frances was receiving only about £100 for the reprint rights and I had a full-time job. I suggested he might get more for rewriting some of his older books and selling them as new, but Frances didn't agree: "Rewriting is, if anything, more wearing than writing something new (at least it is for me)." When I persisted that one story in particular deserved a modern treatment, he said, "If you want to rewrite this story yourself, in your own way, I have no objections whatsoever to you using the plot, and wish you every success with it. I won't do it myself, as you have suggested, because I have no confidence that any publisher today is able to consider accepting manuscripts purely on their contents. All kinds of factors dominate acceptance for publication, mostly based on economics."

It was economics that made Frances suggest his plan to bring over the Hank Janson books and have them seized by customs. *The Obscenity Of Hank Janson* was written in rough, but Frances wanted to generate publicity in the hope that this would get the attention of publishers. In November 1984, Frances penned a six-page outline of the circumstances he felt had turned the Janson trial, thirty years earlier, into something that "amounted almost to a conspiracy among judicial officials to railroad Hank Janson into obscurity."

"I am so weary after writing the enclosed comment on Hank Janson that this letter will be abbreviated brief," Frances wrote in a covering note. He had written with energy and emotion, quoting from bitter memory parts of the trial. "After you read this, you will realise why I believe there is a good newspaper story here," he said. "It is not that times have changed and Hank Janson is no longer obscene that exasperates me. It is that it *wasn't* obscene at the time it was condemned. It was 'made' guilty by Government officials when it wasn't.

"I sincerely believe there is a lot of meat here for a newspaper scoop of Sunday newspaper type. Why not send a fotostat of this letter to your friend at the *Sunday Mirror*?"

A few days later, I had written a suitable covering letter and mailed off photocopies of Steve's comments to various newspapers.

We heard nothing. By the following May, a dejected Frances asked: "After this lapse of time it seems as though the *Mirror* is not interested in Hank Janson?????"

He was still looking for a market: "When next you write, will you let me know if *Weekend* has folded or is still being published?" He had sold stories to *Weekend* in the early 1960s.

I changed jobs, four times in four years, during which time I lost touch with many correspondents. When I was laid off in August 1989, I found myself with a fairly generous golden handshake – more money than I'd previously ever had – and thought it might be enough capital to live on while I wrote a short book about Hank Janson for an American publisher who had shown some interest. Pieced together from old newspaper clippings and from my correspondence with Frances, I wrote what I felt was a reasonably complete history of Hank Janson in November 1989 and despatched it to Frances in Spain.

A letter came back from his agents in London: "Your letter of November 25th to Stephen Frances unfortunately arrived just after he died. I am sorry to have to tell you this sad news."

* * *

His health had not been good for fifteen years. Frances had contracted pneumonia at least three times, which had eventually forced him to give up smoking; but too late. Emphysema wrote "The End" to Frances's life.

Even in the 1980s, a letter addressed to "Stephen Frances, Rosas, Gerona" would reach him without problems. "I remain because it is my home," wrote Frances. "Many of those I met on my very first visit to Rosas are still my friends. We remember Rosas as it was. And we sit together, quietly sipping our drinks, and commiserate nostalgically with one another."

In these appendicies the book number given is that used on the title in question. 'nn' is used to indicate no number. The month and year of release is stated if known, followed by the actual author of the book. If the authorship is in doubt, then this is indicated by the name being in square brackets. If the author is unknown, then no author is listed. r/p indicates a reprint.

Appendix 1

The Hank Janson Novels

Ward & Hitchon
nn • When Dames Get Tough (1946; by Stephen D Frances)
nn • Scarred Faces (1946; by Stephen D Frances)

S D Frances
1 • This Woman is Death • (Jun 1948; by Stephen D Frances)
2 • Lady, Mind That Corpse • (Sep 1948; by Stephen D Frances)
3 • Gun Moll for Hire • (Dec 1948; by Stephen D Frances)
4 • No Regrets for Clara • (Mar 1949; by Stephen D Frances)
5 • Smart Girls Don't Talk • (Apr 1949; by Stephen D Frances)
6 • Lilies for My Lovely • (May 1949; by Stephen D Frances)
7 • Blonde on the Spot • (Jun 1949; by Stephen D Frances)
8 • Honey, Take My Gun • (Jul 1949; by Stephen D Frances)
9 • Sweetheart, Here's Your Grave! • (Aug 1949; by Stephen D Frances)
10 • Gunsmoke in Her Eyes • (Sep 1949; by Stephen D Frances)
11 • Angel Shoot to Kill • (Oct 1949; by Stephen D Frances)
12 • Slay-Ride for Cutie • (Nov 1949; by Stephen D Frances)
13 • Sister, Don't Hate Me • (Dec 1949; by Stephen D Frances)

14 • Some Look Better Dead • (Jan 1950; by Stephen D Frances)
15 • Sweetie, Hold Me Tight • (Feb 1950; by Stephen D Frances)
16 • Torment for Trixy • (Mar 1950; by Stephen D Frances)
17 • Don't Dare Me Sugar • (May 1950; by Stephen D Frances)
18 • The Lady Has a Scar • (Jun 1950; by Stephen D Frances)
19 • The Jane with Green Eyes • (Jul 1950; by Stephen D Frances)
20 • Lola Brought Her Wreath • (Sep 1950; by Stephen D Frances)
21 • Lady Toll the Bell • (Oct 1950; by Stephen D Frances)
22 • The Bride Wore Weeds • (Dec 1950; by Stephen D Frances)
23 • Don't Mourn Me Toots • (Jan 1951; by Stephen D Frances)
24 • This Dame Dies Soon • (Feb 1951; by Stephen D Frances)
25 • Baby, Don't Dare Squeal • (Mar 1951; by Stephen D Frances)
26 • Death Wore a Petticoat • (Apr 1951; by Stephen D Frances)
27 • Hotsy, You'll be Chilled • (May 1951; by Stephen D Frances)
28 • It's Always Eve that Weeps • (Jun 1951; by Stephen D Frances)

New Fiction Press
29 • Frails Can Be So Tough • (Aug 1951; by Stephen D Frances)
30 • Milady Took The Rap • (Sep 1951; by Stephen D Frances)
31 • Women Hate Till Death • (Oct 1951; by Stephen D Frances)
32 • Broads Don't Scare Easy • (Nov 1951; by Stephen D Frances)
33 • Skirts Bring Me Sorrow • (Dec 1951; by Stephen D Frances)
34 • Sadie, Don't Cry Now • (Jan 1952; by Stephen D Frances)
35 • The Filly Wore a Rod • (Feb 1952; by Stephen D Frances[/ Geoffrey Pardoe])
36 • Kill Her If You Can • (Mar 1952; by Stephen D Frances)
37 • Murder • (Apr 1952; by Stephen D Frances)
38 • Conflict • (Jun 1952; by Stephen D Frances)

39 • Tension • (Jul 1952; by Stephen D Frances)
40 • Whiplash • (Aug 1952; by Stephen D Frances)
41 • Accused • (Oct 1952; by Stephen D Frances/Geoffrey Pardoe)
42 • Killer • (Nov 1952; by Stephen D Frances)
43 • Suspense • (Dec 1952; by Stephen D Frances)
44 • Pursuit • (Jan 1953; by Stephen D Frances/Geoffrey Pardoe)
45 • Vengeance • (Feb 1953; by Stephen D Frances)
46 • Torment • (Apr 1953; by Stephen D Frances)
47 • Amok • (May 1953; by Stephen D Frances/Geoffrey Pardoe)
A • Auctioned • (Jun 1952; by Stephen D Frances[/Geoffrey Pardoe])
B • Persian Pride • (Nov 1952; by Stephen D Frances/Geoffrey Pardoe)
C • Desert Fury • (Jul 1953; by Stephen D Frances/Geoffrey Pardoe)
nn • Britain's Great Flood Disaster • (Mar 1953; by Stephen D Frances)

Top Fiction Press

48 • Corruption • (Jun 1953; by Stephen D Frances)
49 • Silken Menace • (Jul 1953; by Stephen D Frances)
50 • Nyloned Avenger • (Aug 1953; by Stephen D Frances)
(51 • Woman Trap • *announced but not issued*)
(52 • Perfumed Nemesis • *announced but not issued*)
(53 • Blonde Dupe • *announced but not issued*)
(54 • Dainty Dynamite • *announced but not issued*)
D • The Unseen Assassin • (Aug 1953; by Stephen D Frances)
E • One Man in His Time • (Aug 1953; by Stephen D Frances)
F • Deadly Mission • (Sep 1953; by Stephen D Frances)
(G • One Against Time • *announced but not issued at this time*)

Alexander Moring

nn • Contraband • (May 1955; by Stephen D Frances)
nn • Untamed • (1955; by Stephen D Frances)
nn • Framed • (Sep 1955; by Stephen D Frances)
nn • Menace • (1955; by Stephen D Frances)
nn • Tomorrow and a Day • (Nov 1955; by Stephen D Frances)
nn • Deadly Mission • (Dec 1955; by Stephen D Frances)

nn • 48 Hours • (Dec 1955; by Stephen D Frances)
nn • One Against Time • (Jan 1956; by Stephen D Frances)
nn • Devil's Highway • (Mar 1956; by Stephen D Frances)
nn • Hell's Angel • (Apr 1956; by Stephen D Frances)
nn • The Unseen Assassin • (r/p; Apr 1956; by Stephen D Frances)
nn • Escape • (May 1956; by Stephen D Frances)
nn • The Big Lie • (1956; by Stephen D Frances)
nn • Cactus • (Jul 1956; by Stephen D Frances)
nn • Bring Me Sorrow • (r/p of *Skirts Bring Me Sorrow*; 1956; by Stephen D Frances)
nn • They Die Alone • (1956; by Stephen D Frances)
nn • Strange Destiny • (Nov 1956; by Stephen D Frances)
nn • Tension • (r/p; 1957; by Stephen D Frances)
nn • Bewitched • (1957; by Stephen D Frances)
nn • Whiplash • (r/p; 1957; by Stephen D Frances)
nn • Conflict • (r/p; 1957; by Stephen D Frances)
nn • Murder • (r/p; 1957; by Stephen D Frances)
nn • Sweet Fury • (1957; by Stephen D Frances)
nn • Hellcat • (1957; by Stephen D Frances)
nn • Persian Pride • (r/p; Sep 1957; by Stephen D Frances/ Geoffrey Pardoe)
nn • Desert Fury • (r/p; Oct 1957; by Stephen D Frances/ Geoffrey Pardoe)
nn • Don't Cry Now • (r/p of *Sadie Don't Cry Now*; 1957; by Stephen D Frances)
nn • Enemy of Men • (1957; by Stephen D Frances)
nn • Sinister Rapture • (Oct 1957; by Stephen D Frances)
nn • Revolt • (Nov 1957; by Stephen D Frances)
nn • Mistress of Fear • (Feb 1958; by Stephen D Frances)
nn • Too Soon to Die • (r/p of *This Dame Dies Soon*; 1958; by Stephen D Frances)
nn • The Amorous Captive Vol.1 • (1958; by Stephen D Frances)
nn • Kill This Man • (r/p of *Deadly Mission*; May 1958; by Stephen D Frances)
nn • Flight from Fear • (r/p of *Pursuit*; 1958; by Stephen D Frances/Geoffrey Pardoe)
nn • Lose This Gun • (r/p of *The Filly Wore A Rod*; 1958; by Stephen D Frances[/Geoffrey Pardoe])
nn • Don't Scare Easy • (r/p of *Broads Don't Scare Easy*; 1958; by Stephen D Frances)

nn • Situation – Grave! • (r/p of *Sweetheart Here's Your Grave*; Sep 1958; by Stephen D Frances)

nn • Sugar and Vice • (1958; by Stephen D Frances)

nn • Hate • (r/p of *Women Hate Till Death*; 1958; by Stephen D Frances)

nn • Avenging Nymph • (Jan 1959; by Stephen D Frances)

nn • Jack Spot • (Dec 1958; by Stephen D Frances)

nn • The Amorous Captive Vol.2 • (Feb 1959; by Stephen D Frances)

nn • Invasion • (1959; by Stephen D Frances)

nn • Silken Snare • (r/p of *Silken Menace*; May 1959; by Stephen D Frances)

nn • Sultry Avenger • (r/p of *Nyloned Avenger*; Jun 1959; by Stephen D Frances)

George Turton

nn • The Amorous Captive Vol.3 • (Aug 1959; by Stephen D Frances)

nn • Wild Girl • (Sep 1959)

nn • Torrid Temptress • (1959)

nn • Bad Girl • (r/p of *Frails Can Be So Tough*; Nov 1959; by Stephen D Frances)

Roberts & Vinter

nn • All Tramps Are Trouble • (1959)

nn • Obsession • (1959)

nn • Cupid Turns Killer • (1960)

nn • Slaves Of Seduction • (1960)

nn • Hell Of A Dame • (1960)

nn • This Wicked Sex • (1960)

E151 • Quiet Waits The Grave • (1960)

E152 • Ripe For Rapture • (1960)

E153 • Sentence For Sin • (r/p of *The Lady has A Scar*; 1960; by Stephen D Frances)

E154 • This Hood For Hire • (r/p of *Vengeance*; 1960; by Stephen D Frances)

E155 • Beloved Traitor • (r/p of *Lady Toll the Bell*; 1960; by Stephen D Frances)

E156 • Come Quickly Honey • (r/p of *Sweetie Hold Me Tight*; 1960; by Stephen D Frances)

E157 • Ecstasy • (Oct 1960)

E158 • Passionate Waif • (1960)

E159 • Secret Mission • (r/p of *Corruption*; 1960; by Stephen D Frances)

E160 • Cutie On Call • (1960)

E161 • Fireball • (r/p of *Amok*; 1960; by Stephen D Frances/ Geoffrey Pardoe)

E162 • Cool Sugar • (r/p of *Baby Don't Dare Squeal*; 1960; by Stephen D Frances)

E163 • Suddenly It's Sin • (r/p of *Torment For Trixy*; 1961; by Stephen D Frances)

E164 • Downtown Doll • (r/p of *Lola Brought Her Wreath*; 1961; by Stephen D Frances)

E165 • Late Night Revel • (Mar 1961)

E166 • Outcast • (r/p of *Angel Shoot To Kill*; 1961; by Stephen D Frances)

E167 • Delicious Danger • (r/p of *Sadie, Don't Cry Now*; 1961; by Stephen D Frances)

E168 • Prey For A Newshawk • (r/p of *Sister, Don't Hate Me*; 1961; by Stephen D Frances)

E169 • Destination Dames • (May 1961)

E170 • Janson Go Home • (1961; by Harry Hobson)

E171 • Scent From Heaven • (1961)

E172 • She Sleeps To Conquer • (1961; [by Harold Kelly])

E173 • Crowns Can Kill • (1961; by Harry Hobson)

E174 • Venus Makes Three • (1961; [by Harold Kelly])

E175 • Don't Scare Easy *(recover, Alexander Moring)* • (r/p; 1961; by Stephen D Frances)

E176 • Lose This Gun *(recover, Alexander Moring)* • (r/p; 1961; by Stephen D Frances)

E177 • Kill This Man *(recover, Alexander Moring)* • (r/p; 1961; by Stephen D Frances)

E178 • Jack Spot *(recover, Alexander Moring)* • (r/p; Oct 1961; by Stephen D Frances)

E179 • Reluctant Hostess • (1961; [by Harold Kelly])

E180 • Short Term Wife • (Oct 1961)

E181 • Lady Lie Low • (1961)

E182 • Master Mind • (1961; by Harry Hobson)

E183 • Hell's Belles • (1961)

E184 • Break For A Lovely • (1961)

E185 • Play It Quiet • (r/p of *Some Look Better Dead*; 1962; by Stephen D Frances)

E186 • Beauty And The Beat • (1962; by Harry Hobson)

E187 • Rave For A Roughneck • (r/p of *No Regrets For Clara*; 1962; by Stephen D Frances)

E188 • Chicago Chick • (1962; by Harry Hobson)

E189 • She Wolf • (1962)

E190 • Crime On My Hands • (1962)

E191 • Uncover Agent • (1962; by Harry Hobson)

E192 • Flight From Fear *(recover, Alexander Moring)* • (r/p; 1962; by Stephen D Frances)

E193 • Vagabond Vamp • (1962; [by Harold Kelly])

E194 • Take This Sweetie • (1962; by Harry Hobson)

E195 • Honey For Me • (1962; [by Harold Kelly])

E196 • Mistress Of Fear *(recover, Alexander Moring)* • (r/p; 1962; by Stephen D Frances)

E197 • Too Soon To Die *(recover, Alexander Moring)* • (r/p; 1962; by Stephen D Frances)

E198 • Run For Lover • (1962)

E199 • Like Crazy • (1962; by Harry Hobson)

E200 • Like Poison • (1962; by Harry Hobson)

E201 • Kill Me For Kicks • (1962; by Victor Norwood)

E202 • Like Lethal • (1962; by Harry Hobson)

E203 • Blood Bath • (1962; by Victor Norwood)

E204 • Twist For Two • (1962; [by Harold Kelly])

E205 • Dig Those Heels • (1962)

E206 • Grapevine • (1962; by Harry Hobson)

E207 • Way Out Wanton • (1962)

E208 • Savage Sequel • (1962; [by Harold Kelly])

E209 • Nymph In The Night • (1962; by Stephen D Frances)

E210 • Uncommon Market • (1962; by Harry Hobson)

E211 • Angel Astray • (1962)

E212 • Dateline – Diane • (1962; by Harry Hobson)

E213 • Exclusive • (1962)

E214 • Go With A Jerk • (1962; by Victor Norwood)

E215 • Passion Pact • (1963; [by Harold Kelly])

E216 • Dateline – Darlene • (1963; by Harry Hobson)

E217 • Second String • (1963; by Stephen D Frances)

Compact Books

F218 • I For Intrigue • (1963)

F219 • Sensuality • (1963; by Victor Norwood)

F220 • Dateline – Debbie • (1963; by Harry Hobson)

F221 • Brand Image • (1963; by Stephen D Frances)

F222 • Heartache • (1963)

F223 • The Love Makers • (1963; by Harry Hobson)
F224 • Strange Ritual • (1963)
F225 • Hilary's Terms • (1963; by Stephen D Frances)
F226 • Nerve Centre • (1963)
F227 • Daughter Of Shame • (1963; by Stephen D Frances)
F228 • Fast Buck • (1963; by Harry Hobson)
F230 • Playgirl • (1963; by Victor Norwood)
F231 • Hot Line • (1963; by Harold Kelly)
F232 • V For Vitality • (1963; [by Harold Kelly])
F233 • Visit From A Broad • (1963; by Harry Hobson)
F234 • Lake Loot • (1964; by Harry Hobson)
F236 • Top Ten • (1964; by Victor Norwood)
F237 • Crimebeat Crisis • (1964; by Harry Hobson)
F239 • Flower Of Desire • (1964)
F241 • Fan Fare • (1964; by Harry Hobson)
F242 • Voodoo Violence • (1964; [by Harold Kelly])
F243 • Will-Power • (1964; [by Harold Kelly])
F244 • Tigress • (1964)
F245 • Doctor Fix • (1964; by Harry Hobson)
F246 • Soft Cargo • (1964)
F247 • Design For Dupes • (1964)
F248 • Pattern Of Rape • (1964; by Jim Moffatt)
F249 • That Brain Again • (1964; by Harry Hobson)
F250 • Depravity • (1964; by Jim Moffatt)
F251 • Square One • (1964; by Harry Hobson)
F252 • The Dish Ran Away • (1964; by Jim Moffatt)
F253 • Sex Angle • (1964; [by Harold Kelly])
F254 • The Last Lady • (1964; by Jim Moffatt)
F255 • A Girl In Hand • (1964)
F256 • The Love Secretaries • (1964; by Jim Moffatt)
F257 • Double Take • (1964)
F258 • Limbo Lover • (1964; by Harry Hobson)
F259 • Jazz Jungle • (1965; by Harry Hobson)
F260 • Backlash Of Infamy • (1965; by Jim Moffatt)
F261 • Counter-Feat • (1965; by Jim Moffatt)
F262 • Model In Mayhem • (1965; by Jim Moffatt)
F267 • Berlin Briefing • (1965; by Harry Hobson)
F268 • Lust For Vengeance • (1965)
F269 • Say It With Candy • (1965)
F270 • Sweet Talk • (1965; by Jim Moffatt)
F271 • Missile Mob • (1965; by Harry Hobson)
F272 • Abomination • (1965)

F274 • Flashpoint • (1965; by Harry Hobson)
F276 • Junk Market • (1965)
F278 • The Devil And The Deep • (1965)
F280 • Tailsting • (1965; by Harry Hobson)
F282 • Why Should Sylvia? • (1965)
F286 • Furtive Flame • (1965)
F288 • Roxy By Proxy • (1965; by Harry Hobson)
F290 • Catch Me A Renegade • (1965)
F292 • Helldorado • (1966; by Harry Hobson)
F296 • Escalation • (1966; by Harry Hobson)
F298 • Physical Attraction • (1966; by Harry Hobson)
F300 • Liquor Is Quicker • (1966; by Harry Hobson)
F304 • Nefarious Quest • (1966; [by Colin Fraser])
F306 • Mayfair Slayride • (1966; by Harry Hobson)
F310 • Krush • (1966; [by Colin Fraser])
F314 • Dead Certainty • (1966; [by Colin Fraser])
F316 • Riviera Showdown • (1966; by Harry Hobson)
F318 • Darling Delinquent • (1966; by Harry Hobson)
F320 • Bid For Beauty • (1966; [by Colin Fraser])
F328 • The Big H • (1966; by Harry Hobson)
F330 • FEUD • (1966; by Harry Hobson)
F332 • Make Mine Mink • (1966; by Harry Hobson)
F333 • Ladybirds Are In • (1967; by Harry Hobson)
F334 • Zero Takes All • (1967; by Harry Hobson)
F335 • Take Two Blondes • (1967; [by Colin Fraser])
F336 • One-Way Split • (1967; by Harry Hobson)
F338 • Operation Obliterate • (1967; by Harry Hobson)
F340 • Casino Strip • (1967; by Harry Hobson)
F341 • Deadly Horse-Race • (1967; by Harry Hobson)
F342 • Hell Brood • (1967; [by Colin Fraser])
F343 • Casinopoly • (1967; by Harry Hobson)
F344 • Same Difference • (1967; by Harry Hobson)
F345 • The Young Wolves • (1967; [by Colin Fraser])
F346 • Love-In And Lamentation • (1968; by Harry Hobson)
F347 • Shalom, My Love • (1968; by Harry Hobson)
F348 • Microkill • (1968; [by Colin Fraser])
F349 • Crunch • (1968; [by Colin Fraser])
F350 • Sprung! • (1968; by Harry Hobson)
F351 • Cat's Paw • (1969; [by Colin Fraser])
F352 • Globe Probe • (1969; by Harry Hobson)

F353 • Covering Fire • (1969; [by Colin Fraser])
F354 • The Spy In My Bed • (1969; by Harry Hobson)
Gold & Warburton
F355 • Frame And Fortune • (1970; [by Colin Fraser])
F356 • Lament For A Lover • (1970; by Harry Hobson)
F357 • Ultimate Deterrent • (1970; by Harry Hobson)
F358 • Twilight Tigress • (1970; [by Colin Fraser])
H359 • The Big Round Bed • (1970; by Harry Hobson)
H360 • Infiltration • (1970; by Harry Hobson)
H361 • Villon Of The Piece • (1970; by Harry Hobson)
H362 • The Long Arm • (1970; by Harry Hobson)
H363 • The Kay Assignation • (1971; by Harry Hobson)
H364 • Caribbean Caper • (1971; by Harry Hobson)
H365 • The Liz Assignation • (1971; by Harry Hobson)
H366 • Grass Widow • (1971; [by Colin Fraser])
(nn • The Sleeping-Beauty Case • *announced but not issued*)
(nn • Date Line – Death • *announced but not issued*)

Telos
1 • Torment • (r/p; July 2003; by Stephen D Frances)
2 • Women Hate Till Death • (r/p; July 2003; by Stephen D Frances)
3 • Some Look Better Dead • (r/p; Nov 2003; by Stephen D Frances)
4 • Skirts Bring Me Sorrow • (r/p; Nov 2003; by Stephen D Frances)
5 • When Dames Get Tough • (r/p containing *When Dames Get Tough, Scarred Faces* and *Kitty Takes the Rap* plus, from *Underworld* magazine, *Double Double-Cross* and *The Dead Guy*; May 2004; by Stephen D Frances)

Appendix 2

Novels by Stephen D Frances

Novels as Stephen D Frances (series: John Gail, Naked City, Spanish Saga)

One Man In His Time. London, Pendulum, 1946; as by Hank Janson, London, New Fiction Press, 1953.

Day of Terror. London, Consul Books, 1962.

Bad Boy. London, Consul Books, 1964.

Twilight People. London, Consul Books, 1964.

Pattern of Life. London, Consul Books, 1964.

Panic in the City (Naked City). London, Consul Books, 1964.

The Day the Island Almost Sank (Naked City). London, Consul Books, 1964.

The Fault in Our Stars (Naked City). London, Consul Books, 1964.

This Woman Is Death (Gail). London, Mayflower Books, 1965; New York, Award Books, 1969.

To Love and Yet To Die (Gail). London, Mayflower Books, 1966; New York, Award Books, 1970.

The Sad and Tender Flesh (Gail). London, Mayflower Books, 1966; as *The Ambassador's Plot*, New York, Award Books, 1970.

Hate Is For the Hunted (Gail). London, Mayflower Books, 1968; New York, Award Books, 1970.

The Sweet Shame of Fury (Gail). London, Mayflower Books, 1968.

The Spanish Saga:

Criminals of Want. London, Mayflower Books, 1968.

Until the Grapes Bleed. London, Mayflower Books, 1968.

Where the Sun Dies. London, Mayflower Books, 1968.

The Bitter Seeds of Hate. London, Mayflower Books, 1968.

La Guerra (complete in one volume). New York, Delacorte Press, 1970.

The Caress of Conquest (Gail). London, Mayflower Books, 1968; New York, Award Books, 1970.
The Illusionist. London, Mayflower Books, 1970.
Cry For My Lovely (Gail). London, Mayflower Books, 1971.

Novels as Hilary Brand (series: Hilary Brand in all, see also Hank Janson)
News Girl. London, Roberts & Vinter, 1963.
Brand T. London, Roberts & Vinter, 1964.
Peak of Frenzy. London, Roberts & Vinter, 1964.
Black Summer Day. London, Robert & Vinter, 1964.

Novels as Simon Burke
Death is the Payoff. London, Scion, 1949.

Novels as Ace Capelli
Get Me Headquarters. London, B Kaye Agency, 1949; New York, Gryphon Books, 1996.
This Man Is Death. London, B Kaye Agency, 1949.
Chicago Payoff. London, B Kaye Agency, 1949.
Death At Every Door. London, B Kaye Agency, 1949.
Never Turn Your Back. London, B Kaye Agency, 1950; as *Deadline Death* by Desmond Corbett, London, Consul Books, 1964.

Novels as Max Clinten
No Flowers For the Dead. London, S D Frances, 1951; as *The Unlucky Break* by Mark Stephens, London, Consul Books, 1964.

Novels as Mark Clinton (series: Hugh Pecker)
Ways of Passion. n/p, Royal Line, 1966.
Oh! Hugh Pecker (Pecker). New York, Lancer, 1973.
Come Again, Hugh Pecker! (Pecker). New York, Lancer, 1973.

Novels as Ullrega de la Garbia
A Study of an Arab Nymphomaniac, translated by D Pendran Charlvia. New York, Pamar Enterprises Inc. (Goldstar), *c.*1971.

Novels as Maria Deluz
In the Hands of the Inquisition. London, Canova Press, 1971.

Novels as Desmond East
Blood on the Sand. London, George Turton, 1959.

Novels as Dael Forest (series: Slaves of Empire)
#1 Barba the Slaver. London, New English Library, 1975; New York, Ballantine, 1978.
#2 Haesel, the Slave. London, New English Library, 1975; New York, Ballantine, 1978.
#3 Brotan the Breeder. London, New English Library, 1975; New York, Ballantine, 1978.
#4 Graccus the Centurion. London, New English Library, 1975; New York, Ballantine, 1978.
#5 Corissa the Vestal Virgin. London, New English Library, 1976; New York, Ballantine, 1978.

Novels as Stefan Frank
Hot Piece. New York, Bee-Line Books, 1970.

Novels as John Glaston Hilt
The Taming of Elsa. New York, Bee-Line Books, 1971?
Wet and Ready. New York, Bee-Line Books/Orpheus, 1972.
Double Header!. New York, Bee-Line Books, 1972.
Swedish Sex Guide. New York, Bee-Line Books, 1973?
Oral Antics. New York, Bee-Line Books, 1973.
Bare Minimum. New York, Bee-Line Books, 1973.
Juicy Lucy. London, Beeline, c1977.

Novels as Hank Janson (series: Hank Janson; Persian)
When Dames Get Tough (Janson). London, Ward & Hitchon, 1946.
Scarred Faces (Janson). London, Ward & Hitchon, 1946.
This Woman Is Death (Janson). London, S D Frances, 1948.
Lady, Mind That Corpse (Janson). London, S D Frances, 1948; New York, Checkerbooks, 1949.
Gun Moll For Hire (Janson). London, S D Frances, 1948.

No Regrets For Clara (Janson). London, S D Frances, 1949; as *Rave For A Roughneck*, London, Roberts & Vinter, 1962; revised as *Cold Dead Coed*, New York, Goldstar, 1964.

Smart Girls Don't Talk (Janson). London, S D Frances, 1949.

Lilies For My Lovely (Janson). London, S D Frances, 1949.

Blonde on the Spot (Janson). London, S D Frances, 1949.

Honey, Take My Gun (Janson). London, S D Frances, 1949; as *Orchids to You*, Toronto, Weldun Pony Book 126, 1949.

Sweetheart, Here's Your Grave! (Janson). London, S D Frances, 1949; as *Situation - Grave!*, London, Alexander Moring, 1958.

Gunsmoke In Her Eyes (Janson). London, S D Frances, 1949.

Angel, Shoot To Kill (Janson). London, S D Frances, 1949; as *Outcast*, London, Roberts & Vinter, 1961.

Slay-Ride For Cutie (Janson). London, S D Frances, 1949.

Sister, Don't Hate Me (Janson). London, S D Frances, 1949; as *Prey For A Newshawk*, London, Roberts & Vinter, 1961.

Some Look Better Dead (Janson). London, S D Frances, 1950; as *Play It Quiet*, London, Roberts & Vinter, 1962.

Sweetie, Hold Me Tight (Janson). London, S D Frances, 1950; as *Come Quickly Honey*, London, Roberts & Vinter, 1960.

Torment For Trixy (Janson). London, S D Frances, 1951; as *Suddenly It's Sin*, London, Roberts & Vinter, 1961.

Don't Dare Me Sugar (Janson). London, S D Frances, 1950.

The Lady Has A Scar (Janson). London, S D Frances, 1950; as *Sentence For Sin*, London, Roberts & Vinter, 1960.

The Jane With Green Eyes (Janson). London, S D Frances, 1950.

Lola Brought Her Wreath (Janson). London, S D Frances, 1950; as *Downtown Doll*, London, Roberts & Vinter, 1961.

Lady Toll the Bell (Janson). London, S D Frances, 1950; as *Beloved Traitor*, London, Roberts & Vinter, 1960.

The Bride Wore Weeds (Janson). London, S D Frances, 1950.

Don't Mourn Me Toots (Janson). London, S D Frances, 1951.

This Dame Dies Soon (Janson). London, S D Frances, 1951; as *Too Soon to Die*, London, Alexander Moring, 1958; as *Fanny*, Derby, Connecticut, Goldstar, 1964.

Baby, Don't Dare Squeal. London, S D Frances, 1951; as *Cool Sugar*, London, Roberts & Vinter, 1960.

Death Wore A Petticoat. London, S D Frances, 1951.

Hotsy, You'll Be Chilled. London, S D Frances, 1951.

It's Always Eve That Weeps. London, S D Frances, 1951.

Frails Can Be So Tough. London, New Fiction Press, 1951; as *Bad Girl,* London, George Turton, 1959.

Milady Took The Rap (Janson). London, New Fiction Press, 1951.

Women Hate Till Death (Janson). London, New Fiction Press, 1951; as *Hate,* London, Alexander Moring, 1958.

Broads Don't Scare Easy. London, New Fiction Press, 1951; as *Don't Scare Easy,* London, Alexander Moring, 1956.

Skirts Bring Me Sorrow (Janson). London, New Fiction Press, 1951; as *Bring Me Sorrow,* London, Alexander Moring, 1956; as *The Sexy Vixen,* Derby, Connecticut, Goldstar, 1964.

Sadie, Don't Cry Now. London, New Fiction Press, 1952; as *Don't Cry Now,* London, Alexander Moring, 1957; as *Delicious Danger,* London, Roberts & Vinter, 1961.

The Filly Wore A Rod (Janson). London, New Fiction Press, 1952; as *Lose This Gun,* London, Alexander Moring, 1958.

Kill Her If You Can (Janson). London, New Fiction Press, 1952.

Murder (Janson). London, New Fiction Press, 1952; as *Expectant Nymph,* Derby, Connecticut, Goldstar, 1964.

Conflict (Janson). London, New Fiction Press, 1952; as *Her Weapon Was Passion,* Derby, Connecticut, Goldstar, 1964.

Auctioned (Persian). London, New Fiction Press, 1952.

Tension (Janson). London, New Fiction Press, 1952.

Whiplash (Janson). London, New Fiction Press, 1952.

Accused. London, New Fiction Press, 1952.

Killer (Janson). London, New Fiction Press, 1952.

Persian Pride (Persian). London, New Fiction Press, 1952.

Suspense (Janson). London, New Fiction Press, 1952.

Pursuit . London, New Fiction Press, 1953; as *Flight From Fear,* London, Alexander Moring, 1958.

Vengeance (Janson). London, New Fiction Press, 1953; as *This Hood For Hire,* London, Roberts & Vinter, 1960.

Torment (Janson). London, New Fiction Press, 1953.

Amok. London, New Fiction Press, 1953; as *Fireball,* London, Roberts & Vinter, 1960.

Desert Fury (Persian). London, New Fiction Press, 1953.

Corruption (Janson). London, Top Fiction Press, 1953; as *Secret Session,* London, Roberts & Vinter, 1960.

Silken Menace (Janson). London, Top Fiction Press, 1953; as *Silken Snare*, London, Alexander Moring, 1959.

Nyloned Avenger (Janson). London, Top Fiction Press, 1953; as *Sultry Avenger*, London, Alexander Moring, 1959.

The Unseen Assassin. London, Top Fiction Press, 1953.

Deadly Mission (collection; Janson). London, Top Fiction Press, 1953; as *Kill This Man*, London, Alexander Moring, 1958.

Contraband. London, Alexander Moring, 1955.

Untamed (Janson). London, Alexander Moring, 1955.

Framed (Janson). London, Alexander Moring, 1955.

Menace. London, Alexander Moring, 1955.

Tomorrow And A Day. London, Alexander Moring, 1955.

Deadly Mission (novel). London, Alexander Moring, 1955.

48 Hours (Janson). London, Alexander Moring, 1955.

One Against Time. London, Alexander Moring, 1956; as by Astron Del Martia, London, Mayflower Books, 1969; New York, Paperback Library, 1970.

Devil's Highway. London, Alexander Moring, 1956.

Hell's Angel (Janson). London, Alexander Moring, 1956.

Escape (Janson). London, Alexander Moring, 1956.

The Big Lie (Janson). London, Alexander Moring, 1956.

Cactus (Janson). London, Alexander Moring, 1956.

They Die Alone (Janson). London, Alexander Moring, 1956; as *The Exotic Seductress*, Derby, Connecticut, Goldstar, 1964.

Strange Destiny (Janson). London, Alexander Moring, 1956.

Bewitched (Janson). London, Alexander Moring, 1957.

Sweet Fury (Janson). London, Alexander Moring, 1957; as *The Affairs of Paula*, Derby, Connecticut, Goldstar, 1965.

Hellcat (Janson). London, Alexander Moring, 1957.

Enemy of Men (Janson). London, Alexander Moring, 1957; as *A Nympho Named Sylvia*, Derby, Connecticut, Goldstar, 1965.

Sinister Rapture (Janson). London, Alexander Moring, 1957; as *Becky*, Derby, Connecticut, Goldstar, 1965.

Revolt. London, Alexander Moring, 1957.

Mistress of Fear (Janson). London, Alexander Moring, 1958.

The Amorous Captive Vol 1. London, Alexander Moring, 1958.

Sugar and Vice. London, Alexander Moring, 1958.

Avenging Nymph (Janson). London, Alexander Moring, 1958.

Jack Spot (fictionalised biography). London, Alexander Moring, 1958.

The Amorous Captive Vol 2. London, Alexander Moring, 1959.

Invasion (Janson). London, Alexander Moring, 1959.

The Amorous Captive Vol 3. London, George Turton, 1959.

Nymph in the Night (Janson). London, Roberts & Vinter, 1962.

Second String (Brand). London, Roberts & Vinter, 1963.

Brand Image (Brand). London, Roberts & Vinter, 1963.

Hilary's Terms (Brand). London, Roberts & Vinter, 1963.

Daughter of Shame. London, Roberts & Vinter, 1963; revised as *The Witch Mark* by S F Roland, London, New English Library, 1977.

Novels as Arthur Kirby (series: Sexton Blake)
High Summer Homicide. London, Fleetway Publications, 1962.

Novels as Duke Linton
Shrouds Are Cheap. London, Scion, 1950; as by Peter Lamont, London, Consul Books, 1965.

Lips of Death. London, Scion, 1950; as by David Steel, London, Consul Books, 1965.

Crazy To Kill. London, Scion, 1950; as *Wild Blood* by Darcy Glinto, London, Alexander Moring, 1956; as *Trouble With A Woman* by Frank Corbett, London, Consul Books, 1964.

Dames Die Too!. London, Scion, 1950.

Bury Me Deep. London, Scion, 1950.

Too Late For Death. London, Scion, 1950; as *Now Is For Dying* by Preston Elliot, London, Consul Books, 1965.

Kill And Desire. London, Scion, 1950; revised as *Hounded* by Darcy Glinto, London, Alexander Moring, 1957; as *To Kill Or Be Killed* by Munro Carson, London, Consul Books, 1964; New York, Gryphon Books, 1998.

Enough Rope. London, Scion, 1950; revised as *Snatched* by Darcy Glinto, London, Alexander Moring, 1957.

Novels as Steve Markham
Lilies for Laura. London, Art Publicity, 1949.

It's Not Easy To Die. London, Art Publicity, 1949; as *Protection Pay-off* by Darcy Glinto, London, Alexander Moring, 1958; as *It's Not Easy To Die* by Steve Coleman, London, Consul Books, 1964.

Novels as Desmond Reid (series: Pinkerton, Sexton Blake)
The Deadlier of the Species (Blake). London, Mayflower Books, 1966.
The Babcock Boys (Pinkerton). London, Mayflower Books, 1966.
Death Waits in Tucson (Pinkerton). London, Mayflower Books, 1966.

Novels as David Roland
Red Star Over London. London, Hutchinson, 1971.

Novels as Tex Ryland
Bushwhacked. London, B Henry, 1948; as *Bushwacked*, London, Alexander Moring, 1956?; as *On the Vengeance Trail* by Carl C Hanson, London, Consul Books, 1963; as *Trail of Revenge*, London, Mayflower Books, 1968.
A Grave For A Coyote. London, Scion, 1949; London, Alexander Moring, 1956?; as *A Grave For Coyotes* by Stephen Frances, London, Consul Books, 1965; as *Keep the Wagons Rolling*, London, Mayflower Books, 1968.
Death Rides A Bullet. London, Alexander Moring, 1957?.

Novels as Peter Saxon
The Disorientated Man. London, Mayflower Books, 1966; as *Scream and Scream Again*, New York, Paperback Library, 1967.

Novels as Link Shelton
Dead Men Don't Love. London, S D Frances, 1949.

Novels as Sid South
Adventures of a Plumber's Mate. London, Mayflower Books, 1978.

Novels as Dave Steel
Lady Take the Chair. London, K Publications, 1949; as *Call Her Savage* by Johnny Grecco. London, Kaye Publications, 1953; as *Lady Take the Chair* by Stephen Coleman, London, Consul Books, 1964.
Lovely But Deadly. London, Comyns, 1952.
Beauty Found A Grave. London, Comyns, 1952.
Too Tough For Death. London, Comyns, 1953.
You'll Live to Talk. London, Comyns, 1953.

Novels as Danny Stephens
The Whore of Dalsburg. London, Consul Books, 1964.
Not Everyone Died, introduction by F Daniel Stephens. London, Consul Books, 1964.

Novels as Richard Williams (series: Sexton Blake in all)
Vendetta!. London, Fleetway Publications, 1961.
Torment Was A Redhead. London, Fleetway Publications, 1962.
Somebody Wants Me Dead!. London, Fleetway Publications, 1962.
The Slaying of Julian Summers. London, Fleetway Publications, 1963.
The Man With the Iron Chest. London, Mayflower, 1965.
The Sniper. London, Mayflower, 1965.

Non-fiction
Britain's Great Flood Disaster (as Hank Janson). London, New Fiction Press, 1953.
Costa Brava Guide. London, Charles Skilton, 1964.

Anthologies
Editor, *Stories For All Moods.* London, Pendulum, 1945.
Editor, *Stories For All Moods 2.* London, Pendulum, 1945.
Editor, *Stories For All Moods 3.* London, Pendulum, 1946.

Others
Hess, The Man and His Mission, by J Bernard Hutton (ghosted), London, Bruce & Watson, 1970; New York, Macmillan, 1972.
Women Spies, by J Bernard Hutton (ghosted). London, W H Allen, 1971; as *Women in Espionage*, New York, Macmillan, 1972.
The Subverters of Liberty, by J Bernard Hutton (ghosted). London, W H Allen, 1972; as *The Subverters*, New York, Arlington House, 1972.
Lost Freedom by J Bernard Hutton (ghosted). London, Bruce & Watson, 1973.
Healing Power. The extraordinary spiritual healing of Mrs Leah Doctors and 'Dr Chang', her spirit guide, by J Bernard Hutton (ghosted). London, Leslie Frewin, 1975.
Step Into the Unknown. A study of all aspects of parapsychology, by J Bernard Hutton (ghosted). London, Leslie Frewin 1976.

Appendix 3

Destruction Order issued against Hank Janson titles: 1950-1953

The following table lists the combined number of destruction orders issued against Hank Janson titles up to and including 1953.

Title	Destruction Orders
When Dames Get Tough	-
Scarred Faces	-
This Woman Is Death	41
Lady, Mind That Corpse	47
Gun Moll For Hire	22
No Regrets For Clara	20
Smart Girls Don't Talk	11
Lilies For My Lovely	32
Blonde on the Spot [124]	7
Honey, Take My Gun	23
Sweetheart, Here's Your Grave	27
Gunsmoke In Her Eyes	42
Angel, Shoot To Kill	49
Slay-Ride For Cutie	27
Sister, Don't Hate Me	44
Some Look Better Dead	49
Sweetie, Hold Me Tight	33
Torment For Trixy	41
Don't Dare Me Sugar	30
The Lady Has A Scar	32

[124] Also listed in one instance as *Blondie On The Spot*

Appendix 4

Schedule of Successful Prosecutions: 1935-1956

Year	Number of Destruction Orders	Books & Magazines	Photographs	Postcards	Miscellaneous	No. of persons found guilty	Total amount of Fines	Range of Sentences
1935	39	900	8347	78	176	39	£1048.15s	6w—12m
1936	33	1506	11492	7784	705	18	£244	6m—2y
1937	44	5314	8737	0	622	31	£675	1m—6m
1938	66	24727	2064	17	5006	39	£370.15s	1m—2y
1939	11	3006	344	0	7	7	£69	12m
1939	67	40404	7182	297	160	19	£451	3m—12m
1950	271	65277	28956	11662	2150	51	£5938	6w—2y
1951	115	31842	8329	16029	2546	34	£906	6w—18m
1952	154	44130	20131	32603	1950	49	£2786	3m—12m
1953	132	167293	10903	16646	18609	111	£12677	3m—18m
1954	38	3056	7142	1214	151	43	£1830	2w—3y
1955	38	2110	3019	22448	1745	42	£1724	2m—1y

324

Select Bibliography

Branson, Noreen & Margot Heinemann, *Britain in the Nineteen Thirties*. London, Weidenfeld and Nicolson, 1971.

Brockway, Fenner, *Towards Tomorrow*. Frogmore, St. Albans, Hart-Davis, McGibbon, 1977.

Carr, Raymond, *The Spanish Tragedy*. London, Weidenfeld & Nicolson (2nd edition), 1986.

Chibnall, Steve, "Pulps vs. Penguins: Paperbacks Go to War", in *PBO #5*, Summer 1997.

Chibnall, Steve, *Reginald Heade: England's Greatest Artist*. Richmond, Kentucky, Books Are Everything, 1991.

Craig, Alec, *The Banned Books of England and Other Countries*. London, George Allen & Unwin, 1962.

Dodson, Sir Gerald, *Consider Your Verdict: The Memoirs of Sir Gerald Dodson Recorder of London, 1937-1959*. London, Hutchinson & Co, 1967.

Ferris, Paul, *Sex and the British*. London, Michael Joseph, 1993.

Gold, Ralph, *Good as Gold*. London, Robson Books, 1997.

Greenfield, George, *Scribblers For Bread. Aspects of the English Novel Since 1945*. London, Hodder & Stoughton, 1989.

Griffin, John (uncredited), *Hank Janson File*. Np. [Privately published], 1985.

Harbottle, Philip, *The Multi-Man: A bibliographic study of John Russell Fearn*. Wallsend, P J Harbottle, 1968.

Holland, Steve, *Gaywood Press, Compact Books and Hank Janson Publishers*. Scunthorpe, Richard Williams, 1986.

Holland, Steve, *The Trials of Hank Janson*. Richmond, Kentucky, Books Are Everything, 1991.

Holland, Steve & Bill Lofts, "The Pulp Fiction of Hank Janson", in *The Book and Magazine Collector #17*, August 1985.

Hyde, Douglas, *I Believed: The autobiography of a former British Communist*. London, William Heinemann, 1950.

Hyde, H Montgomery, *A History of Pornography*. London, William Heinemann, 1964.

Loth, David, *The Erotic In Literature*. London, Secker & Warburg, 1962.

Orwell, George, *The Collected Essays, Journalism and Letters of George Orwell Volume 1: An Age Like This, 1920-1940*, edited by Sonia Orwell and Ian Angus. London, Secker & Warburg, 1968.

Rolph, C H, *Books in the Dock*. London, Andre Deutsch, 1969.

Scaffardi, Sylvia, *Fire Under the Carpet: Working for Civil Liberties in the 1930s*. London, Lawrence and Wishart, 1986.

Smith, Arthur, *Lord Goddard: My years with the Lord Chief Justice*. London, Weidenfeld & Nicolson, 1959.

Stableford, Brian, "Hank Janson", in *Million #7*, January/February 1992.

Stevas, Norman St. John, *Obscenity and the Law*. London, Secker & Warburg, 1956.

Stevenson, John & Chris Cook, *The Slump*. London, Jonathan Cape, 1977.

Thomas, Donald, *A Long Time Burning. The History of Literary Censorship in England*. London, Routledge & Kegan Paul, 1969.

Thomas, Hugh, *John Strachey*. London, Eyre Methuen, 1973.

Contemporary Authors, Dictionary of National Bibliography, Who Was Who.

ABOUT THE AUTHOR

Steve Holland has been collecting books and comics since childhood and wrote his first article in 1981. Since then he has had over 1,250 features published and has written and co-written a number of full-length books, including *Vultures Of The Void* (with Phil Harbottle) and the Anthony Award-nominated *The Mushroom Jungle*.

He has had a varied career in and out of writing, working at a local hospital, a frozen food warehouse and as an office manager in London. He has edited magazines on subjects as diverse as comics and 4x4 cars, and books on everything from science fiction to movies.

"I have always had a fascination with the backwaters of popular literature, from penny dreadfuls to paperbacks, and I've always tried to get some of that enthusiasm over in everything I've done, whether it's radio, TV or in articles," he says. "Thankfully the books I've had a hand in have been well received.

"I've wanted to write *The Trials Of Hank Janson* for some years but always held off because I knew it would be quite a gruelling experience. I corresponded with Stephen Frances, Hank's creator, for some years before his death and looking through his letters you realise just how angry and sad his experiences with Hank made him.

"When I read the books twenty years ago I knew from the start that they were more than simple crime thrillers. Frances threw himself into them – he *was* Hank when he was writing them. To hear a Judge describe your work as obscene in the highest court in the land, to see your friends imprisoned and have newspapers baying for your arrest and conviction – it must have felt as if his whole world had caved in. And then, after the dust had settled, he lost control of the character he had created and the novels he had written. You can only imagine how that must have made him feel."

Index

using a dictation machine for writing, 78, 86-87; edits *Underworld*, 85-86; death of mother, 91-92; obtains a divorce, 92; moves to Spain, 92, 116; precautions taken against prosecution, 115; a more relaxed pace of writing, 117; questioned by Scotland Yard, 128; prosecuted at Darwen, 129; writes *Britain's Great Flood Disaster*, 132; interest in science fiction, 136-137; outrage at sentences passed at Old Bailey, 196-197; offer to return to England to stand trial, 198; warrant issued for arrest, 199; prosecution at Guild Hall, 200-203; begins writing Hank Janson novels again, 218; purchases the rights to Darcy Glinto, 220, 256-257; on *Success Story*, 227; doubts over relationship with Carter, 229; reaction to sale of Hank Janson, 234; post-Janson novels, 235-238, 245-246; creation of John Gail, 250-257; writes *La Guerra*, 257-264; return to UK to write *The Avenging Sun*, 268-273; collaborations with J Bernard Hutton, 273-278; writing pornography to keep off the breadline, 279-281; writes Hugh Pecker humour novels, 281-282; writes the 'Slaves of Empire' series 282-283; writes *Adventures Of A Plumber's Mate*, 285-286; edits *Caroline Newsletter*, 288-294; life in Spain, 295-296; attempts to revive interest in Hank Janson, 297-301; death, 302

Frances, Stephen Daniel (novels): *Adventures Of A Plumber's Mate* (as Sid South), 286; *Alicia The Concubine* (unpublished), 283; *Bad Boy*, 236; *Barba The Slaver* (as Dael Forest), 283; *Beauty Found A Grave* (as Dave Steel), 95;

The Bitter Seeds Of Hate, 263; *Brotan The Breeder* (as Dael Forest), 283; *Bury Me Deep* (as Duke Linton), 81; *A Butterfly In Pamplona* (unpublished), 283; *Chicago Payoff* (as Ace Capelli), 77; *Come Again, Pecker* (as Mark Clinton), 281; *Corissa The Vestal Virgin* (as Dael Forest), 283; *Criminals Of Want*, 263; *Cry For My Lovely*, 253, 278; *Day Of Terror*, 236; *Dead Men Don't Love* (as Link Shelton), 77; *Death At Every Door* (as Ace Capelli), 77; *The Disorientated Man* (as Peter Saxon), 237, 278; *Double Header* (as John Glaston Hilt), 281; *Get Me Headquarters* (as Ace Capelli), 77; *Gracus The Centurion* (as Dael Forest), 283; *A Grave For A Coyote* (as Tex Ryland), 79; *Haesel, The Slave* (as Dael Forest), 283; *Hate Is For The Hunted*, 253, 257; *The Healing Power* (ghosted for J. Bernard Hutton), 276; *Hess: The Man And His Mission* (ghosted for J. Bernard Hutton), 275; *High Summer Homicide* (as Arthur Kirby), 235; *In The Hands Of The Inquisition* (as Maria Deluz), 280; *It's Not Easy To Die* (as Steve Markham), 79; *Lady Take The Chair* (as Dave Steel), 79; *La Guerra* ('The Spanish Saga'), 257-264, 278-279; *Lovely But Deadly* (as Dave Steel), 95; *Never Turn Your Back* (as Ace Capelli), 77; *No Flowers For The Dead* (as Max Clinten), 85; *Not Everybody Died* (as Danny Stephens), 237; *The Obscenity of Hank Janson* (unpublished), 278, 296-298, 301; *Oh! Hugh Pecker* (as Mark Clinton), 281; *One Man In His Time*, 27, 35, 54, 58, 70, 136; *Oral Antics* (as John Glaston Hilt), 280; *Pattern Of Life*, 236; *Pecker's Arabian Nights* (unpublished), 282;

HANK JANSON TITLES AVAILABLE FROM TELOS PUBLISHING

SOME LOOK BETTER DEAD
Hank Janson

A seemingly innocuous visit to a fashion show leads *Chicago Chronicle*'s ace reporter Hank Janson into a web of murder and intrigue with dark secrets from the past.

112pp. A5 paperback reprint.
Includes an introduction by
pulp historian and writer Steve Holland

ISBN 1-903889-82-0 (pb) £9.99 UK $9.95 US $14.95 CAN

SKIRTS BRING ME SORROW
Hank Janson

Murder, blackmail, a femme fatale and switched identities
... just everyday problems for Hank Janson.

The Telos edition reinstates the previously-unpublished
original cover artwork by Reginald Heade, which was
censored when the novel first appeared in 1951.

144pp. A5 paperback reprint.
Includes an introduction by
pulp historian and writer Steve Holland

ISBN 1-903889-83-9 (pb) £9.99 UK $9.95 US $14.95 CAN

A Telos Classic

TORMENT
Hank Janson

Chicago Chronicle reporter Hank Janson is caught up in a convoluted web of intrigue involving telepathy, murder, grave robbing, pornographic photographs, infidelity and suicide! He is faced with having to uncover the links that bind all these disparate and seemingly unconnected events together and discover what really lies behind them.

Telos' publication of *Torment* marked the 50th anniversary of the book.

144pp. A5 paperback reprint.
Includes an introduction by
pulp historian and writer Steve Holland
ISBN 1-903889-80-4 (pb) £9.99 UK $9.95 US $14.95 CAN

341

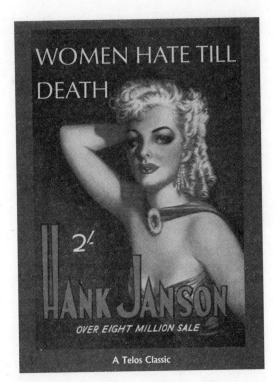

A Telos Classic

WOMEN HATE TILL DEATH
Hank Janson

At a promotional event for a revolutionary new car, Hank Janson encounters cousins Doris and Marion Langham, whose wartime experiences in a Nazi concentration camp haunt them still. When a subsequent journalistic assignment leads Hank to investigate the gruesome shooting of Joe Sparman, who worked for the experimental car's manufacturer, he starts to suspect that the harrowing events of the past are having even more tangible consequences in the present ...

144pp. A5 paperback reprint.
Includes an introduction by
pulp historian and writer Steve Holland
ISBN 1-903889-81-2 (pb) £9.99 UK $9.95 US $14.95 CAN

WHEN DAMES GET TOUGH
Hank Janson

This anthology of ultra-rarities reprints the first three Hank Janson novellas – *When Dames Get Tough, Scarred Faces* and *Kitty Takes The Rap* – which initially appeared in 1946 over two volumes (with the latter two collected together under the *Scarred Faces* title). Literally only a handful of copies of the original editions now survive. Also included in this Telos anthology, as a bonus, are two Hank Janson short stories from the scarce *Underworld* magazine.

**144pp approx. A5 paperback reprint.
Includes an introduction by
pulp historian and writer Steve Holland**
ISBN 1-903889-85-5 (pb) £9.99 UK $9.95 US $14.95 CAN

The prices shown are correct at time of going to press. However, the publishers reserve the right to increase prices from those previously advertised without prior notice.

TELOS PUBLISHING
c/o Beech House,
Chapel Lane,
Moulton,
Cheshire,
CW9 8PQ,
England
`Email: orders@telos.co.uk
Web: www.telos.co.uk

To order copies of any Telos books, please visit our website where there are full details of all titles and facilities for worldwide credit card online ordering, or send a cheque or postal order (UK only) for the appropriate amount (including postage and packing), together with details of the book(s) you require, plus your name and address to the above address. Overseas readers please send two international reply coupons for details of prices and postage rates.